CLASSROOM BEHAVIOUR

CLASSROOM BEHAVIOUR

A practical guide to effective teaching,
behaviour management and colleague support

William A. Rogers

P·C·P
Paul Chapman
Publishing

© William A. Rogers 2002
First published in 2000 by Books Education 2000
Reprinted 2001, 2002 (twice)
This edition published 2002 by Paul Chapman Publishing

 Paul Chapman Publishing
A SAGE Publications Company
6 Bonhill Street
London EC2A 4PU

SAGE Publications Inc
2455 Teller Road
Thousand Oaks, California 91320

SAGE Publications India Pvt Ltd
32, M-Block Market
Greater Kailash - I
New Delhi 1 10 048

British Library Cataloguing in Publication Data

A catalogue record of this book is available from the British Library

ISBN 0 7619 4017 0
ISBN 0 7619 4018 9

Library of Congress catalogue record available

Designed and typeset by Kate Williams, Abergavenny
Printed and bound in Great Britain by Cromwell Press Ltd., Trowbridge, Wiltshire

Contents

Scope

Chapter 1 explores the dynamics of children's behaviour; how both student and teacher behaviour affect each other, for good or ill. The issue of "control" and management is developed as it relates to the purposes of management, teaching and discipline.

Chapter 2 addresses the critical phase of the year, the "establishment phase", covering those first meetings that help define and shape our leadership, authority, discipline and relationship with the class (as a group) and the beginnings of workable cohesion. Particular emphasis is given to the importance of a classroom agreement for behaviour and learning, developed with the students.

Chapter 3 develops a framework for behaviour management and explores key behaviour management and discipline skills within that framework. A number of case examples are noted to illustrate those skills.

Chapter 4 explores the fundamentals of effective teaching and outlines core understandings and skills. Case studies are again noted to illustrate aspects, features and skills of effective teaching.

Chapter 5 discusses behaviour management in terms of behaviour consequences and "punishment". A framework for planning and utilising consequences is developed. School-wide consequences such as detention are also discussed.

Chapter 6 addresses challenging behaviours and children who present with emotional and behavioural difficulties. A school-wide framework for supporting teachers and students is developed with an emphasis on an educational model of support.

Chapter 7 addresses the issue of anger: our own anger as teachers and how we manage and communicate it; and how we can better communicate with and support others when they are angry.

Chapter 8 discusses how we can support each other, as teachers, when things get difficult. Issues such as the hard to manage class, harassment, stress and coping are discussed in the context of colleague support.

Acknowledgements

Putting a book together is time consuming for more than the author. I want to thank my wife Lora – closest friend and fellow teacher – who gave ongoing support and tolerated an overly papered dining room table. Thanks, too, to our daughter Sarah; we shared the dining room table many, many times (homework and book writing). Thanks also, Sarah, for the book cover and the cartoon in Chapter 8.

To all my colleagues whose stories and accounts are detailed herein and to all the students who (although names are changed) would be surprised to read that their behaviour has been the subject of the many cases studies utilised in this book.

To Richard Myers whose encouragement and support enabled this project.

To Dr John Robertson, friend and colleague, for advice, wisdom and support over the years.

My thanks, too, to Felicia Schmidt who patiently transcribed my handwriting (yes – handwriting) into readable text.

My thanks, lastly, to my many colleagues who put up with me as a mentor teacher in their classrooms and whose accounts form the interactive examples about teaching, behaviour and behaviour management in this book.

All the best to my first-year colleagues embarking on their teaching journey (particularly our daughter Elizabeth).

Introduction

"I never thought I'd become a teacher"

Education is simply the soul of a society
as it passes from one generation to another.
G. K. Chesterton, 1924

A teacher's response has crucial consequences ...
it creates a climate of compliance or defiance, a mood
of contentment or contention, a desire to make amends
or to take revenge ... Teachers have the power to affect a
child's life for better or worse. A child becomes what
he/she experiences. While parents possess the original key
to their offspring's experience, teachers have a spare key.
They, too, can open or close the minds and hearts of children.
Haim Ginott

I never thought I'd become a teacher

I never thought I'd become a teacher; I had mixed success at school. It wasn't the work; I could handle that (by and large) – it was the culture of control and authority. Few teachers encouraged or allowed students much expression of their views or ideas. I also had many "run-ins" with petty, mean-spirited and, at times, cruel teachers. Being chastised – even hit and caned – was an occupational hazard in those days. On one occasion, at the age of 11, I was caned for breaking a pencil that another pupil had snatched from me. I was blamed in the ensuing fracas, and later caned. I also was caned for "answering back" on a number of occasions, and for going to the shops at lunchtime (a major crime in those days).

I survived – we all did – but I never thought I'd become a teacher. In the 1950s (after the Second World War) many of the male teachers in my school would have served in the forces, and they didn't take kindly to students appearing as even mildly challenging to adult authority. I suppose I was "heralding" the view that I had basic rights. At the heart of these rights was the desire to be treated with fundamental dignity and respect. I had no problems with the teachers who gave such (strangely).

I can recall one particular teacher walking up to me, in front of the class, and grabbing my shirt so I faced him. (I'd been whispering something to a friend behind me.) He then pushed me with his fingers in my chest and said, "Were you brought up or dragged up, Rogers?" He didn't like me. I stood up, heart thumping, and said, "It's none of your bloody business!" (I was a little taller than him at 15). No one was going to "have a go" at my progeny or parenting. I then turned and walked out of the class. The class was hushed – *waiting*; it was all very dramatic. I didn't see "the git" (as we'd nicknamed him) for a week. He didn't even put me on detention – he must have realised he'd gone too far (even then). He merely kept out of my way until the end of term.

I left school at 15. It wasn't an uncommon thing to do. I left because I'd been caught putting up a large picture of all the teachers I disliked on the central school notice board. It was 1962, with two days to go until the end of term. I'd spent a long time on this painting – in oils – the faces painted in the manner of Salvador Dali; "melting", merging into the darker, swirling, background. I had come in to school early, that particular day, with the unsigned painting. It was my message, my "statement"; a *coup de grace*. I was observed by a prefect as I surreptitiously pinned up the painting. He reported me, although he didn't have to. At the form assembly our senior master held up the painting (thereby giving it a second public viewing), looked at me and said, "You know what is going to happen to you, don't you Rogers?" Well, I'd been caned before. I sighed, frowned, shrugged my shoulders. He hadn't seen the joke.

He rolled up the painting and as he dismissed the class I saw him put it on the desk in his office area adjacent to the classroom. When he wasn't looking, I sneaked in and retrieved my property, stuck it under my school jumper and, *en route* to Period 1, put it back on the notice board again (surreptitiously). Later that morning the Form 4 students were watching a film in the upstairs double classroom; a black and white nature film (*Otters in Canada* or something like that). It was probably a "filler activity", it being within the last two days of term. We were whispering in the darkness, pretending to be absorbed, when a knock on the door heralded yet another prefect. The teacher turned off the film, a chink of light fell across the room and a voice said, "Mr Smith wants to see Billy Rogers *immediately*". The teacher said something like, "Alright, if he's here I'll send him as soon as the film has finished". The door closed, and the darkness and the noise of the film gave me enough "cover" to sneak out. I whispered to my friend, "Don't say anything, I'm off – home". I tip-toed quietly, my back pressed along the wall, moving carefully in the darkness. I opened the door as little, and as quietly, as possible and found partial freedom.

We had a letter a week later, from the headmaster (after school closure for the term – we didn't have a phone). "We are deeply disappointed with your son's behaviour …" it went on, or words to that effect. My parents asked me what I wanted them to do about "all this". Wisely they let me go to another school – for six months or so, and we emigrated to Australia when I was 16.

Many years later on one of my trips back to England to lecture on behaviour management and discipline issues in schools, I met a teacher whose father had taught me at the high school where I had painted "the picture". I relayed the story of the painting episode and he shared it with the local press (I didn't know he had passed on the story). The following is an extract from that article:

EXPRESS, FRIDAY, 8 SEPTEMBER 1995

SIX-OF-THE-BEST DAYS OF HIS LIFE

Now rebel Bill lectures on school discipline!

TURBULENT times – that's how Bill Rogers describes his 1960s adolescence at a Government High School in Hemel Hempstead.

When he failed his 11-plus exams Bill believed he would never achieve academic success.

And his strongest schoolday memories are of the canings he received for rebellious behaviour.

Former head of discipline at the school remembers the incident that heralded the end of Bill's schooldays when Bill showed off his artistic talents and mounted a display of caricatures of the least popular teachers.

When the cartoons were confiscated by the senior master they later mysteriously disappeared from his office.

Bill left school in 1961 and emigrated to Australia one year later.

Now the self-proclaimed academic failure is an educational consultant who regularly jets back to England to give university lectures on school discipline and behaviour management.

Bill explained: "I eventually went back to night school and did it the hard way ..."

I was a little annoyed at the line "self-proclaimed academic failure ..." (I've never said that or believed that): journalistic licence, I suppose. But there is a lesson in this trip down memory lane. You can't predict where a student will go or what he or she may become. Some of my teachers had said in effect, and sometimes in words, "You won't amount to anything ..." and then had added the *because* statement of the day: "because you didn't listen", or "won't listen"; or "because you won't concentrate or apply yourself". There is also the lesson that learning is lifelong, that education doesn't finish at school, or with school.

I recall looking out of classroom windows many, many times (particularly when bored or when the teacher droned on and on). I could see, in the distance, the green fields and trees of Hertfordshire. The window seemed to say, "Come!" I couldn't.

I eventually became a teacher – many years later. Many of my teachers at least taught me how *not* to discipline: how not to embarrass, criticise and shame children. They also taught me how *not* to teach. I had good, kind and generous teachers too. We always remember such teachers. They affirmed, encouraged and believed in me and enabled me to continue learning to this day.

In my journey as a teacher I have had to rethink many aspects of classroom behaviour, teacher behaviour, the purposes and limitations of discipline and management and how we can establish more cooperative classrooms where rights and responsibilities work together for the benefit of all.

This book is the outcome of many years of in-service training with teachers and countless hours in the classroom with colleagues as a mentor-teacher in Australian schools.

Having made 14 visits to the UK to conduct INSET in schools, education authorities and universities I hope the link between my Australian teaching and consultancy experiences and my in-service work in the UK will find a receptive (and useful) audience here.

Tactical pausing (...)

In many of the dialogue exchanges between teacher and students throughout the book, you will find a set of brackets with an ellipsis (...). This refers to a typical teacher behaviour I choose to describe as "tactical pausing". This is conscious behaviour whereby the teacher briefly pauses in their communication to emphasise the need for student attention, or allow some processing by the student of what the teacher has just said. It can also communicate (to older children) a sense of expectant "calming".

For example, if you beckon, or direct, a student to come across to you, in the playground, from several yards away, you need to get eye contact first. This is easier (obviously) if we know the student's name. If we don't we probably lift the voice (as we look in their direction) and say, "EXCUSE ME (...)! EXCUSE ME (...)!" Do we want to be excused? Or we may say, "Oi (...)! Oi (...)!" We might use a generic, "FELLAS (...)! Fellas (...)!", or "Guys (...)!" The tactical pausing (...), in directional language, is our attempt to initiate and sustain some attention.

In the classroom we frequently include tactical pausing when engaged in management and discipline. Several students are chatting away as the teacher seeks to explain a point on the whiteboard. She scans the room; she tactically pauses (saying nothing). As the restlessness settles she says, "Looking this way and listening (...) ...", and she tactically pauses (again). Lowering her voice she repeats, "Looking this way and listening, thanks (...)". Sensing the class attention she then refocuses on the task at hand. Tactical pausing is a small aspect – but an important small aspect – of overall teacher behaviour.

No disclaimers There are books whose disclaimer reads: "All characters are fictitious ... any resemblance to ...". It's the opposite in this book. Every example and case study, even the "snatches" of teacher–student dialogue, are drawn directly from my teaching/mentoring role in schools.

My own teaching, these days, comes out of periodic peer-mentoring – working directly in a team-teaching role with primary and secondary teachers who are seeking to be more consciously reflective of their day-to-day teaching and management. Mentoring is a joint professional journey: there is no superior–inferior relationship. The aim is to build *reflective* professional practice.

In this book each skill or approach suggested is supported by case examples (and studies) taken from recent teaching situations that I have been involved in as a mentor teacher.

I have changed the names of colleagues (teachers) and students wherever ethical probity demands. I have even changed grade and subject allocations and gender where I thought necessary, without changing the behavioural context and meanings of the real examples and situations noted. As I wrote each case example, each "snatch" of dialogue, the memories of particular classes, and particular students, on particular days, came back – easily, quickly. I could even "relive" some of the emotion that occasioned some of the more difficult discipline situations I have had to address.

In sharing these case examples with you my aim is always to draw forth concepts, approaches and skills of effective teaching and management. As I write, I am also acutely aware of the fact that you – as a teacher – are constantly on the go the moment you walk in the school gates. Being acutely aware of what the day-after-day-after-day of teaching can be like I have sought to address ineffective as well as effective teacher practice; always distinguishing between what one *characteristically* does and what one does as a result of bad-day-syndrome.

There is never a stage when we stop being a reflective teacher (or learner). I hope this book enables your own professional reflection and supports and encourages you in your teaching journey.

Chapter 1
The dynamics of classroom behaviour

A few years ago I met an old professor at the
University of Notre Dame. Looking back on his
long life of teaching he said, with a funny twinkle
in his eyes, "I have always complained that my
work was constantly interrupted until I slowly
discovered that my interruptions were my work".
Henri Nouwen

Day-to-day school teaching normally takes place in a rather unusual setting: a small room (for what is asked of it), often inadequate furniture and space to move, a 50-minute time slot (or less) to cover set curriculum objectives, and 25–30 distinct, and unique, personalities, some of whom may not even want to be there. Why would there not be some natural stresses and strains associated with a teacher's day-to-day role?

We teach each other

Into that rather unusual setting, where students and teachers bring personal agendas, feelings and needs, and where certain obligations and rights have to be balanced, both teacher and student are "teaching" each other through their daily behaviours.

It is not simply enough to detail student disruption as a discrete issue only pertaining to the student. In any school the same students may behave differently, in different settings, with different teachers. The teacher's behaviour and the student's behaviour have a reciprocal effect on each other and on the ever present "audience" of peers.

The case examples that follow (as noted earlier) are taken directly from my recent work with colleagues as a mentor teacher and observing colleagues widely across the schools in which I have been working.

As you read these case examples I encourage you to reflect on how teacher behaviour and student behaviour act reciprocally on each other. The nature, extent and effect of disruptive behaviour, in this sense, is not simply the result of students acting disruptively; behaviour is also "learned" within its context.

"Overly vigilant" management

Corey has been described as "a bit of a lazy lad". Any support from home for basic organisational skills and the application of day-to-day responsibility is "limited". In the classroom he is leaning back in his seat, a vacant look in his eyes – he's looking out of the window (to partial freedom perhaps?). His attention is hardly gripped by the task requirement in his maths class. It's his third lesson with this teacher.

The teacher walks over to him and, standing next to his table, asks, "Why haven't you started any work?"

"I haven't got a pen, have I?" Corey, at least, is honest at this point.

"Don't talk to me like that!" The teacher doesn't like Corey's tone and manner ("lazy sod").

"Well I haven't got a pen, have I? What d'you expect me to say?!" Corey folds his arms sulkily, averting his eyes.

"Well *get* a pen." At this, Corey gets up and walks out of the classroom. The teacher hurriedly catches up with him.

"Oi! Where do you think you're going? Get back in here!"

Corey, with feigned exasperation, says, "You *asked* me to get a pen! Gees – I'm just going to get one from me locker." He clicks his tongue.

"I meant get one from a classmate – if you've got one." The teacher adds the tempting – but unnecessary – sarcastic barb.

Corey slopes off towards the back of the classroom to a mate.

"Hey Craig, give us a pen."

Craig answers, "I'm not giving you a pen – gees I didn't get the last one back".

Corey walks back to the teacher (most of the class is now enjoying this little *contretemps*). "He won't give me a pen." He grins.

Corey's teacher says, "Look I'm sick of this. You know you're supposed to bring pen and paper ..."

Corey butts in, "Yeah well people forget sometimes y'know!"

"Look if you can't come to my class prepared to work, you can leave and go to Mr Smith (the year head).

"Yeah – well I'm leaving. It's a shit class anyway!!" Corey storms out.

The teacher calls after him. "Right! I'll see you in detention!"

Corey (now half-way down the corridor) calls back. "I don't care!"

A small incident like a student without a pen (almost unbelievably) becomes a major fracas. I've seen this too many times. Maybe the teacher is having a bad day (maybe the student is too). Maybe the teacher is characteristically petty, churlish, pedantic, sarcastic – whatever. What can be seen is that the teacher's behaviour contributes as much to this incident – and its management – as that of the student.

In another classroom a similar incident is taking place. The teacher walks across to a student who has been un-engaged in his learning task for several minutes. She has given him some take-up time – after all, he may be thinking, he may just need a few minutes to get his idea formed, he may be another lad with ADD (attention deficit disorder).

She greets him and says, "Bradley, I notice you're not working ... can I help?" She avoids asking why he hasn't started work yet.

He says, "I haven't got a pen".

"You can have one of mine", replies his teacher.

As it is still the first few lessons, the teacher still has not sorted out which students are genuinely forgetful, or maybe lazy, or maybe just seeking attention or indulging in some "game-playing". She has a box of blue pens and red pens, some rulers, some spare erasers and some pencils (all taped with a 1cm band of yellow electrical tape around the tip – to track them back to the box – itself yellow). On the box, in large letters, it reads: RETURN HERE – THANKS IN ADVANCE Ms Brown. [ENGLISH].

The offer of a pen is met with "Yeah – but I haven't got a red pen have I?"

"There's one in my yellow box," (she points back to the teacher's table).

"Yeah, but I haven't got any paper," (he grins).

"Bradley – there's A4 lined and plain paper next to the yellow box." She finishes with a wink and, "OK, Bradley – I'll come and see how you're going a little later". She walks away giving Bradley some "take-up time". Her tone and manner indicate that she is aware of Bradley's avoidance "game-playing" but is confident that he will get what he needs and actually start some work. She comes back to chat with Bradley later (in the on-task phase of the lesson), to re-establish and check on the progress of his work.

Overly vigilant behaviour

A special-needs Year 3 student has a small soft toy on her table next to her daily diary writing task. The teacher walks over and in an unnecessarily stern voice says, "You know you're not supposed to bring toys to your table don't you!?" He snatches it up and walks off. The girls (naturally) protests and he adds, "Get on with your work or you'll finish it at recess ...". Who would speak to a student like that? He did.

He could have walked over, looked at the toy (even smiled – miserable sod!) and given a fair and simple "directed choice". For example:

"Danielle, it's a nice toy but I want you to put it in your locker tray or on my table" (here he could use a softer directional voice) "and carry on with your diary writing. I'll come and see how you're getting on soon ...".

This leaves her with both a behavioural choice, a "task-focus" and expectation of cooperation.

A female student walks in to class a few minutes late. Melissa likes a bit of attention, she's grinning at a few of her friends as she enters. She is wearing long, "dangly" earrings (non-regulation).

Teacher: Come here [in a sharpish voice – clearly frustrated with Melissa's lateness and "*grand dame* entrance"]. Why are you late?

Student: I'm just a *few* minutes late.

Teacher: Why are you wearing those ... things?

Student: What?

Teacher: *Those* things – you know what I'm talking about – those stupid earrings.

Student: Mrs Daniels [the tutor teacher] didn't say anything. [Melissa's tone is sulky, indifferent – she averts her eyes. The teacher senses – yet annoyingly "creates" – a challenge.]

Teacher: Listen, I don't care *what* Mrs Daniels did or didn't do – get them off. You know you're not supposed to wear them! [He's clearly getting rattled now. He believes it's an issue on which he has to not only exercise discipline – he has to win.]

Student: Yeah – well how come other teachers don't hassle us about it, eh?

Teacher: Who do you think you're talking to?! Get them off now and sit down or you're on detention!

What message do the "audience" and Melissa really get from the way the teacher dealt with this "uniform misdemeanour"?

If a teacher's management style is this "vigilant" – unnecessarily and overly vigilant –there are many students who will naturally challenge and even "bait" the teacher (I was often tempted to myself, at that age!)

Non-vigilance   Walking across the playground at the end of period six, I noticed a couple of students riding their bikes towards the school gate doing mini-wheelies on the gravel (most students, most times, walk their bikes as per the school rule). I also noticed a colleague on end-of-day duty who couldn't have failed to see the two lads. In the brief glance I gave him (en route to the staff room) he looked wistful, oblivious to the bike riders. Perhaps he was singing – to himself – one of the favourite ditties of teachers, "How many days till the end of term …?" I was about 30–40 metres away from the lads and I called them over.

"Fellas (…), Fellas (…)" – eventually getting some eye contact from distance. "See you for a few minutes over here (…) Thanks."

They stopped, akimbo their bikes, near the school gate. I thought they might just ride off (that's happened before).

"What? What d'you want?!"

They called out across the playground. They looked annoyed with a "we're-in-a-hurry-don't-hassle-us" look. I wanted them to come across to me so that I could briefly chat with them away from their immediate audience. This approach is often preferable in playground settings. It avoids audience participation and the "Greek-chorus syndrome" (no offence to Greeks, you understand). I called them over again.

"Gees, mate What?! What d'we do?!" they called back. ("Mate" is a typical "Australianism" – even used by some students to teachers.)

"You're not in trouble – a brief chat (…) now. Thanks." I turned aside, walked a few paces and stopped, to convey expectation (from distance) – take-up time (p. 68).

The whole "episode (one of countless we engage in on our teaching and management journey) hadn't taken long at all.

I saw them walking across the playground in my direction (out of the corner of my eye). I didn't want to message a visual stand-off; I've seen teachers call students over with fists curled on hips, legs astride, messaging (no doubt) a kind of "show-down".

They came over and stood nearby, with their bikes.

"Yeah? What?" (sighs, eyes averted, seriously wry mouths). I tactically ignored the sighs (etc.) so as to keep the focus on the main issue – bike riding in school grounds.

I introduced myself and asked their names.

"Adam (…) Lukas (still sulking and sighing).

"Adam and Lukas (…) what's the school rule for bike-riding in school grounds?" Avoid asking *why*.

"What?" Adam wasn't sure what I was getting at initially. I repeated the question.

"What's the school rule …?"

"Other teachers don't hassle us …" He now knew what I was on about.

"Maybe they don't." I smiled – a brief "partial agreement" (p. 60) What's the school rule?" I asked again. This time Adam looked at me, grinned.

"It depends who's here …"

That's the point. The students tend to know which teachers are "non-vigilant".

It does make it harder to exercise reasonable consistency in a school when teachers ignore, or choose not to address, "small-beer" issues like "hats on in class", "chewing gum in class", "running in corridors", "testosteronic play-punching and bonding around the neck", "bike riding in school grounds", and so on.

It is easy to fall into a kind of jaded tiredness when it comes to addressing such behaviours. If such "non-vigilance" is typical across a school it makes it doubly hard for others in the team to exercise "*relaxed* vigilance".

Relaxed "vigilance"

As Melissa enters (late), to a little coterie of grins, the teacher acknowledges her with a smile, a small frown, and a welcome.

"Welcome Melissa" (her friends laugh). "I notice you're late; please take a seat." The teacher does not make an issue of the lateness (2–3 minutes) or the fact that she has on dangling earrings *at that point* in the lesson. As Melissa walks to her seat (was that the gait of a supermodel?) the teacher is reclaiming group attention and focusing on the lesson almost "as if nothing serious had happened at all". The teacher's confident calmness and focus has minimised Melissa's initial audience-seeking entry.

Later in the lesson, when the students are "working", she calls Melissa aside (quietly) from her immediate peer audience.

"Melissa – you were late last period and the one before that; we'll need to have a brief chat after class."

Melissa moans, "Why? I couldn't help it!"

"Well perhaps you can explain to me after class – I won't keep you long. Nice earrings." She quickly changes the focus.

"What?"

"Nice earrings ..."

Melissa grins with ill-concealed suspicion. "Yeah!"

"What's the school rule about earrings, Melissa?" The teacher avoids the point-less interrogative "*Why* are you ...?" or "*Are you* wearing earrings?" What's the point of asking a student "why" they're doing something inappropriate if we, and they, know they're doing it?

Melissa appeals to a well worn student ploy, "But Mrs Daniels didn't say anything in tutor group about them." Here Melissa sighs, folds her arms and gives a sulky grimace.

"Maybe she didn't." The teacher doesn't call Melissa a liar, nor does she pass judgement on her colleague's possible ignoring of jewellery rules. "I can check that with her." The teacher's tone is pleasant, not sarcastic or in any way provocative. She repeats the question. "What's the school rule about earrings?" By using an imperative form ("what?") the teacher is directing the ownership back to Melissa. Melissa, again, mentions Mrs Daniels. The teacher "partially agrees" (briefly) but refocuses to the rule question.

"What's the rule for ...?"

Melissa sighs, "Yeah – well ... we're not supposed to". She says it, sighing, in an "I-can't-believe-why-we've-got-this-petty-rule ..." kind of voice.

The teacher then says, "Alright Melissa, it's my job to remind you, you know what to do." She smiles, "I'll come and see how your work is going later".

The teacher becomes task-oriented now. She signals an end to this brief rule reminder, conveying the expectation that Melissa will take the earrings off. By giving the student some take-up time (p. 68) she also minimises any forced "showdown" such as forcing Melissa (Year 9) to hand over the jewellery. If Melissa doesn't take them off then the teacher knows the underlying issue is a potential power-struggle and rather than force her to take them off will use a deferred consequence (p. 103).

The "tribal tom-toms" convey the message around the class that this teacher will always address issues that matter (even earrings) but they also appreciate the *way* this teacher does it.

Is it worth the teacher's brief effort to address the student's lateness and earrings in *this* way? The "simple" answer is yes. *Relaxed* vigilance enables workable consistency – we'll never get perfect consistency just reasonable and workable consistency. This teacher sends the clear (fair) messages about arriving to class on time and jewellery rules but in a least-intrusive way that keeps the workable and respectful relationship between teacher and student intact.

Swearing: inappropriate language

I was teaching in a maths class a couple of years ago. My colleague and I had finished the "instructional part" of the lesson and we were moving around the room to encourage, assist, refocus … on-task time.

Out of the corner of my eye I saw a student throw an eraser, parabolically, to another student who missed the catch. Cassie called across the room – quite loudly – to the student who had dropped it.

"Gees, you silly bitch!" She said this in a laughing, "matey", kind of way (had she meant her friend to catch it?).

The other girl laughed – as did many in the class. My colleague was closer to the fracas than I was but hadn't taken any action on the swearing incident so I called to Cassie, across the room, to come over to me (away from her immediate coterie). She stayed seated.

"What?! What do you want?!" She gave me a sulky, frowning look.

I repeated, "See you for a minute over here thanks."

I had said this in a firm (but relaxed) way while working with another group of students. She stood up, arms folded.

"What did I do then, eh?"

I wasn't going to discuss anything across the distance of several rows of students. I had directed her *away from her immediate class mates* to avoid unnecessary embarrassment (to her) and also to speak to her (briefly) about her behaviour. Cassie certainly knows how to "play to the gallery".

I added for a third (and last time), "I want to see you over here. Now (…)." I turned my eyes away from Cassie and turned aside to the group I was working with to convey my "expectation".

She came over and stood next to me, with folded arms, skewed eye contact, eyes raised to the ceiling and sighing.

"What do you want?" she said, in a careworn, "I'm-doing-you-a-favour-by-coming-across-to-you" tone of voice.

It's hard to keep the focus on the "primary" issue or behaviour. Ignoring the sulky non-verbals, I said, "I called you over so I wouldn't embarrass you in front of your classmates."

"What?" She seemed oblivious as to any reason why I'd need to speak to her.

"You threw an eraser at Melinda and she dropped it. You called across the room to her that she was a silly bitch." I'd said all this quietly. She looked at me, incredulously.

"What!? She don't care if I call her that. She's my friend anyway. Gees!!" (… the social injustice of it all!)

Should we simply accept "street" language, as some social commentators suggest we should? Should we accept "friendly banter" expressed in language that includes words like bitch, slut, a— hole, dickhead, poofter, wanker, and so on? If I do let such language go I've tacitly said, "I don't care if you speak to each other like that" (and I do care).

I *partially* agreed with Cassie.

"Maybe Melinda doesn't care. I do." (I meant it.)

She sighed and said, "So-reee!" (sorry).

I *briefly* reminded her of our classroom agreement about respectful language.

"Can I go back to my seat now?" Her tone and manner continued to evidence sulky indifference.

It would have been pointless at this point to add, "Look you don't really mean you're sorry! Say it properly, as if you mean it!" (I've seen teachers force students like Cassie into face-losing, or verbal slanging matches, because of the tone of voice in which a "sorry" is given.

As Cassie was leaving the class later that morning she said to me, "This class was OK till you came". That was probably true (as her version of "OK" goes.) The class had got used to being very noisy, with frequent calling out, cross-talking and a lack of focus in work tasks. There were several students like Cassie who hadn't had the issue of friendly "banter" addressed until this occasion. She was more amenable in the following lessons. We developed a basic, respectful understanding about expectations, about 'focus', and why we are here together in this place. It took time, effort and continued goodwill.

Being a reflective practitioner

However many years we have been teaching we can always benefit from some reflection on our teaching and management practice. I once heard a teacher say, "You can't teach an old dog new tricks". My colleague was in a small group of teachers discussing behaviour management practice and skills. I knew my colleague had management problems in a number of classes (but unfortunately found it hard to share those concerns). The discussion group was a collegial forum to enable such general sharing of concerns. When she had said, a little too defensively, "You can't teach an old dog new tricks", I replied, "But you're not a dog; you're a human being". My wry smile was returned. "If we're willing, and see a need for fine-tuning, even change, in our management practice and if we are aware of more effective management practice we *can* always learn ... with support ..."

"Primary" and "secondary" behaviours

In many of the exchanges between teacher and students in this book, you will note a frequently recurring theme: that of a student's non-verbal and verbal be-haviour potentially increasing the stress a teacher faces when seeking to manage student behaviour. Elsewhere I have described such behaviours as *secondary* behaviours. The student's pouting, sulking, tut-tutting and huffing behaviours and their procrastination and argumentative stance are *secondary* to the primary issue that the teacher addresses (Rogers 1998). These secondary behaviours are also often more stressfully annoying than the primary issue or behaviour.

A student has not cleaned up his work area, and it is getting close to the "bell" (breaktime). The teacher reminds the student to clean up. The student says, "Alright, alright ..." but sighs as he says it, rolls his eyes to the ceiling, leans back in his seat, leans forward again, but makes no initial move to start cleaning up. It is as if he's saying, "Here-we-go-again".

The *primary* issue (litter on the floor) is hardly on the radar screen of teacher concern. Even the words the student uses ("alright") are almost amenable. It is the *tone* of the voice, the expelled sigh, the upward turn of the eyes; those body language signals appear to say, "I don't care – don't hassle me!" It is these *secondary* behaviours that appear (quickly) as more disconcerting, or frustrating to the teacher than the issue of the litter itself.

I was teaching a Year 10 social studies class. It was my first session with them. During the instructional part of the lesson a student in the back row leaned back in her seat and sprayed a small can of what looked like perfume around the room. It annoyed some of the class. Others (her friends and her audience) laughed. It was behaviour that couldn't be ignored. I called across the room to her, by name.

"Anne (…) Anne (…)" I'd remembered her name from roll call. She looked across the room at me with a look of (feigned?) surprise.

"Yes – what?" She leaned back in her chair, the can of perfume spray still on the desk. She grinned.

"You've got a can of Impulse (that's what I thought the brand was) and you've sprayed it around the room." It helps to be specific and focus on the student's behaviour. "I want you to put it away in your bag or on my desk. Thanks." I gave her a directed choice rather than walk to the back of the room and either tell her to hand it over or just take it.

"It's not Impulse, it's Evoke," was her response. No doubt she said it to garner group attention ("Notice me, all!") and in a tone of voice that suggested "Let's play verbal ping-pong shall we?"

These kinds of secondary behaviours are much more annoying to teachers than the primary behaviours that trigger them: the sighs, the head movements, the averted eyes or the eyes to the ceiling, the supercilious grin and, of course, the annoying time-wasting things that some students say.

Rather than argue with Anne about the spray perfume ("I don't care if it's Chanel number bleedin' 9!! Put it away now or …!"), I said, "I want you to put it in your bag or on my desk", repeating the "choice". The bag was under her table.

"But it stinks in here!" She still wanted to play verbal ping-pong. A bit of brief, partial, agreement can help avoid pointless argument.

"I know it stinks." She was actually right on that score. Local factories produce some awful smells that, on a hot day, waft, almost palpably, into the classrooms. "And I want you to …" I repeated the choice.

At that point I took the minimal risk of leaving Anne with the directed "choice", as it were, and reclaimed group attention by saying something like, "Looking up here everyone (…) Thanks", and going back to the diagram and topic I had started to address earlier. Out of the corner of my eye I noticed her slowly (ever so slowly) put the Evoke in her bag.

If she hadn't I'd have spoken to her later in the lesson, during class time, away from her direct audience. If she had refused, full stop, to put it away, a deferred consequence would have been made clear to her (see p. 103, 104).

The hard thing always, in such situations, is to display some sense of calmness and personal control when dealing with such secondary behaviours. Yes, there are times when it is appropriate and necessary to communicate one's frustration and anger (Ch. 7), but in this case, with this silly game-playing, a directed choice, avoiding argument and refocusing the class are more effective. Of course, I could have:

- walked over and grabbed the perfume off the table, "Right! I'll have that!"
- demanded she hand the perfume over, "Right … give it to me … give it to me *now*!" (What if she doesn't, what if she says, "No!! – can't make me!")
- said, "Don't you ever speak to me like that! Who the hell do you think you are?" (or words to that effect)
- been sarcastic or rude, in order to embarrass her in front of the class
- told her to leave the room.

Some of these options are no doubt transitionally tempting! What I am trying to

This is a drawing of a Year 10 class I worked with. You can see one lad throwing ("I was only passing") a ruler to a mate. Another has a personal stereo plugged in. Anne is into serious seat-leaning and task avoidance. It took some time to refocus this class (p. 142)

say is that we, in effect, teach each other in these episodic transactions. Anne is learning something about appropriate teacher authority and leadership and (where necessary) about facing the consequences of her behaviour. So are the audience of her peers.

There are many things I *could* do or say. There are always many "ifs", "could-bes" and "what-ifs" in behaviour management with challenging students. There is also no guarantee that any approach will always work in all situations. Behaviour is complex at times; situational and relational behaviour also has its audience-seeking effect, which can either work for the teacher's (and class's) benefit or work against the teacher.

We can ill afford to lose the 80% of cooperative students by forcing the challenging student to lose face and thereby making it easy for the 70–80% to "side" with the disruptive student or, conversely, allow ourselves to be backed-into-a-psychological-corner.

In another Year 10 class (last year) I was moving around the room during on-task time and noticed a student with a personal CD player – tiny earphones in his ears and clearly enjoying the music that I could hear, faintly, as I worked with students nearby. Walking over to him I made eye-contact and beckoned with my fingers for him to take the earphones out. He did. I could hear the pulsating, heavy metal buzz more intensely now.

"It'll help if you turn it off," I suggested. He did.

"Nice CD player," I observed.

"Yeah," he agreed.

"Brock," I asked, "What's the school rule about personal stereos in class?" (Students are allowed to bring personal stereos or handheld electronic games or mobile phones to this school but they're not supposed to use them in class – for obvious reasons one would think. It's hard to communicate to a student who – in Brock's case – has serious heavy metal going on "upstairs".

Instead of answering the question I had asked ("What's the school rule about personal stereos in class?") Brock pointed to the teacher and said, "Ms Snaggs doesn't mind if we have them on – long as we're doing our work ..." He didn't say this rudely, even cockily (some do); he was stating it as a matter of fact.

In my team-teaching-mentoring role in this school, I had noticed that a few teachers didn't seem to care if students brought, and played, their personal stereos as long as they got their classwork done as well. No doubt at all – of course students can work with Walkmans in their ears (even head-banging music ...) that's not the issue. The school rule is clear (and fair) – "no personal stereos in class time".

Some teachers "overservice" this verbal secondary behaviour by entering into a pointless discussion about the veracity of what the student has said, or they try to defend the reasons for the rule (generally a most unwise course); "Brock ... look ... I don't make the rules do I?" Some teachers almost sound like they are "pleading". They present with a defeated if affable and well-meaning tone, suggesting that whatever happens the student will have their way despite what the fair rules may say. "Other teachers might let you play personal stereos but they're not really supposed to, are they?" It is pointless *asking* the student to reason about something he may see as unfair; besides it is a time-wasting exercise distracting away from the business of teaching and learning.

Some teachers become overly vigilant and defensive, and will cast ineffective aspersions on other colleagues. "Look I don't care what Ms Snaggs does or doesn't do! In my class you don't have personal stereos on – *full stop!* Give it to me." When students want to appeal to "what other teachers do (or let us do)" a *brief* partial agreement is helpful followed by a refocusing to the right or rule affected, or a refocusing to the task.

"Miss Donkin lets us have personal stereos in social studies"

"Maybe she does (partial agreement) (...) however in this class the rule is clear. I want you to put the personal stereo in your bag or, if you like, on my table ..." The teacher beckons to the teacher's table.

Whenever I've given this directed choice (at primary or secondary level), I've never had a student (yet) say, "OK, I'll put my expensive personal stereo", or other *object d'art*, "on your table".

Residual secondary behaviour

Jaydon is chewing a largish, viscous, fruity-smelling chewing gum. The teacher walks over and quietly says, "Jaydon (...)". Brief eye-contact is established.

"Yeah, what?"

The teacher says, "The bin is over there".

"What?" he asks.

The teacher repeats, "The bin is over there". This *incidental* direction in part "describes the reality" (there is a bin) and invites some "cognitive shortfall" (put the chewing gum in the bin) by reminding the student where the bin is. It is said respect-fully, a little tongue-in-cheek, as if to say "You know that I know that you know what you should do ... "

If the student engages secondary dialogue "But other teachers don't hassle us ...!" (blah, time-wasting, blah), the teacher will *briefly* acknowledge with partial agreement and refocus.

"Other teachers may let you chew. Here, in this class, the rule is clear and the bin is near ... Ta." The teacher walks off expecting cooperation by giving the student some take-up-time (p. 68).

Ten seconds or so later the student shuffles off to the bin sighing and muttering, "I'll put it in the bin, I'll put it in the bin n'yah, n'yah (in a *sotto voce* whine) ..."

The teacher *tactically* ignores this residual secondary behaviour and observes (out of the corner of his eye) that the student has slumped in his seat, sighed, and slowly restarted work (more residual secondary behaviour). A little later he goes over to the student and re-establishes the working relationship by focusing on the task. "So, how's it going then? Let's have a look. Where are you up to?"

You can imagine what could happen if the teacher overservices all those residual behaviours. "Look!! When you put chewing gum in the bin, you put it in the bin *without* a fanfare – alright?!" That would unnecessarily re-escalate any residual tension.

Some teachers try to ameliorate what they see as the perceived upsetness of the student; they take the huffing and puffing and muttering as an indication they've upset the student. "Troy, Troy, I don't make the rules do I ... be reasonable ...". This kind of good intent only overservices the sulkiness and pouting. It is generally better to tactically ignore such behaviours *until* the student is back on-task, as it were, and then have a brief "re-establishing" that focuses on the task (the classwork) at hand.

If a student's secondary behaviour is too disturbing, or rude, in tone or manner, it will need to be addressed, briefly and firmly, and with a focus on the unacceptable behaviour and a refocus back to the task or expected behaviour: "I'm not speaking to you like that, I don't expect you to speak to me like that". This to a student whose tone of voice is rude, cocky or arrogant. At this point it is prudent to give take-up-time as the student sulks off back to his seat.

If such sulking and pouting is *characteristic* of the student's behaviour, an after class chat that involves some modelling and feedback may be a helpful way to help the student become aware of his typical behaviours and then work on a "plan of understanding" (p. 71). If such follow-up is carried out early in the teacher–student relationship, and with supportive respect, it can go a long way to seeing a reduction in residual secondary behaviours.

We will also come across students who, through their behaviour, say (in effect), "You can't make me!" or "I don't have to do what you say ...". I have seen some infant students really upset their teachers by turning aside and refusing to look at them after the teacher has specifically given a direction: "Bronson (...) Bronson (...) Look at me. Look-at-me!!" I've seen teachers put their hand under a child's chin and force it up to engage attentional eye contact. I've seen teachers bodily turn young children around so they are facing their teacher. I can understand such teacher behaviour and in some carefully thought-out behaviour modification contexts, such teacher behaviour may be appropriate. But if the teacher is getting frustrated and forcing the child's head up the resistant child may be saying (through his behaviour) "You can't make me!", or "I can do what I want and you can't stop me". The child's "private logic" is, at this point, correct; annoying, but correct. Who is controlling whom? The issue of challenging children is addressed more fully in Chapter 6.

- Sometimes secondary behaviours are the result of habit; the student may be unaware that their non-verbal behaviours appear as sulky, pouty, indifferent, testy, having a "chip on the shoulder" (with some students there is "a bucket of attitudinal chips"!). In these cases early and thoughtful follow-up to acknowledge the teacher's concern and gain some shared understanding, and then work on changes, is crucial (p. 71).
- Sometimes such behaviour is the student's bad-day syndrome; sensitivity in the teacher will acknowledge this (privately) and encourage the student to be aware of their behaviour in the future.

- Sometimes such behaviour is provoked by the teacher through their own insensitive, petty, even confrontational behaviour.
- Sometimes the student, too, will use their secondary behaviours in a provocative way …. Shakespeare speaks of *"some kind of men … that put quarrels purposely on others … to test their valour …"* (Twelfth Night [iii] [iv]) Such behaviour is often used as a territorial posturing.

One of the harder messages I had to learn as a younger teacher was that I cannot simply and easily "control" others' behaviour. I can control myself *in* the teaching and management situation. To the extent that I thoughtfully control myself, my language, my "manner" and my approach to the students, is the degree to which I can invite cooperation *or* conversely find my students becoming difficult, or even resistant. The skills addressed later in Chapters 2 and 3 specifically address the issue of effective teaching management, and discipline.

I have also learned not to make demands on reality that reality won't bear.

Our "explanatory style" in behaviour management

Some teachers bring an *overly* demanding "explanatory style" to classroom management and discipline; a *characteristic* way of defining and explaining reality. One's explanatory style can not only affect how one relates to others, but it can also affect one's emotional state and well-being (Seligman 1991; Bernard 1990; Rogers 1996).

When stressful events come to us it is not only, or *simply*, the stressful event that directly causes how we feel, and how effectively we cope and manage. Our "explanatory style", our "working beliefs" about behaviour, what students *should*, and *shouldn't* do, also contribute significantly to how effectively we manage situations.

Some of the unhelpful, assumptive, beliefs that, of themselves, can increase one's stress are directly related to how we perceive and explain what is happening when a student is rude, arrogant, lazy or indifferent, and so on. Secondary behaviour is a typical case in point. When a student slouches, sighs, rolls his eyes to the ceiling or gives a malevolent grin some teachers will automatically react to the secondary behaviours in a stressful way, often saying (later) that "Children must not question or disagree with their teachers" (their superiors), or "Children should do what I say the first time", or "Children should not answer back". The most common belief statement I hear is, "Children should respect their teachers" (full stop).

The "should" and "must" part of the explanatory style is often the problem. There is an imperative here; a demand on reality that is often unrealistic – unrewarded in reality. There are many children who show disrespect, who do not respond or "obey" the first time, who answer back, who are uncivil. It is unpleasant of course, and frustrating when this happens. However when we say, "students *must* obey me …", "*must* not answer back …" or "*must* respect me …" we are making absolute demands that, if not met, contribute to the level of our stress and also to how effectively we handle management situations. If we say, "He *shouldn't* answer back to me" when he did, the internal self-speech can increase the amount of stress one feels at that point, particularly if the intensity of cognitive demand (shouldn't!) is a *characteristic* way that one explains such stressful reality.

I have seen different teachers, managing the same student, in much the same situations, and seen quite different degrees of effectiveness in management and teacher coping that are not explained simply through personality style alone

(Rogers 1996). A more *realistic* belief avoids absolutistic imperatives: "I can't stand it when ...!!" is different in kind from "It's annoying, frustrating, unpleasant when ... but I can cope if I do *X, Y, Z*". We might still feel stressed holding this belief, *and* explaining difficult events in this way, but we won't be *as* stressed for *as* long. Of course our beliefs need to be buttressed and supported by skills of coping in management contexts. It is the *balance* between realistic beliefs and management skill that enables less stressful, more positive coping.

A cognitive fixation about receiving respect can alter how we perceive, interpret and manage the sorts of secondary behaviours noted earlier. Whether we like it or not, we have to "earn" respect by the effectiveness of our teaching (Chapter 4), our confident management and by the effort we make to build and sustain workable relationships with our students.

Beliefs and standards

The belief "Children *must* not swear ..." is not the same as having a standard about respectful language. Having a more realistic and appropriately flexible belief about swearing – "I *don't like most swearing* however I won't let it unnecessarily stress me, while at the same time I will need to address it accordingly to situation, and circumstance" – will occasion a less stressful state of mind and (with some prior skill) enable a more effective management of swearing (see pp. 91–3).

It can help to "dispute" unhelpful, self-defeating beliefs and explanatory styles that are often couched in "must", "should" ("I *should* be able to control these kids!!"). By "reframing" the demands to preferences based in reality we tune into workable reality without "dropping our standards". We also reduce insistence-focused statements about reality ("He *must* ...", "I *must* ...", "Others *must* ...") that can increase emotional stress levels. At the end of the day, reality has no obligation to obey our demands.

This is not mere badinage. Talking, even self-talking, is an action, and actions have effects. If I say "I'm no good", that is overgeneralising. If I have a demand behind it ("I *must* get it right all the time"), I'll set an impossible pace. If, however, I say "Look, I'm having difficulty with (a given student or class group)" and "What skills and support do I need?", that is *accurate* self-talk. Being more accurate and reasonable about reality will help me in addressing my goals and managing inevitable, natural stress.

Inaccurate, inflexible, demanding and negative self-talk may become a habit. If not addressed, it may become so *characteristic* that it is no longer a conscious activity. And while past performance and past experience may have interred our characteristic self-talk, it is in the present that we are using it and in the present that changes need to be made.

The bad-day syndrome

There will be days (naturally) when normative tiredness and concerns arising from one's personal life, the issues of the day and one's state of health will affect the quality of our day-to-day teaching and behaviour management. Even those days when we just feel "out-of-sorts" will have this effect. It is easy on those days for *our* frustration to spill over into our behaviour. We may become short-tempered, snappy and even angry.

It is important to telegraph to students when we're having a bad day. "You can probably tell I'm not feeling the best today. It's not your fault. ('Well it is a bit', you might be tempted to say!) I don't want to go into it all – but I'm a bit annoyed, or cheesed off. If you see me getting a bit 'snappier' today you'll know why ..."

If we are unwell it will be important to briefly explain we've got a bad headache, or .... If it is a more personal issue it is normally unwise to share details; it is enough to just telegraph the fact we're having a bad day. Most students cannot really cope with such personal information (nor should they have to). I am amazed at how much personal information some teachers are apparently willing (and comfortable) to share with children – even primary aged children: information about their relationships, their divorce details, their financial hassles and even concerns they have about their fellow teachers!

Children enjoy the sort of sharing about childhood experiences ("When I was a boy we did ...") but it is inappropriate to use the teacher–student relationship to either "off-load" one's personal frustrations or to make students inappropriate *confidantes*.

We don't need to go into details on our bad days; it is enough to let them know so that they can have some basic awareness of how we're feeling, even occasion some sympathy with our shared humanity! Children understand that *everybody* has bad days.

There are bad days where we might say something inappropriate, or thoughtless, to a student; a throwaway line that we didn't intend to use; a sharper tone even an insensitive, churlish or petty comment. Tiredness, stress, being rushed and hurried (and harried) by others can easily chip away at our goodwill and patience. On such days we are wise and professional – human – to remember to acknowledge and apologise. Having done so, it will then be important not to engage in self-blame and to move on.

This is to be distinguished from teachers who *characteristically* discipline and manage in petulant, mean-spirited ways, destined (it seems) to create, even sustain, unnecessary anxiety or control over their students. While such teachers may still (in some schools) get "results", they do so at a great cost to student well-being and self-esteem. I have worked with teachers who have refused to forgive students (even students who have made an attempt to apologise). I have seen teachers refuse to apologise when it was the right and proper thing to do, or who nurse a grudge. They forget that we are all fallible. Such teaching and management behaviour needs (in my view) to be confronted where it exists.

Coping with our personal psychological junk-mail

Bad days, failure and self-criticism often go together. We can at times be quite hard on ourselves, unfairly hard, when we don't perform well.

I've sat and talked with teachers who, having got angry with a student or a class, say "I *shouldn't* have got angry like that ...". Why ever not? There are many situations where we will get angry with our students. Yes, there are more effective ways of managing anger than shouting or yelling, but we *did* get angry. We are not a failure for that. We can always do something about poorly handled anger (Chapter 7).

Psychological junk mail comes loaded with global, stable self-talk: "I shouldn't have" (we did); "It's not fair" (really?); "I always get it wrong" (always?); "I'll never get through to them" (never?). Maybe we shouldn't have done, or said, X, Y, Z, but we did; that's the reality. If we add to such self-talk repetitions of and ruminations about our failure ("I shouldn't!", or comments such as, "I'm an idiot", "I'm stupid, a failure") we will naturally feel worse and cope less effectively with our failure, and our struggle.

I'm not suggesting a kind of cognitive shrugging it off by saying it doesn't really matter when it does; it can hurt. It *does* matter when we fail, when we get things wrong, but repetitive self-talk (like that above) acts like psychological junk-mail and we feel worse than we need to feel.

Natural feelings of failure are normal, and even appropriate. Learning to fail meaningfully means we acknowledge our fallibility (in ourselves *and* others). Label the failure for what it is – a mistake, a lapse in judgement (even a lack of skills) – and instead of excusing the failure ask what can be learned from it: "Do I need to apologise to anyone?" (probably); "What do I need to do?"; "Do I need support or help to move beyond this?" We can learn as much, at times, from what goes wrong as what goes right (a message we frequently tell our students).

By *relabelling* failure – "OK, I did get it wrong. I should have done *X, Y, Z*" – and then asking "What can I do now and what can I do *next time* in a similar situation?", we redirect the emotional energy that can easily be eaten up by "mentally kicking oneself" (Edwards 1977). Tuning into negative self-talk is not easy; like any skill it needs to be acknowledged and practised as a kind of "norm" whenever we catch ourselves posting psychological junk-mail upstairs. Maybe we can't take control of the first thought that comes in to our head but we can *learn* to take control of subsequent thinking and internal dialogue.

We're likely to be using negative self-talk when we're experiencing emotions such as frustration, anger or on-going anxiety, or jadedness towards someone or some situation. The reason for disputing erroneous and self-defeating thinking is that it can bring about a more effective way of coping; emotional and practical coping. We will need to ask ourselves if our current thoughts, the way we explain hurtful or bad events to ourselves, is actually helping to deal with our struggle; our failure. What are the consequences, the outcome, of *this* kind of thinking?

Failure

Noel Coward once said, "The secret of success is the ability to survive failure". Professor Martin Seligman, a leading researcher on *learned* helplessness and *learned* optimism has said:

> Failure makes everyone at least *momentarily* helpless. It's like a punch in the stomach. It hurts, but the hurt goes away – for some people almost instantly … for others the hurt lasts, it seethes, it roils, it congeals into a grudge … they remain helpless for days or perhaps months, even after only small setbacks. After major defeats they may never come back.
>
> (1991: 45)

According to Seligman *learned* helplessness derives from an explanatory style that believes, and explains, difficult and bad events in several dimensions: permanence, pervasiveness and personalisations. "It's *me* … I *never* get it right … it will last *forever* … it will affect *everything* I do …".

An *optimistic explanatory style* acknowledges the annoyance, even pain, in failure, but avoids using abiding traits to explain the failure and bad events. Using qualifiers like "Yes, I do *sometimes* get it wrong", "*lately* I haven't been up to scratch with my lesson plans" and "it is *annoying* that I missed out on my promotion, so what do I need to do to improve or change? ". The more optimistic explanatory style acknowledges frustrating reality, but reframes it, seeing the failure as having transient rather than permanent and pervasive causes. Further, the optimistic explanatory style avoids recumbent self-blame, or other blame: "It's *me* …", "*I'll* never change …" and "I'll *never* get it right …". Acknowledging one's *temporary* stupidity, ineptness, laziness, lack of forethought and planning is, in short, acknowledging one's humanity!

It is the *habits* of explanation that lie at the heart of explanatory styles and personal self-talk. It is not the explanation we make in interpreting our episodic stresses; it is the *residual* explanatory style one falls back on in seeking to cope with stressful events. Seligman's research into learned helplessness and learned optimism is a positive and very practical resource in stress management and coping.

Contrast "I *never* …", "I *always* …", "I *can't* stand it …" and "*Everybody* in this class is …" with "I *sometimes* fail; *however* …", "*Some* people are *difficult* to work, with while others are not …", "It may be *difficult* (rather than "I *can't* stand it") … *but* when I …", "It *will* get better *when* …", "If I do *X* and *Y*, things will improve …" and "Even if *I've failed* I am not a failure …". Private (internal) speech has a self-guiding and self-regulatory function.

Failure doesn't mean we're *a* failure. Defining failure in global and stable terms rather that in situational and specific terms changes our perception of both ourselves and those areas in which we failed.

Adaptive, and maladaptive, thinking behaviours are learned (Rogers 1996).

You control us!

Working with a new Year 9 class once, I struggled to communicate the difficult message that it was *their* job to control *their* behaviour. Apparently their previous teacher (on stress leave) had battled with this class, week in and week out, and now it was my turn.

At the classroom meeting I conducted (p. 143), I raised the issue of their perception of "control". Many students indicated that it was "the teacher's job to control the class"; "the teacher's job to make us behave".

I asked "how?" and in the ensuing (and lively) discussion students' comments about teacher control ranged from "shouting" behaviours through to "intimidation" and "detentions". I further asked if they *liked* that kind of behaviour; and if they believed such behaviour was fair and helpful.

As we teased this out they agreed that it wasn't helpful to anyone really – being forced to behave through the "controlling" behaviour of teachers. What it amounted to is that these students effectively wanted the teachers to "control us" but part of *that* arrangement meant that they would make it a challenge for the teachers to control them: "you've got to prove you can control us". When students talk like this there is also the underlying message of security: they expect their teachers to be able to lead, manage and direct the day-to-day complexities of 25–30 students in a small room, engaged in teaching, learning and socialisation. To this extent their "cry of control" is valid; but our role is also to lead the students beyond mere simplistic, external control, to appropriate "self" and "shared" control.

It took a while but we finally managed to shift their thinking and their game-playing towards a new understanding: "As students … we control ourselves … you (our teacher) lead, guide and support us to manage ourselves. We give you that right and that responsibility to lead us in that way."

This shift is not a simple teaching exercise. Teachers need to be able to call on student cooperation through:

- shared understandings of core right and responsibilities. This was expressed through a collaborative classroom agreement. (See Chapter 2.)
- the teacher's effort to teach with some enthusiasm, skill and willingness to address a wide range of student ability and to consider a range of teaching approaches (Chapter 3).
- the teacher's effort to communicate respect and care, even when they discipline (Chapter 4).
- the teacher's willingness to reach individuals as well as class groups (even a brief effort to get to know, and assist, an individual has a powerful effect on teacher–student cooperation).

I have many, many times discussed the issue of teacher management and discipline with students. They seem very able to sum up how confident, sure, "together", able and so on a teacher is. They seem to gain this knowledge by *how* a teacher *initially* expresses themselves in a management, discipline and sense, and how effectively the teacher manages to teach (Chapters 2 and 3). Those first impressions, in those first meetings in front of the group largely determine how the group defines the teacher's subsequent role.

As one student wrote about taking teachers on the first impression:

When you can see that you can get away with things with a teacher you often be stupid and go to other people's desks and don't take any notice of them (the teacher ...)

This student is saying, in effect, that a "good" teacher needs to control the *situation* in which students behave. They normally then discuss (as this student does) how and why students do (or don't) "take notice" of teachers. Having notice taken of one's leadership and authority is primarily related to how relaxed one appears, how confident one's leadership style appears when *encouraging* and *directing* group and individual behaviour.

One's confidence is increased by having a plan for those first meetings. This is discussed in the section on the establishment phase (p. 25f.) and in the later section on language skills of behaviour management (p. 55) and effective teaching (p. 75f.).

Don't smile until Christmas

This is not the clearest maxim! I remember being told a version of this years ago. *Imagine* standing in front of a group (in the corridor or in the classroom) with a tense, frowning, face – heavy impatient breathing – rocking back and forth on the toes ...

Such non-verbal behaviour will more than anything indicate a lack of confidence in one's authority and "status". It may even provoke unnecessary, contestable behaviour in some of our students. If a teacher stands in front of a class group looking anxious, arms folded in a protective – closed – body language, or a hesitant and sheepish smile that says, in effect, "please be nice to me ...", students may well read "indecisiveness", "non-assertion" or lack of confidence.

A confident, pleasant, relaxed smile, *while* we are communicating (not a sycophantic smile) can telegraph a *potential* confidence in student cooperation.

Of course, what the maxim is meant to say is that one needs to be firm and clear at the outset in those first meetings about behaviour and learning. There is truth in this. It is much harder to reclaim unfocused, off-task, behaviour than to *establish* positive, clear, norms from day one – first meeting.

I have heard many teachers say that they, in effect, "lost" the class because they tried to be "too friendly" from the first meeting.

The 70–80%

I have seen teachers lose the goodwill and potential cooperation of most of the class by the way they treat individuals and the group. Some teachers are surprised when the bulk of the class becomes resentful if the teacher treats any *one* individual with characteristic disrespect or unresolved conflict. I have seen teachers use whole-class detentions to seek to put pressure on several disruptive students only to initially frustrate and then alienate the 70–80% when they continue to use such detentions.

While it is natural to get frustrated by some individuals in a class group we need the cooperation of the 70–80% to successfully manage and support the 20–30% of more difficult or challenging students.

What we can, and can't "control"

When I write, here in this book, about managing or disciplining students I'm not speaking about *controlling* the students; the ease, the facility, with which we say, "I *made* the student put his hand up …", or "I *took* the student aside and told him to …". We can't simply *make* a student do anything, or *take* a student anywhere, unless of course he or she is either naturally cooperative, highly compliant, or obedient, or unquestioningly compliant or obedient (which are not necessarily healthy traits at all). I have always discouraged my own children to "simply obey your teacher because they are a teacher". (Mind you – I've taught them skilful ways to address unfair or even unjust teaching behaviour.)

Rather than asking myself how can I more effectively control "my" students, it is more appropriate, and much more constructive, to ask "How can I be a more effective teacher and manager?" and "What can I do to bring more effective control to the teaching situation and learning context?" The way I manage myself, and my thinking and attitude (p. 17), have a significant (even lasting) effect on how students behave (cooperatively or uncooperatively) when I am with them.

The approaches, and skills, developed in this book are a means to *that* end.

Intent and relationships

Students hear and see the teacher's intention in a teacher's discipline and management behaviour. If the *intention* read is one where the teacher is perceived as wanting to embarrass, shame or "hurt" the child then the acceptance of such discipline will be resented and often lead to an unworkable teacher–student relationship. For example, where a teacher emphasises the severity of the consequence, rather than the certainty, then that is all the child will focus on (p. 99).

If it is our intention to enable a student to take responsibility for his or her behaviour and to actively consider others' rights, and if our discipline has that as its aim, the child will more likely hear and see that intention in the kind of language and manner we use. The degree of cooperation, even compliance, also depends on the kind of relationship existing between teacher and student.

In the establishment phase of the year the teacher is seeking to build a workable relationship with the whole class, as a group, and also with the individuals. Even deceptively mundane expressions of humanity such as learning (and using) a student's name (at all times), positive greetings to the group and individuals (even out of class), remembering aspects and details of their individuality (a student's hobbies, special interests, events, and birthdays) are all indicators of a teacher's effort to build and sustain positive working relationships.

Being pleasant (not sycophantic) to unlikable students, going out of one's way to say "hello" (to an unreturned or muttered response), not holding grudges and starting each day afresh are all aspects of relational teacher behaviour that children soon acknowledge, affirm and respond to in a positive way.

When students get to know that you care about them as individuals, (as persons with needs, concerns, feelings) then the teacher's discipline is judged and accepted within the understanding that the teacher cares about them.

Building relationships

It is, generally speaking, the positive relationships we develop with our students that we remember long after they have forgotten the history of the Tudors or positive and negative integers. I've often asked my own children, "What was maths (or French, or history) like today?" Sometimes they'll talk about the subject matter, but more often they talk about the *kind* of teacher they have and what happens in the relational dynamics of the classroom. My children have quickly "sorted" out which teachers can manage which classes (and why); which teachers teach well (and interestingly); which are fair and considerate; and which are normally patient, have a sense of humour and, above all, care.

I went to a high school in St Albans for six months (aged 15). I was running late for science class one morning. The bus was late. I arrived at the classroom door huffing and puffing, anxious because Mr Brown was not the most empathetic teacher in the school. Entering the classroom I saw a *new* teacher; a supply teacher. He approached me at the door, smiling, and said, "You look a bit puffed out ..." (I'd been running). "I'm Mr Ryland. What's your name?" His tone and manner immediately put me at ease. He spoke to me quietly, away from the door (and the immediate hearing of others). "Who do you normally sit next to?" Having told him I sat next to Roger, he explained we were doing an experiment on Archimedes' principle (displacement of water). "Roger will fill you in, eh? Catch your breath. I'll come over and see how you're going later." Not only did I feel better (less anxious and less embarrassed) but I was also more motivated in a subject that wasn't a favourite). Not only did I remember Archimedes' principle, but I remembered the difference a teacher can make to how one feels and works.

Contrast Mr Ryland's treatment of my lateness and this account from my oldest daughter when she was in high school (Year 9).

Vicki and I were sitting on the wall (where we usually wait for the lift home from Vicki's grandpa) at the end of the school day. Miss Green (Vicki's maths teacher) came over to us and said, "Have you made any effort to get that maths book yet?" And before Vicki could answer she said, "No, I don't think you have. I told you to wait behind on Friday and someone told me you *only* waited 5 minutes!"

"I couldn't wait because my Grandpa didn't know I was staying behind and he would be worried."

I chipped in at this point, trying to help out. "And it's a bit hard to stay behind because we go home in a car pool."

And Miss Green said, "I don't think this has anything to do with you! I don't think you know what this is about so I think you should just keep out of this!"

Well I just shut up (being the generally angelic and compliant student I am) but the truth is I knew a damn sight more than she did and instantly made up my mind I did not like this teacher.

A colleague of mine found this missive on the worldwide graffiti board (you know – the Internet). It describes so well the normative frustrations of a teacher; frustrations that even Jesus must have felt.

The joy of teaching

Then Jesus took his disciples up the mountain and gathering them around him, He taught them saying:
Blessed are the poor in spirit, for theirs is the kingdom of heaven.
Blessed are the meek.
Blessed are they that mourn.
Blessed are the merciful.
Blessed are they that thirst for justice.
Blessed are you when persecuted.
Blessed are you when you suffer.
Be glad and rejoice for your reward is great in heaven.
Then Simon Peter said, "Are we supposed to know this?"
And Andrew said, "Do we have to write this down?"
And James said, "Will we have a test on this?"
And Phillip said, "I don't have any paper."
And Bartholomew said, "Do we have to turn this in?"
And John said, "The other disciples didn't have to learn this."
And Matthew said, "May I go to the toilet?"
Then one of the Pharisees who was present asked to see Jesus's lesson plan and inquired of Jesus, "Where is your anticipatory set and your objectives in the cognitive domain?"
And Jesus wept.

(Anon)

Chapter 2

New class, new year: the establishment phase of behaviour management

Habits change into characters.
Ovid (45BC – AD17)

New year, new class, new start

As you stand in your classroom on the one, pupil-free day, before Day 1, Term 1, you scan the room and furniture (sometimes inadequate and uncomfortable). You think, "Tomorrow there will be 25–30 students in here, each with their unique personality, temperament and needs. Phew!"

For some of you it will be your first class "on your own" as it were; for others it will be another fresh new year that (at times) will soon develop into the daily, hourly, minute-by-minute juggle of demands that make up normative teaching.

Most teachers can remember their first class – and even their entire first day.

One of the important, fundamental, questions at this stage of the year is "What can I do (and what can we do as a collegial team) to *minimise*, and prevent (where possible), unnecessary hassles or problems in establishing positive behaviours in our classes?"

The answer to this question will focus on the necessary procedures, routines and rules to enable the smooth running of quite a complex community. It will be important to integrate routines and rules into a workable system and then consciously teach that system through discussion, modelling, encouragement and teacher-management.

There is ample research to show that effective and positive teachers are acutely conscious of the importance of the first lesson, the first few days, the first few weeks and how they establish the shared rights and responsibilities of classroom behaviour with their students (see Doyle 1986; Kyriacou 1986, 1991; Rogers 1997, 1998; McInerney and McInerney 1998; Robertson 1997).

Establishment phase (practices and skills)

The establishment phase of the year is a crucial time in the development of a class group (and even the school as community). In terms of basic group dynamics there is a psychological and developmental readiness in the students for their teacher to explain how things will be *this* particular year with regard to expectations about behaviour and learning. The three basic phases of the life of a classroom community are set out in Figure 2.1

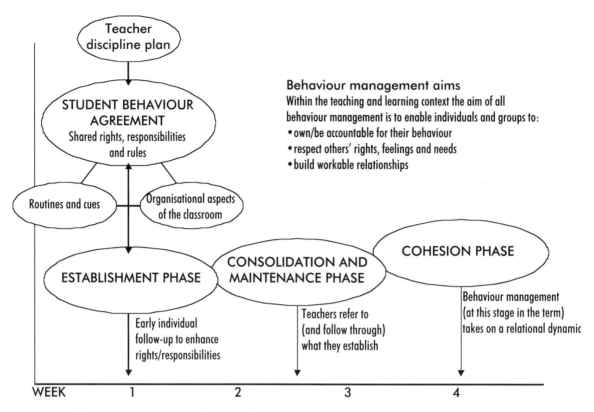

Figure 2.1 The fundamental phases of life in a classroom

Students expect their teacher to clarify:

- Lining up and room entry procedures.
- Seating plans and student grouping for Week 1, and possibly Term 1. Such planning needs to include whether seating should occur in rows, pairs or table groups.
- Student entry to class and settling at workplaces or "carpet space" for infants. Cues will need to be explained, modelled and monitored. With infants, it will also be important to explain, and model, personal space, place when "on the carpet" and keeping hands and feet to oneself (although adolescents can benefit from a clear message about testosteronic bonding also!)
- Organisation of locker space/place. At primary age level where locker trays are in the classroom, consideration needs to be given to how they are sited for ease of student movement.
- Use of cues for whole class discussion and questions.
- Use of teacher cue(s) to initiate whole class attention at any stage.
- Appropriate movement patterns between instructional and on-task learning time (transitions).
- Use of appropriate cues to get teacher assistance during the on-task phase of the lesson/activity.
- Routines for tidying work space/place.
- Cues and procedures for lesson closure and exit from the classroom.

These are, of course, the basic – foundational – routines/cues. Teachers also need to establish routines for lunch (dinner times), for monitor systems, for home-work procedures, distribution of notices, use of school diaries, quiet reading time procedures, toilet/drink rules, dealing with students who are frequently

(rather than incidentally) late to class, and so on. Most schools plan such routines and procedures on a team, or faculty, basis.

When raising student awareness about behaviour and learning (and their impact on each other) we need to emphasise the fundamentals of our learning community:

- "We share the same place, time, space, resources, every day. We have to learn to get on with each other for our own good and the good of others and to help each other in our learning here."
- "Everyone here is individual – we have our own feelings, needs, concerns."
- "As we would want others to think about us and our feelings so we, in turn …"
- "The rights and responsibilities we *all* share here: the right to be treated with respect, the right to learn, the right to feel safe here …"

It can help to discuss with students the common issues and concerns about shared space, time and resources, and basic, respectful relationships. With younger children, a practical discussion on basic manners will be initially important (and revisited many times in the first few weeks): "please"; "thank-you"; "excuse me"; "asking if you want to borrow …"; "giving/putting things back where we borrowed …"; "sharing and cooperative behaviour …". For some children the classroom environment (notably at infant level) presents expectations and norms of behaviour they are not used to, or that they do not easily accommodate to; it can help to run mini role-plays on manners and helping behaviours.

These early discussions about behaviour and learning can be developed into a *student behaviour agreement* that can form the basis for the teacher's behaviour management and discipline on the one hand, and student–teacher cooperation on the other.

Developing a student behaviour agreement with the class: rights, responsibilities and rules.

Many schools now develop classroom behaviour agreements in the first week or two of the school year. Building on the natural readiness, and expectation of students (about teachers developing rules and routines), grade teachers set aside some classroom time to develop a more collaborative model of classroom management through the establishment of shared rights and responsibilities. Students participate, with their teachers, in an agreement addressing common rights, responsibilities and rules for behaviour and learning, core consequences for unacceptable behaviour and a framework of support to assist students when they are struggling with their behaviour and learning (Fig. 2.2).

At secondary age level such an agreement is best developed by tutor (or form) teachers who set aside one full timetabled period early in the first week to discuss, with their form groups, the key understandings about behaviour and learning (Fig. 2.2). A common framework for such discussions across all form groups is noted in Figure 2.2. Once established such an agreement forms the basis on which subject and specialist teachers can fine-tune rules and routines pertinent to particular needs and contexts.

This agreement is published within the first fortnight of Term 1 and a copy is sent home to each family. At the primary level this classroom agreement (sometimes called a behaviour plan) has a cover page with a photo of the grade teacher and the students (Fig. 2.3).

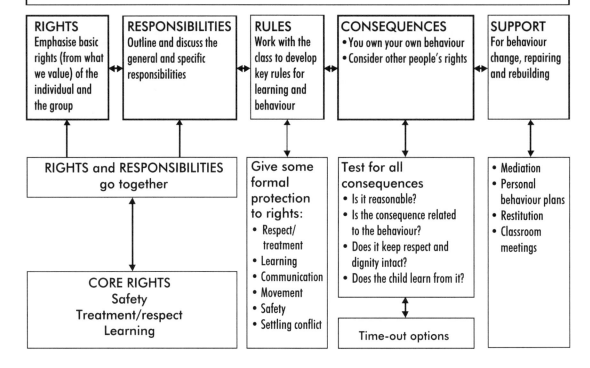

AWARENESS RAISING
Discuss with the class the issue relating to (concerns about) behaviour and effect on learning. Invite their understanding, cooperation and support for the need for a common plan or agreement

RIGHTS
Emphasise basic rights (from what we value) of the individual and the group

RESPONSIBILITIES
Outline and discuss the general and specific responsibilities

RULES
Work with the class to develop key rules for learning and behaviour

CONSEQUENCES
• You own your own behaviour
• Consider other people's rights

SUPPORT
For behaviour change, repairing and rebuilding

RIGHTS and RESPONSIBILITIES go together

CORE RIGHTS
Safety
Treatment/respect
Learning

Give some formal protection to rights:
• Respect/treatment
• Learning
• Communication
• Movement
• Safety
• Settling conflict

Test for all consequences
• Is it reasonable?
• Is the consequence related to the behaviour?
• Does it keep respect and dignity intact?
• Does the child learn from it?

Time-out options

• Mediation
• Personal behaviour plans
• Restitution
• Classroom meetings

PUBLISH the outcome as a classroom agreement (behaviour) plan for students and teachers. Use user friendly language and include a class photo. Send copies to the administration office and to parents

Figure 2.2 Class agreement – behaviour plan (adapted from Rogers 1997: 41)

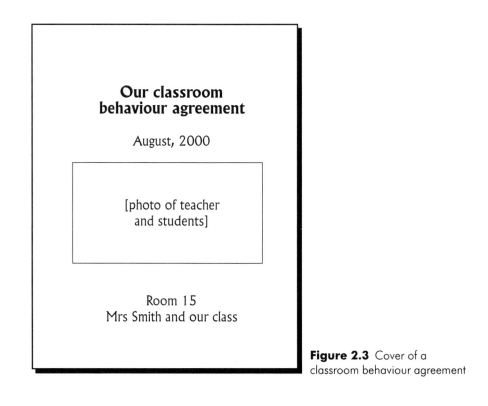

Our classroom behaviour agreement

August, 2000

[photo of teacher and students]

Room 15
Mrs Smith and our class

Figure 2.3 Cover of a classroom behaviour agreement

Any classroom based (or year-level) behaviour agreement needs to reflect the values and aims of the whole-school policy on behaviour. The advantage of a classroom based policy or agreement, notably at primary and middle-school level, is that it raises a school-wide awareness and consciousness about behaviour, learning, and relationships, and does so in a class-by-class, age-related and developmental way. This gives reasonable school-wide consistency on the common, and essential, aspects of behaviour policy.

A framework for such a plan or policy is set out in Figure 2.2. Each teacher, from infants to junior, junior to senior, follows the same framework, modifying the language and concepts to age and comprehension so that all students across the school share the same understandings.

The process is as important as the outcome. On the first day the class teacher sets aside time to raise whole-class awareness about behaviour and learning, inviting student participation, understanding and cooperation for a plan or agreement about fair and proper behaviour that enhances positive working relationships and learning. Some teachers will take a more discursive approach, perhaps through a classroom meeting (or circle time); other teachers are more comfortable with a formal approach that outlines the key areas of the plan and invites student discussion.

The policy, plan or agreement begins with a general statement:

"Our behaviour plan has been discussed and developed by the children and the teacher in Year [X]. It is a record of how we seek to behave towards each other. It applies to all the people who come into our class and will be used throughout the school year."

Our common rights

The key elements of a student behaviour agreement

Non-negotiable rights are the basis of a classroom agreement: the right to feel safe at school; the right to learn; and the right to be treated with respect. Rights such as the right to play, the right to equality, the right to have my say, the right to be an individual and the right to teach are all subsumed within these core rights. These core rights are based on the value of mutual regard, without which no group or community could effectively cohere and work together for mutual benefit. A right, in this sense, is that which we believe is fair, *right*, and proper about the way we should relate and work together.

Even very young children have an emerging concept of fundamental "rightness". Obviously they behave in contradistinction to that rightness (as do we all), but they hold to it strongly. It is the "natural law".

Simply stating that we have a right to something is not the same as enjoying that right.

We might include in our policy, for example:

The right to safety doesn't just mean being safe – it is about feeling safe too. Put-downs, cheap shots at others, excluding others on purpose, harassment and swearing are all ways that take away someone's right to feel safe here.   (From a Year 6 classroom agreement)

In this sense rights imply, and necessitate, responsibilities. If we have a right to learn it implies that the teacher enables the best – most effective – learning that is *reasonably* possible. (This further implies that when we're tired, and it's cold and wet, and we're stuck in the "excuse for a classroom" that looks like a shed we still do our best.)

In discussing these rights with our students we provide a common focus for the way that we look at, understand and address behaviour.

Responsibilities flow from our rights

Individual and group responsibilities overlap:

> Shared responsibilities mean that we care for ourselves and others here. Responsibilities and respect go together; when we respect others we are thinking about how our behaviour affects others.

Whole class "brainwaving" ("surfing the collective brain space" sounds less violent than brain*storming*) will quickly elicit norms about the responsibility to, for example: get to class on time; have the relevant materials; share (ideas, resources and even our time); do one's best; help out; listen to others; manage our whole class noise level(!). A discussion on responsibilities will also need to address respect in terms of basic manners. Basics such as saying please and thank-you, asking when we borrow, returning when you've finished, saying excuse me when moving around others, being aware and respectful of others, allowing personal space, using first names (rather than 'he', 'she' or 'them'), taking turns, lining up without pushing, and so on, are all aspects of self-awareness as we interact with others day after day.

The *core* responsibilities can be summed up in cooperative and respectful behaviour: the consideration of others as well as oneself.

Rules: protecting rights and encouraging responsibility

The primary purpose of a rule is to give a formal, recognised and public protection to one's rights. Fair rules also highlight and encourage one's responsibility.

In the first few weeks teachers can be heard across all classes, using rule-reminders: "remember *our* rule for asking questions", "*We've* got a rule about respectful language". In the playground teachers will be heard going up to students inviting some cognitive, behavioural awareness, by asking questions such as, "What's *our* rule about playing ball games?" and "What's *our* rule for safe play on the climbing frame?"

In framing rules it is important to remember some basics:

1. Have rules that focus on the core rights: a safe place and safe behaviour; a respectful place and respectful behaviour through the way we treat others; a learning place where we give our best and cooperate to learn. Rules should be few in number but address the necessary behaviours. I have seen classrooms where teachers have posted 20 or more rules on the wall; rules often stated negatively ("You must not ...", "You shall not ...", "You can't ...") and not outlining the desired behaviour. Simply telling a child what he should *not* do is hardly helpful; a helpful rule should at least contain the negative within a positive. For example, "In whole-class learning time we put our hand up to ask questions and to contribute (the positive rule) *without calling out* (the negative caveat).

   I have usually found it helpful to have 4–6 rules covering:
   - treatment (courtesy, manners, respect);
   - communication (hands up, "partner-voices", positive language, active listening);
   - learning (cooperation and support, use of resources, how to fairly utilise teacher assistance);
   - movement (walking not running, orderly entry/exit to classroom, personal space, sensible movement);
   - problem solving (settling problems peacefully, using teacher assistance, using classroom meetings for resolving common concerns).

2. Express the rules behaviourally and positively where possible:

> To show *respect* in our classroom we are courteous, and use our manners. We use positive language with each other. This means no teasing or put-downs.

> When we solve problems in our classroom we talk it over or ask the teacher to help. We do not fight with words or fists or feet. If we fight we will have to go to time-out.

It can help highlight the key behaviour focus of the rule by having a rule heading such as: Our *communication* rule; Our *respect* rule; Our *learning* rule; Our *safety* rule.

3. Use inclusive language in framing the rules: "In *our* classroom *we* …".
4. Publish the rules in both the classroom agreement and on bright classroom posters (even at middle-school level). This can help with a teacher's verbal reminders about appropriate behaviour. Cartoon motifs can help the visual effect of the posters. At infant level teachers can further illustrate the relevant behaviour through photographs attached to the rule poster.

Consequences Students need to know that consequences follow inappropriate and irresponsible behaviour. Consequences are directly related to rules and rights. Students will need to understand that when a rule is broken, in effect a right is affected or even abused.

If a student is *repeatedly* disruptive by calling out, butting-in, talking really loudly, interfering with others' workspace or materials or acting unsafely or aggressively, he or she is affecting others' rights to learn and, of course, the teacher's right to teach. The necessary, fair, and appropriate consequence in such a case will need to be "time-out" (in-class or even out-of-class) (see p. 100).

Students, therefore, can (temporarily) lose their right to be a part of the learning community through a consequence such as time-out.

Students need to know that beyond rule reminders (as a verbal consequence) they may be: directed to work away from others; take cool-off-time or be directed (even escorted) from the classroom for time-out; stay back to discuss their behaviour with their teacher; or stay back after class time to "fix-things-up"; be directed into a mediation process; or be part of a parent/teacher/student meeting.

All consequences operate on a least-to-most intrusive basis. Students need to know they will always have an appropriate right-of-reply as part of the consequence process (see p. 73).

Support of students

It is important to balance the *corrective* and *consequential* aspects of the classroom agreement with the offer of teacher support (Fig. 2.2). Here is an example of support from a Year 5/6 (composite) classroom behaviour agreement.

Supporting each other in our classroom

There are many ways we can support each other here. Most of all we support others when we take time to think about others – to help, encourage and cooperate. Of course there are days when things don't go right; we recognise this. It is important though, to explain to your teacher, or classmate, when you're having a "bad-day". If we don't let others know they might get confused as to why we look (or sound) annoyed, upset, or angry.

Sometimes we have concerns, worries or problems outside and inside school. It can help to talk about this. Your teacher or school counsellor is always willing to help in any way we can.

If we are making poor choices, or wrong choices about our behaviour our teacher will help us with:

- discussing our behaviour;
- personal behaviour plans;
- a chance to put things right (restitution) – sometimes we may need to put things right by talking things through with a fellow student (mediation).

On some occasions our parents may need to be involved in helping us with our behaviour at school.

Many teachers also include an extended note (in the classroom agreement) on classroom meetings (circle time). Some parents may not be aware of this concept so a brief note about the positive and educational features of classroom meetings will assist in the understanding of basic classroom democracy:

We have regular classroom meetings (circle time) in grade [X]. These meetings give all students an opportunity to explore common concerns, needs and problems. These meetings allow shared understandings, active problem solving and student-assisted solutions to common issues of concern.

The last page of the classroom agreement is signed by the students and their grade/tutor/form teacher:

We have discussed, drafted and edited our behaviour agreement with our teacher. We agree to use it and support it.

The classroom behaviour agreement is a document for parents as well as students. A copy will be sent to all parents/caregivers of all children in each grade or class group. A covering letter from the headteacher goes home with the classroom agreement/plan.

Dear _____ ,

This behaviour agreement has been discussed, and developed, by the teacher and the children in Year 6 … It outlines the way we address behaviour and learning in our school. We ask you to read through this agreement/plan with your son/daughter. We look forward to your understanding and support this year …

As the year plods on, all behaviour issues are, one way or another, referred back to this behaviour agreement.

Non-negotiable rules and consequences

There are rules, in a school, that are non-negotiable across all ages – all classes. These relate to issues such as health and safety, aggression, bullying and violent behaviour. These rules need to be made known in the first meetings with students, in the school diary, in classroom agreements and school policies.

For example in Australian schools there is a "no hat, no outside play" rule in the hot summer months. It is a rule directly related to health and safety.

When schools have a common framework for classroom behaviour agreements, each successive year group becomes increasingly conscious of "the way we do things here", enabling some sense of common understandings and expectations about appropriate and fair behaviour and also some reasonable consistency in behaviour management by adults across the school.

As noted earlier, there are several phases in the ongoing life of a class group (p. 26). If the teacher has thoughtfully established "the way we need to work here", and has developed positive routines and rules for classroom learning and social interaction, the class, as a group, becomes habituated into workably cohesive "norms".

Cohesive phase During the "cohesive" phase, the routines and rules become the norm; "the way we do things here". At the beginning of each term we might need to revisit the student behaviour agreement (p. 27) and some of the routines (such as noise monitoring) that we have established in the first few weeks. Students "forget" during term breaks, or are "resocialised" in non-school settings. A brief and positive re-establishment can help start each term with a shared focus.

In this phase of the year, most of our behaviour management occurs within a *relational dynamic*. Hopefully we have built a positive working relationship with the individuals as well as the group. We rely less on the rules and routines now and the students are more self-aware and self-directed in their behaviour and learning. Students are taking appropriate "ownership" of classroom life.

During these phases, teachers can utilise classroom meetings (circle time) to discuss issues relevant to individual and group needs and concerns.

Communicating the rules to students

In communicating the necessary rules to students it is important to emphasise the purpose of rules: protection of rights and expectation of basic responsibilities.

In communicating the rules to a new class group (or year group) some teachers are more directive – outlining the expected rules, their reasons, and the normal consequences when rules are broken. Other teachers are more discursive in their approach, emphasising shared dialogue and engaging a *process* of agreement (Fig. 2.2). Some teachers begin the year with a classroom meeting (circle time at infant level)and use the meeting to address the need for rules and consequences.

The approach taken will depend, in part, on one's comfort zone about class dialogue and classroom discussion. I have been in schools where the rules are read out almost perfunctorily by tutor teachers, or (more pedestrian) the students are directed to read the rules in the school diary – full stop.

If your preference is for a more directive approach to communicating the rules it will be beneficial (at least) to gives the reasons for the rules and invite student questions.

Visual reminding of routines and rules

In the establishment phase of the year the process of rule encouragement and maintenance can be assisted by visual posting of key rules and routines (p. 31). At infant and early years levels these could include:

- A photo and name card can be used for coat hooks.
- The key classroom rules can be illustrated as a visual *aide-mémoire* posted in a prominent place at the front of the classroom. So could routines such as: partner-voice (working noise), what to do when you have finished the set work, how to set out a piece of writing, and use of wet areas.
- At infant level teachers often take photos of the children working cooperatively – tidying the room, communicating respectfully, sharing cooperatively, – and these photos are displayed with the relevant rules the teacher has established.
- I have seen teachers use a name board with an in/out space for students who need to leave the room to use the toilet/washroom.
- Simple signs for cupboards, quiet areas and the library corner enable association of place, space and purpose.
- I have even used simple posters to remind students at *secondary* level about tidying work space: chairs under table; straightening furniture; chairs *on* tables at the end of the day; cleaning up any residual litter; and leaving the room in an orderly way (p. 51).
- Baskets can be used for "finished work here", and there can be an "early finishers box" with worksheets or activities.
- A noise-meter can be used to establish and monitor working noise (p. 48).

Discussing rules within the wider social context

When discussing rules with students (even up to Year 8) it can help to discuss them within the students' experience of rules in many different places and contexts: the highway code, clubs they belong to, road signs, their families, and even board games. The purpose of and reasons for fair rules can be helpfully discussed within these familiar contexts and a natural transition of understanding can be made to the classroom and playground.

Students have already learned that rules *help* govern behaviour, *help* protect people (at least potentially) and *encourage* shared responsibility (thinking of others), and, when broken, rules occasion consequences. They have seen the yellow card used with adult footballers (and they have also seen adult footballers throw tantrums).

Maintenance and consolidation

It is crucial to maintain and consolidate the rules and routines that are established Day 1, Week 1 (Fig. 2.1). Effective teaching and management in the establishment phase also includes planning for the typical disruptions to day-to-day teaching and learning and developing a workable "system" for the smooth running of the classroom in terms of behaviour and learning. (This is discussed in Chapters 3 and 4.)

Simply stating, or even publishing, fair rules and routines is not enough. Teachers need consciously to address issues and behaviour such as lateness, unsuitable noise levels, calling out, time off-task and task avoidance and inappropriate language on a day-to-day basis until there are "norms" of expected behaviour present in the classroom life and learning.

A teacher's discipline plan (pp. 56, 57) forms a key feature of a workable system that thinks through typical (or likely) disruptions and plans the sorts of responses (even one's language) that are likely to invite student cooperation – not as a formulaic system but rather as an enabling framework.

None of us would ever teach a lesson or activity without some kind of plan, but I'm still surprised by how many teachers continue to teach without planning for typical distracting and disruptive behaviours that can affect the quality of teaching and learning.

As noted earlier (p. 27) students expect the teacher to clarify rules, routines and cues in terms of "how things are expected to be here ...". It is important to thoughtfully plan how we will communicate, establish and monitor these rules, routines and cues, not as an end in themselves (teacher control), but as a means to an end (teacher–student cooperation in a shared learning community). In this sense this establishing *enables* effective management, teaching and learning.

Seating plans and student grouping

When planning room organisation we will need to ask what the purpose of the physical seating layout serves ('U' shaped, rows, pairs, table groups) and also student placement (who sits where and with whom).

In some classes, allowing friendship groups on Day 1 may create unhelpful power cliques and habituated patterns of behaviour that are difficult to refocus later in the term. While it is important that teachers allow some freedom in seating arrangements, this freedom is better given later in Term 1.

On Day 1 it will assist in general management to have students seated in random allocation (with a name sticker on each table). This allows easy learning of students' names by the teacher and allows some early classroom socialisation outside the natural friendship groupings. Random allocation may also need to include gender mix and, possibly, ability mix. Also if we know that some students do not work or relate well together that knowledge will need to be translated into student seating arrangements.

In a Year 7 class I worked with recently two students who had robust and motoric expressions of ADD had promised their teacher that they would work well if they sat together. "Really Miss! We'll be good if we sit together please Miss; please!!" It was a time-wasting mistake. After several frustrating promises we relocated their seating arrangements, and moved the whole class into rows. They settled down and actually became more focused in their learning behaviour.

While socialisation is an important feature of classroom life and learning, it is also important that the students understand, from Day 1, that the classroom is not merely an extension of playground socialisation; *this* place is set aside for teaching and learning. Some children are very easily distracted, for example, when sitting in table groups, so in the establishment phase of the year it may be wiser to use a more formal seating plan (rows, or paired seating, facing the front) to minimise unnecessary distraction.

Simply placing the students in table groups does not facilitate (of itself) cooperative learning behaviour. It can help to use small group seating for more focused cooperative activities and retain seating in rows for the core teaching and learning activities.

I have seen many teachers give up the positive benefits of cooperative learning by early expectations that table group seating will, of itself, engage cooperative learning; it won't. Cooperative learning needs to be structured, and taught, over time and is normally more effective when the class is more relationally cohesive.

Welfare of our students (establishment phase)

Students new to a school can often be anxious about settling in, particularly at reception level and first year at high school. It is important for teachers to be aware of and considerate for a student's natural concerns about how they will fit in; whether other students will accept and befriend them; whether they will be able to cope with the demands of the work, the timetable, the different teachers. In short whether and how they will "belong". The need to belong, to feel accepted and part of a group, is an important aspect of day-to-day existence at school.

Even basic considerations such as who they will be asked to sit next to and for how long (will it be every lesson?) can concern some students. It can be helpful to rotate seating pairs, or groups, over the first few weeks to enable basic group befriending. It is also important to keep an eye on students who appear to be loners or students who have difficulty befriending others, particularly at play-times and in sports sessions. Many primary schools (and some secondary schools) now have "buddy" programmes for reception age, for pupils in Year 8 (transitional year) and for students new to a school. Older students take on a peer support role that enables the younger (or new) student to settle into the classroom group and social climate of a playground. The "peer-buddy" receives basic training beyond the natural skills and personality that equip them for such a role.

Group activities that involve games, activities and discussions, can all assist in the settling-in process and in terms of getting to know each other. Name games can sometimes lose their novelty at upper primary level but a basic seat-rotation and getting-to-know-you time can enable a *basic* sense of group cohesion and bonding.

One's welfare obligations to one's students are not confined to primary teachers. As part of a secondary year level team, the house heads and year advisors (home-room tutors) have a particular responsibility to liaise with subject colleagues to keep the lines of communication open about how their students are coping with settling in.

When seating plans don't work

I've worked with teachers who have allowed the friendship-seating option to create little coteries or cliques; the row of students down the back whose *esprit de corps* creates contestable, time-wasting, behaviours; the little group of girls (or boys) who won't let anyone else sit with them.

I've found it helpful in such situations to change the seating plan by partial cooperation with the students. The teacher's concern about noise-level, and time off-task (as it relates to learning) is briefly set out in a *pro forma* with an invitation to assist in a seat change :-

> As your teacher I am concerned about the level of noise, and time off-task, during class work-time. I believe a change of seating-plan will help. I would appreciate your cooperation. Please write down the names of two students you know who will make it easier for you to get on with your classwork and get the best benefit out of your time in this class/subject.
> While all fair suggestions will be taken on-board I will be the final umpire. I will let you know next class period.
> Thanks for your co-operation.
>
> Mr Rogers.

This needs to be developed in a spirit of good-will wherever possible. With a particularly difficult class it can help to have a supportive colleague come in and conduct the exercise with you (see also p. 142).

The first meeting with the students

The first meeting at secondary level is normally in the corridor (outside the classroom). I've had some students in more challenging classes immediately start hassling me: "Who're you?", "What's yer name?", "You going to be our teacher today?", "Eh ... where's Mr Smith ...? He was our teacher last time – he's a donk!" (guffaws). Several students are talking over each other and there's some pushing, shoving or playful "testosteronic bonding".

I've seen teachers enter into long time-wasting responses to such group banter; smiling and answering their questions, no doubt hoping they are building an early friendly relationship. The students' definition is different; they are seeking to define how they will "work" the teacher–student relationship.

It is wiser to tactically ignore most of the multi-student banter and questions with a brief, polite statement: "I'm not answering personal questions – now. We need to be ready to go into our classroom. Thanks." Our tone is pleasant, but

I did this drawing of a middle-school class arriving outside their classroom. The girl on the right, Donna, is letting the group know who the new teacher is: "Yooooo, Mr Rogers. I seen you before in another class. Yoooooo, Mr Rogers!" She had a "notice me" kind of voice, often used in wearing teachers down. I tactically ignored her. Be careful when tactically ignoring that you don't enjoy it too much!

businesslike, enabling some group "attentional focus" by a relaxed, non-verbal, "blocking hand" indicating such questioning is not on the agenda *now*. Direct group attention quickly so that the core business (teaching and learning) becomes the immediate focus, rather than whether you have a boyfriend, or are married or are new here, and so on.

As Robertson (1997) reminds us, it is important to *define* the first meeting(s) in your own terms as teacher; to be confidently secure; pleasantly firm, without any overtones of "force", perception of threat or perceptible anxiety.

The brief "corridor-settling" by the teacher conveys the change in pace and setting: between *outside* the classroom (play, high motoric, noisy, behaviour, which is natural and OK for the playground) to *inside* (quieter, sitting – mostly focused thinking, cooperating in our learning and social interaction). It will be important to create (even here) an expectant tone, quickly, before going into the classroom.

Scanning the group outside the classroom the teacher will often have some expectation of "lining up" or "considerate one-at-a-time entry" to the classroom. A *reminder* to this effect can calm and focus natural student restlessness:

> "Settling down everyone (…). Before we go into our classroom I notice a few hats on; if you have a personal stereo on remember we're going into a classroom learning environment. Thank you." The teacher smiles and nods as he gives brief, positive, feedback to the individuals as they settle. "When we go in I want you to remember …" Here the teacher briefly outlines the protocol about where students will sit, where their bags go, and so on.

Teacher confidence and authority

Robertson (1997) notes that "relaxed behaviour" is consistent with "high-status" and also implies that one is not threatened. Of course we may have natural anxiety but we need to project an approach, a manner, that in effect says, "I expect your cooperation and compliance in student behaviour". Of course such a leadership style needs to convey respect, good-will and humanity.

When a teacher's manner, body language, posture and communication appear confident and authoritative, and when such confidence is further maintained in both teaching and management, students are likely to cooperate with the teacher's leadership.

There is a reciprocity at work here:

> If the teacher feels confident the pupils are noticeably more responsive and this in turn reinforces his own assurance; if the teacher lacks confidence, the process can begin in reverse and he can quickly become thoroughly demoralised.
> (Robertson 1997: 66)

Confidence (not cockiness) is a crucial feature in the teacher's overall communication with a group of students.

Confidence, in part, derives from being well prepared and knowing what one intends to teach (Chapter 3) but it also derives from one's characteristic presentation of self: open, relaxed body language; not appearing easily flustered (yet willing to accept fallibility without going to pieces); the ability to regain composure quickly when one has made a mistake – not being easily flummoxed (Rogers 1997); a confident, pleasant, engaging voice; being able to assert where necessary (pp. 56, 60); effective use of eye-scanning, eye contact (p. 66); being aware of one's body language when engaging students' personal space. These are basic but significant features of a confident teacher's personality.

Establishing whole-class attention

It is important to establish, at the first group meeting, the importance of whole-class attention and focus. Developing the habit of whole-class attention is crucial to an effective beginning to class learning.

Verbally focusing attention

Once the individuals are in their seats the teacher needs to cue for group attention. This can be initiated through a combination of non-verbal cues (p. 40) and verbal direction(s).

- It can help to use an imperative form: "Settling down everyone (...)" Allow some, brief, tactical pausing to give the students take-up time to process the teacher's cueing (p. 3). "Looking this way and listening (...). Thanks."

  Avoid questioning phrases: "Would you please look this way everyone?"; "Can you settle down please?"; "Would you stop talking?"; "Why are you talking?"

  "Thanks" at the end of an imperative form of words implies expectation.

  Think about your language for addressing a *group*: "Class ..."; "Folks ..."; "Everyone ..."; "Guys ..."; "6D ..."? "Guys ..." seems to be favoured as a unisex generic by younger teachers. It's not one of my favourites.

  Some teachers find a non-verbal cue helpful *before* they give a verbal direction. With new classes I often "ting" a small drinking glass with the tip of my metal pencil, then follow with the whole-class direction.
- Be aware of posture. An "open", expectant, confident posture and a positive, expectant, tone in one's voice will convey our meaning ("settle", "look", "listen') as much as anything else will.
- Step the voice down with the *part* direction. The initial words (e.g. "Settling down folks ...") are said a little louder to gain initial attention; it may be necessary to repeat the first part of the direction.

"*Settling* down everyone (...)"	a little louder
"Looking this way thanks	softer
and listening (...)"	softer (in concert with increasing attention and focus)

This verbal form ("Settling down ...") is a variation of "*Stop* (what you're doing), *look* this way, and *listen*".
- Scan the eyes and faces of your class as you speak (it can communicate one's positive manner as well as giving the teacher feedback about student attention and focus). Allow time for the residual noise to settle (...), then proceed with the rest of what you want (or need) to say when the class are attending (e.g. a class welcome and the instructional phase of the lesson).

Some teachers will use a raised voice to initiate group attention and, when only half the class are listening, continue to talk to the group while the rest are still whispering or chatting. All this does (of course) is to emphasise that such talking or "chatting" is OK. It is important to scan and wait for whole-class attention. While scanning the group, it will be important to non-verbally (or verbally) affirm students who do settle, face the front and listen with readiness with a smile, a nod, a brief affirming comment: "Thank you, John, Damien, Lucien, Susan ... you're ready"; "Nuyen, Tran, Bilal ... thanks."

At infant level teachers will often give several such encouragers to emphasise the fact the students *are* listening, *are* sitting, *are* facing the front, *are* ready, and so on.

Teacher movement

It doesn't help group attention and focus if the teacher telegraphs too much motoric restlessness by pacing up and down at the front of the classroom; the undiagnosed "ADD students" will tend to over-focus on the teacher's movement only half listening (if at all) to what the teacher is saying. I've watched teachers bouncing up and down on their toes while reading to the class, unaware that their overly motoric movement telegraphs an unconscious restlessness in the students whose eyes involuntarily track the bouncing up and down.

Stand at the front of the room to initiate and sustain group attention: a centre-front position, facing the class group, standing relaxed and scanning the faces of the students while cueing for attention will normally signal the teacher's readiness and expectation.

Non-verbal cues to gain group attention

One of the non-verbal cues to initiate or signal for group attention is the raised hand. When the class is seated the teacher faces the class (from the centre-front of the classroom) and visually scans the room with one hand raised. He or she does not speak; the raised hand is a *cue* to which the students respond by, likewise, raising their hand in a kind of domino effect across the room. Students look around and, in effect, copy. It is a cue to focus and refocus attention (as is necessary during the lesson) and can be quite effective at primary age level and lower secondary level. When the class has responded (15–30 seconds) the teacher lowers his or her hand, thanks the class for their cooperation and continues with a class greeting and the session's activity.

One of my post-grad students had been told this was a good signal for settling a class and proceeded to try it with a new Year 6 class. She had her hand up for a few minutes when a student finally said, "Yes, Miss ... how can we help you?" When using non-verbal cues for the first time it will be important to verbally associate the expectation carried by the cue with directional words. In the case above the teacher could have raised her hand *and* verbally directed the group, "Settling down everyone (...), looking this way (...) and listening (...) ...". When they were quiet and listening she could have then explained that the next time she puts her hand up *like that* at the beginning of the lesson ... So much for hindsight!

Typical non-verbal cues used by teachers include ringing a small hand-bell; a sound from an instrument (many years ago I used my guitar – strumming a chord to signal to my, then, early years class to come and sit on the mat); a hand-clap rhythm copied by all infant students (the teacher then reducing the clap to a two-finger clap , and finally a single finger "quiet clap" and hands resting in the lap). Even standing still, relaxed, scanning the class – waiting – can, *itself*, be a non-verbal cue.

Re-establishing group attention

There are occasions when a teacher needs to re-establish group attention beyond the initial lesson establishment. There may be an occasion when the noise level of unnecessary off-task behaviour occurs, or the teacher may need to refocus an aspect of the lesson task. The most obvious re-establishing needs to occur before lesson closure. It is important to allow appropriate time for packing up, lesson summary (if necessary) and orderly and calm exit (see pp. 51–2).

A primary teacher stops her class 3 or 4 minutes before the closing bell. The students are still busily colouring in or writing on their worksheet. She gives several instructions about materials and where to put finished work, adding, "Stand behind your chairs when you've finished". The problem is that the teacher is speaking over significant residual noise and activity. A third of the class is still working with pencils in hand while she is talking. She "allows" this behaviour to continue where she should have briefly refocused the class, and individuals, for whole-class attention.

Whenever we give *group* instructions, directions or reminders it is important to wait for whole-class attention to enable focus and processing of even routine directions.

A further problem can occur. If the teacher frequently talks *over* talking and kinaesthetic noise the students get used to it, and there is a group habituation that is not easy to change.

- Have a signal or cue for group attention (verbal or non-verbal see pp. 39, 40).
- Use a brief tactical pause (p3) so students can process the direction. Repeat the group instruction if necessary: "Everyone (...) eyes and ears this way now. Thank you (...). Paul (...), Simon (...), Simone (...) Donna – pencils down." This to the several who are still not attending. "(...) Eyes and ears this way (...) Thank-you." Firm, confident and pleasant, it sets the norm; the routine.
- Visual cue reminders can help at primary level (see p. 48).
- A word of acknowledgment and encouragement of appreciation can help: "I appreciated the way in which you all packed up at your tables and put the lids on felt-tip pens – that'll help them to live longer"; "Thank you for listening, and concentrating, when I asked you all to ".

Sustaining group attention

The ability to *sustain* group attention depends on the teacher's ability to engage the students in the teaching and learning focus – at that point. The ability and skill to teach effectively and to manage disruptive behaviours is crucial to the effectiveness of any group learning. This is discussed in some detail in Chapters 3 and 4.

The seemingly non-responsive, non-attentive class (first meeting)

This phenomenon is more common at secondary than primary level. The teacher enters the class with a group of restless and noisy students. It seems that they are in a world of their own (and they probably are). The teacher stands at the front of the room waiting, waiting ... students are having private conversations, fiddling with *objets d'art*, rearranging class furniture. Does the teacher exist? What should he or she do?

It will be counter-productive (if tempting) to shout. It might, temporarily, stop the noise and the motoric restlessness, but it will probably restart or, worse, they will react in a hostile way.

It is also unhelpful to stand there *just* waiting.

Ideally if such a class is known to behave like this (even from Day 1), the establishment phase (first few lessons) should involve a team-teaching approach with one of the teachers well known by the students in that group as a teacher with credibility and respect. The new (ongoing) teacher plans the first few lessons (establishment) with this colleague; this allows a kind of "credibility by proxy" (Rogers 1997). It has to be genuine teaming and well-planned. This collegial teaming could also include some ongoing monitoring of students' behaviour in (and out of) class. What is to be avoided is any *known* "difficult class" being given to a beginning teacher or a teacher new to the school without initial and ongoing colleague support.

When faced with a seemingly unresponsive class, rather than stand at the front of the room waiting, or even cueing for group attention (pp. 39), I've found it helpful to leave the centre-front of the room (where students expect the teacher to try to establish some class attention and control) and move around the room initiating conversations with individuals and pairs. This is a kind of mini-establishment, in "their" space. It initially unsettles some of the students. They don't expect *this*. No doubt they're thinking, "You should be up the front where we can make life difficult for you ...".

As I walk up to students and initiate conversations (beginning with a mutual name introduction) I sometimes get cocky, smart-alec responses. I find *tactical ignoring* of such behaviour (wherever appropriate, pp. 66–7) quite effective. I seek to indicate I'm no threat, nor am I threatened by their behaviour, but at the same time I am initiating and establishing my leadership. I ask a few questions about the sorts of things they might expect in *this* English class and assure them that our time together will be worthwhile: the process is brief, excursive, roaming and establishing. Walking back to the front of the classroom I try to hold some key student names in my short-term memory and *then* go to the centre-front of the classroom. Using the remembered names I can now cue for whole class attention, "... settling down, thanks (...), Paul ..., Dean ..., Damien ..., Troy ...". Most students are settling, calming down and facing the front. They are affirmed (briefly), "Thanks, Crystal (...), David, Donna ...". Having had some brief relational chats and introductions I can use the names with some early, relational confidence. After a few minutes, and several tactical pauses, the class is substantially settled. It isn't easy, but it is an approach I have found helpful to initiate group calming and focus.

If a pattern of non-attentiveness is typical it will be important to seek immediate, senior colleague support:

- It may help to see if the problem is wider than your own class.
- It can help to work with the key ring leaders; those students who trigger non-attentive or provocative behaviour in their classmates. Follow-up will need to emphasise the effect of their behaviour on the class and on the shared rights of all, and then work on their responsibility and commitment to change. The follow-up will also be helped by senior colleague support, but it is crucial that the class teacher engages in any one-to-one follow-up with these students.
- It can help to run a classroom meeting outlining the major concerns the teacher has about general noise level, inattention and students talking while the teacher is talking, and then invite student responses about the need for change and developing a class plan to address these concerns about behaviour and learning. Such a meeting, though, will benefit (again) from colleague support (p. 142).

Learning and using students' names

This may sound like a mundane point, but it is crucial – from Day 1. I have worked with secondary teachers who still haven't learned the names of their students by Term 3! I know it takes effort but it is significant in relational and management terms.

At primary level – at least for the class teacher – the names can be assigned and tagged to the desk itself for Day 1, seating plans can be organised and name-games utilised (even at secondary level).

As a mentor/teacher with every new class I work with I ask a student to draw me a classroom plan of the furniture and note down the first name of the students in relation to their desk, or table group. I then use that name plan during the on-task phase of the lesson. I also find it helpful to double check the *sound* of students' names so I don't cause unthinking offence (or embarrassment). I use these hand-drawn plans *at every* lesson until I've learned the names.

Some colleagues have a class list with a small photo of each student – this assists the short-term memory in each lesson as we build those workable relationships. It is also important to use the students' names in non-classroom settings (corridor and playground), and even in brief, civil, exchanges.

Small aside

It isn't easy learning students' names at high school (or if you are a 'specialist' teacher at primary level). I've found that when I do forget a name I'm trying to remember it sounds a bit nicer to say to the student, "I'm trying to remember your name" (the truth), rather than, "I've forgotten your name" or even "I don't know your name".

Addressing disruptive behaviour during instructional time

When students call out, butt in or talk across the room

Like any aspect of classroom management we need to:

- discuss such behaviour within the class agreement (p. 27);
- have an age-related established routine (at junior level it might be "hands up without calling out", whereas at senior level it might be "one at a time in class discussions");
- be able to confidently manage the calling out when it occurs.

In the first few lessons the teacher will need to define, establish and maintain the fairness of one person speaking at a time and others consciously making an effort to listen. Before any group discussion we can *preface* any question-time by reminding students: "Remember our rule (or agreement) for …". We might add, "I know some of you will be really keen to contribute; however if you just call out, or talk over someone, that is unfair to the other person if they are waiting. If you are waiting to make a point or contribute and others call out, you, too, would feel their behaviour is unfair."

If students do forget, or call out to gain some attentional advantage, then a brief reminder of the rule will be important to the several or the individual.

When giving directions or reminders it is important to be brief, giving a few seconds of take-up-time, and then re-engage whole group attention to and focus on the activity. If we accept calling out and validate such behaviour in the first few meetings we will find it difficult to re-train the group later.

It is important not to ignore such behaviour in the illusion that it will go away or that the students will naturally settle.

I have seen teachers teach *through* such noisy, disparate behaviour as if they are teaching when, in fact, several or more students are actively ignoring the teacher through their cross-talking. If we accept a student's butting in, calling out or cross-talking we ratify that such behaviour is OK.

A "hands up" correction is a necessary correction in most classes – even in some Year 11 and 12 classes – particularly in the establishment phase of the year.

Some basic cues to correct and refocus calling out are:

- *A non-verbal reminder:* (At infant or middle primary level). The teacher raises his or her hand (to simulate hands up) and, briefly, covers his or her mouth (to indicate hands up *without* calling out). She then acknowledges a student with their hand up.
- *Incidental direction:* The teacher describes what the student is doing: "Jason (…), you're calling out and clicking your fingers". The teacher then gives some take-up time, then acknowledges other students with their hands up, and names them – "Jason …, Dean …, Carla …, I see your hands up 1, 2, 3" – and responds in turn to their questions or contributions (p57).

If several students are calling out it will be important to stop the class – a blocking hand – and scan the room, waiting for quiet: "Folks (…), several students are calling out (…). We have a class rule. Thank-you". The teacher then, in a positive, expectant manner, resumes the class discussion. "I don't mind *which* hand, as long as you have a hand up [teacher smiles]. Alright … let's go for it …"

Other examples of verbal cues to a group or individual:

- "Hand up without calling out, thanks …"
- "Remember our class rule for asking questions."
- "Hands up so I can see your voice."
- "I can hear questions; I can't see hands up."
- "I get concerned when several of you call out (…) *we* end up not able to hear anyone." (This is a brief, whole-class reminder.)

If a student, has persistently called out during Day 1 it will be worth following-up with them after class time, perhaps even making some form of verbal agreement (one-to-one) about hands up behaviour (p. 49).

Like any corrective management, we need to have the preventative focus in place, and will need to have thought through simple, brief, positive forms of corrective language to remind students of their responsibility and to bring students back on task. Avoid negative or interrogative corrections like: "Don't call out!"; "Are you calling out?"; "Why are you calling out?"; and "You're not supposed to be calling out are you!?"

Transitions

When a teacher moves from the instructional to the on-task phase of the lesson it is natural for the noise level of the class to rise; some students who were not listening earlier now tend to be unfocused and want teacher assistance (quickly!); many start talking to their classmate (which is acceptable providing such talking is not loud or significantly non-task in focus); there will also be students who do not have the appropriate equipment.

More than anything teachers need to make the transition between instructional time and on-task time clear and definite. I've worked with teachers who have a fuzzy, inchoate transition, where the students are unclear what they are supposed to be doing *now*. The teacher may just tail off a series of task instructions, or even start answering individuals' questions, leaving the rest of the class uncertain as to where the focus of the lesson is *at this point*.

Basic, but crucial points like having the work task/activity written-up as a question, or series of points/steps and having monitors for distribution of materials (particularly with group work) need to be established from Day 1.

It will be important to plan for these behaviours and contingencies by explaining to the class what is meant by "working noise" and *why* a reasonable level of working noise is important. It will also be important to discuss reasonable and acceptable movement *around* the classroom (this will, naturally, vary according to subject area and context). If students need teacher assistance they will need to know how they can, fairly, get teacher help in a classroom of 25–30 students.

It will also help to have some spare pens (blue and red), some spare rulers, pencils and erasers, and some lined (and plain) A4 paper, just in case. Initially the teacher will not know if a student without a pen is being difficult, lazy, indifferent or genuinely forgetful. A box of necessities is essential in the first few lessons at upper primary level onwards (p. 6).

In developing such routines, cues and procedures with their students, teachers will find it helpful to plan ahead with colleagues who teach similar ages of students and in similar teaching/subject areas.

Cater for the visual learners in the group

Some teachers over-rely on an auditory approach to teaching. We might (sometimes) be critical of the so-called "chalk and talk" days, but then many teachers did understand the importance of visual cueing: writing key points on the board, building up concepts from main concept to subsidiary points, or using the "well-known to less-known" principle. Long before the modern emphasis on "multiple intelligences", visual, auditory and kinaesthetic learning, and so-called left brain/right brain learning, effective teachers were using "mind-map" concepts[1] and catering for visual and experiential learners.

I was team teaching with a senior teacher in an English class a few years ago. She was discussing (with a Year 10 class) aspects of positive communication. As she developed some quite complex ideas I noticed (ten minutes into the session) that a third of the class were restless and unfocused. I asked my colleague (casually) if I could "write a few of these points on the board". She replied (pleasantly), "… of course, Mr Rogers". As I wrote her key points up I noticed the students re-engage, almost straight away. It was as if the words on the board had given them a framework for the flow of the lesson as well as their own thinking.

If, for example, I'm conducting a classroom discussion I like to have a student write up key points so the class can have a visual focus (it also validates a student's contribution). I also like to have another student record the points down (as a class scribe) so I'm free (as the teacher) to manage and chair the class dialogue and discussion.

Noise levels

In an old *Punch*[2] magazine I read an unusual word: "charivari". I couldn't figure out its meaning from the context so I looked it up. It's French in origin: "A serenade of rough music made with kettles, pans, tea-trays, etc. Used in France in derision of incongruous marriages … hence a babel of music …" (Oxford Shorter Dictionary). I've had quite a few Year 7–10s exhibit charivari! Some students are not (seemingly) aware of how loudly their voices carry (along with 25–28 others) and may be unaware of the chair scrapes, the kinaesthetic movements, that all add up to a "charivari".

Teachers have differing levels of tolerance regarding noise levels. Some can tolerate very high levels of noise whereas the teacher next door may (rightly) find the next door's classroom noise inhibiting their own classroom teaching and learning. To ask a colleague if they are aware of how loud their normal classroom is can be a sensitive and touchy issue.

When 25–30 students are grouped several times a day in small rooms with tightly orchestrated furniture and space and are, then, expected to cohabit, think, discuss, cooperate, work and move, there is bound to be noise. How do we manage the environment, and student behaviour, so that we have reasonable and fair levels of noise proper to the place and activities we set?

We could try Cardinal Hume's approach when he was a school master: "I don't mind you making noise if you don't mind me stopping you" (Mortimer 1984).

It is important that the students understand and appreciate the difference between "outside the classroom space", "inside the classroom space" and the purposes of *each* "space" and "place". Some children bring all their kinaesthetic energy and louder (outside) voices into the classroom context and do not adjust and monitor their movement and voices accordingly (p. 38).

A calm, quieter atmosphere inside a classroom will enable attention, focus and effective teacher–student communication:

- Explain why we, as a class group, need to have inside or "partner-voices" as distinct from louder, outside voices. The classroom is, principally, a teaching and learning place: "we (therefore) use our voices, and the level of our voice, differently in here".
- Teach the difference between the levels of voices to emphasise whispering and appropriate partner-voice (Robertson 1997). One of the ways I've found helpful is to point out to the class that at any time during the on-task phase of the lesson, "I should be able to speak in a normal voice from the front of the room to the back of the room – without raising my voice – and be heard". Teaching by modelling can help. I have modelled partner-voice by, say, asking a student for a pen in different levels of voice to qualify, to the whole class, the meaning and extent of partner-voice. When I ask students (even at secondary level) to describe partner-voice they invariably use qualifiers such as "soft", "close", "using eye contact", "first name", "using manners – please, thanks, etc.".
- Monitor and encourage conscious habits of appropriate and reasonable working noise. There are a number of simple, visual ways to give students feedback about working-noise (see later).
- Review noise levels with the class during the first few weeks to maintain positive, and conscious, habits of voice moderation.

I prefer, and use, the terms "partner-voice" and "working-voices" rather than "working noise": I try to get away from the "noise" motif where possible.

We remember to use our partner voices at our table groups

The teacher's voice

Sometime the teacher's normal – characteristic – voice level and volume are UNNECESSARILY HIGH(!), raising the residual noise level of the students' voices and creating a kind of normatively louder classroom. Most often the teacher is unaware that this is a feature of their NORMAL VOICE LEVEL. The problem is that when they need to project a firmer, or slightly louder voice (for emphasis) it is not effectively heard. If a teacher's normal voice is particularly loud, or it sounds as if he or she is frequently annoyed or irritated, the classroom will be an unnecessarily tense place that will inhibit learning, even if the teacher falsely believes he or she has "good control".

If the teacher has an overly controlling voice, and "peppers" his or her remarks with negative language (overusing "don't", "mustn't", "shouldn't", "why?" and "are you?"), the class becomes an unpleasant group to be part of. I've seen older students, eventually, react against such teachers by overt or covert sabotage.

Keeping our tone and volume of voice pleasant, confident and adult will aid group calmness and enable student attention.[3] Then when we need to raise our voice for *particular* attention, or to communicate our frustration, or even anger, (Chapter 7), it will have an appropriate effect. When we raise our voice to *emphasise*, or to gain *attention*, it helps to drop the voice (de-escalate) to a calmer or more controlled (firmer) voice. This reduces residual tension.

Teaching partner-voice(s) to early years (age 5 to 7)

Like many social experiences that involve self-control we cannot assume that all the children in our classes understand what we mean by "working noise", "partner-voice", "taking turns", "lining up", "hands up without calling out" and "moving *carefully* and thoughtfully around the room"; even basic manners can't be assumed.

In the establishment phase of the year (Day 1, Week, 1) it will be important to explain why we need to use our partner-voice inside our classroom; and to teach and monitor working noise. A classroom is a physically small environment in which to creatively house and engage 20–30 young children. If poor habits of working noise develop it can be stressful for the teacher, who will frequently have to use a raised voice to regain group attention. It can also affect the attentional behaviour of children during on-task learning time.

The children are sitting on the carpet area at the front of the classroom. Before the first on-task session for the day the teacher talks about the large room and 25 (plus) voices sometimes all talking at the same time. She hypothesises with them about what could happen if we talked loudly during work time at our desk. She models with her hands apart as far as she can stretch to indicate a loud voice. She speaks about places in the school where we would use loud(er) voices (such as the playground), and why. She asks why we need quieter (much quieter) voices inside our classroom. She discusses what a partner is and introduces the concept of partner-voice or inside or working voice (Robertson 1997; Rogers 1997). Here she indicates a smaller, quieter voice with a non-verbal cue of hands close together.

She invites a few students to role play partner-voice with her in front of the class. A table has been set aside and she sits at the table with a couple of students, asks to borrow a coloured pencil, modelling partner-voice, and asks the children what they noticed. She soon has class feedback on observed behaviours such as "softness" and "manners". She models "whisper", and "quiet-work talk" as features of partner-voice. She invites modelling from the other children in the role play. As a contrast she models "playground-voice", and the children laugh.

"Imagine if I used that kind of voice if I was asking to borrow a pencil or scissors or even if I was talking to someone about the work we were doing ..."

The noise meter

The teacher introduces some large drawings (at least A3 size) depicting children in classroom situations. The first picture illustrates the key behaviours during "carpet-time", and depicts children sitting facing the teacher and listening. Some of the children in this picture have their hands up (they are not calling out). The children and the teacher look relaxed and are smiling.

"When we sit together on the carpet we face the front and listen ('eyes and ears') and we sit comfortably."

It will help to explain sitting options that do not annoy others: sitting space. The teacher also discusses other behaviours such as "taking turns"; "listening when others speak" and "hands up without calling out if you want to ask a question or share".

By having the picture, as a visual cue, the teacher can refer to it during instructional time or class discussion time, and can simply say, "Remember our rule about hands-up ..." and physically point back to the rule reminder poster.

The second picture illustrates a table group during work time. In the background are a few faces, and in the foreground the table group are portrayed using partner-voices.

The third picture is similar to the second picture but the children at the table group are clearly using loud voices. The children in the background are frowning, indicating social disapproval.

As with all teaching about social behaviours we emphasise the effect of individual behaviour on others and that we don't just live to/for ourselves.

The fourth picture is the same as the third picture but has a circle encompassing the loud-talkers and a diagonal line through the circle.

The teacher explains what each picture means.

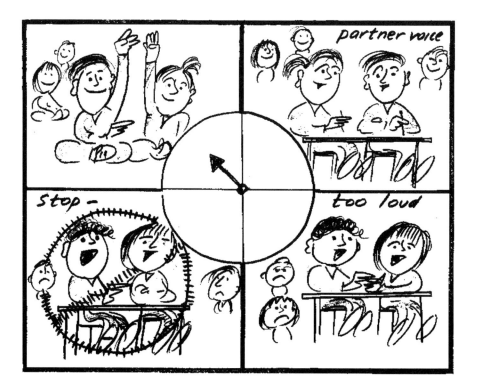

These pictures are portrayed together with a coloured meter (a circle of cardboard about 30 cm in diameter) in the centre. Each quadrant is coloured: white (carpet-time voices), green (partner-voices), orange (partner-voices getting too loud – this signals a reminder/warning) and red for stop. The meter has an arrow (with split pin) that can rotate to any of the four pictures. The teacher explains the arrow and colours. He or she has the arrow on white during carpet-time, and on green for partner voice.

If children become too loud during on-task learning time the teacher can put the arrow on orange as a non-verbal and visual *aide memoir*. He or she will wait to see if students pick up on this cue. If necessary he or she will cue for class attention (wait) and point to the warning picture and either non-verbally cue for partner-voice (p. 66) or will give a brief, positive, verbal reminder, "Remember your partner-voices. Thank you", before putting the arrow back to green.

If the teacher puts it on red it signals stop and everyone has to refocus back to partner-voices. This involves a *brief*, whole-class, reminder about partner-voices. Like any routine it takes time to develop general habituation about inside partner-voices.

At Year 1 to 3 level it can help to appoint noise monitors on each table group. Their role is to keep an eye on the noise meter from time to time. The teacher can assist their role by cueing the noise monitor with a brief reminder. It can also help to rotate this role in the first few weeks.

As the teacher roves the room he or she will also encourage students when they are using their partner-voices.

"You're keeping your voices soft and I noticed you're looking at each other when you speak and you're remembering your manners … That all helps us to get our classwork done. Thank you."

In this way the teacher describes what they do that helps their table group (brief, descriptive feedback) and encourages group members.

The noise meter and picture cues are means to an end; they are props and prompts. They have their acute focus in the establishment phase of the year and can be shelved as the behaviour generalises.

The noise meter is both an establishment teaching device and a monitoring *aide-mémoir*e. In time it can be replaced by a tablecard reminder: "At out table group we use our partner-voices" (p. 46).

Partner voice feedback (Rogers, 1998)

Personal reminder plan for Travis

If an individual student is still struggling with his voice level, and use of voice, it can help to develop an individual behaviour plan with him. This plan attempts to teach him (one-to-one) the "why" and "how" of a quiet working voice (in effect it teaches him individually what most students have adapted to normatively). In teaching a child one-to-one (in non-contact time) the teacher can:

- use simple picture cues to illustrate how individual, noisy voices affect others;
- mirror the child's typical noisy voice (ask permission, "Do you mind if I show you how it sounds when you …?", and keep the mirroring brief (p. 72));
- model appropriate partner-voice;
- practise partner-voice with the child (one-to-one);
- let the child know this is his or her (personal) reminder plan (a small card illustrating the student using his partner-voice).

As with any individual plan for behaviour or learning it is developed away from other children, one-to-one, with an emphasis on support and encouragement (p. 122).

It can be helpful with middle-school aged students to give some non-verbal feedback on how the students are using their partner voice during the lesson. A simple way to do this is through a graph on the board.

The teacher uses a simple histogram. The vertical axis runs from 0 (silence), through 2 (whisper zone) and 5 (the upper limit of partner voice) to 10. Any noise in the 5 to 10 region is too loud (10 being House of Commons on a normal day!).

The horizontal axis is divided into five minute sections. Every five minutes during the on-task phase of the lesson the teacher goes to the board and draws in the vertical line denoting the level of partner-voice.

Students are often unaware of how loud they are when conversing and working during on-task time. This simple graph gives the students visual feedback every five minutes (or more often if necessary). I've heard, and seen, students (many times) nudging each other as I go to the board and give the "histogrammatic" feedback.

If their noise level creeps above the 5 mark (vertical scale) it can help to see if the class picks up the visual feedback cue and brings the level down by themselves. If they do a visual scan of the room with a non-verbal OK sign indicates your encouragement.

This approach is an "establishment routine": it is a means to an end, like the noise meter (p. 26); the end being reasonable working noise.

- Explain and discuss partner-voice with the class on the first day or session.
- Explain the graph and the feedback cues.
- At the end of each class period give the class some descriptive feedback on how they performed across the on-task time period: "Folks, you kept your partner-voices well below 5 for most of the lesson (...) a couple of times you crept over 5, but you remembered when reminded. Thank you ... I appreciated your efforts".
- As with any establishment routine it can be phased out as positive group behaviour generalises.
- With particularly loud, and kinaesthetically robust classes, I've used a points system whereby the teacher grants points for students (as a group) keeping their partner-voices below 5 (and awards more points if the level is below 4 or 3). If the class has achieved 20 points five minutes or so before the bell, the teacher packs up the class early and students chat quietly until "bell time".

Giving assistance to students during the on-task phase of the lesson

The main point behind any cue, or routine, for giving students assistance *during class time* is the rational fairness and distribution of teacher assistance for so many over a short period of time.

- The teachers should explain, even discuss, how he or she can equitably support students who ask for assistance during work/task time. The explanation will include the obvious point (humourously made) that a teacher is not an octopus!
- The teacher should discuss the importance of "checking set work yourself – read through, ask yourself: what am I asked or required to do here and now; where should I start; how do I set the work out?" These self-monitoring questions can be taught as part of a class discussion on positive learning habits.
- For set work procedures it can help to have a class poster with the basic reminders about drafting a piece of writing, page lay-out, and the writing process.

- The teacher could remind students that they can quietly check and discuss the work with their immediate classmate (not a classmate on the other side of the classroom!)
- When the class group is well established it can help to appoint classroom mentors (peer-mentors) who can assist their fellow students with conferencing about their classwork. Such students need to be well received by their class peers and possess natural social skills such as effective listening and communication.
- The teacher could establish a routine: "Check (quietly) with three (directly near you) before you check with me". This can also help students to gain peer assistance before easily, and quickly, seeking out the teacher.
- At primary age level it can help to have the key learning tasks for the day set out on a separate board, as a visual focus, so that students can rotate between tasks as they complete each appropriate phase or stage.
- At upper primary onwards it can help if students go on with other work while they wait for teacher assistance or conferencing. One way of visually focusing the teacher assistance process is to have a teacher help board where the students note down their name if they need to conference with the teacher. Of course before they note down their name they will need to have:
  (i) checked the set work requirement/task/activity themselves;
  (ii) checked with their classmate or working partner;
  If they note down their name they can go on with other set work (or other options) *while* they wait for the teacher. This avoids having children just waiting with their hands up until the teacher gets around to them.

Lesson closure

It is important to plan ahead for lesson closure, particularly in the first few lessons. The teacher will need to discuss with the students routines such as:

- packing up and straightening the furniture; chairs under the table (or *on* the table at the end of the last class period of the day);
- picking up any residual litter and putting it in the litter bin on the way out;
- leaving the classroom in an orderly fashion (this may need to involve dismissing the class row by row, or table group by table group).

Remember there is a natural readiness on Day 1, Week 1, for the teacher to make these expectations and routines clear. It is also important to finish the lesson, or activity, positively (even if it has not been the best lesson in the world). Aim for a calm, positive closure with a reminder that, "Another class is coming in after us, let's do them a basic favour. Chairs under ...; litter in the bin ...; we leave quietly, row by row (teacher nominates the rows). Thanks ..."

Homework cues are best written up on the board or printed reminders handed out. Auditory reminders about important topics are miscued by many students in the last few minutes of a lesson as most students are just waiting for the bell. In fact some students will already have packed up well before the bell; it will be important to speak to such students (one-to-one) and encourage them to recheck their work, or read the class novel, or ...

It may be important to remind the class politely that the bell is a reminder to both the class, and the teacher, that *this* lesson has ended; it is the teacher's responsibility to dismiss the class.

Caveat: There are some occasions when a *brief* 'stay-back' of the class may be warranted.

A quarter or more of the class make a bee-line for the door on Day 1 (Lesson 1) as soon as the bell goes. The other 70 per cent or so hold back. The teacher calls the two or three students who have left the room back inside (she does this quickly, firmly, confidently, "hopefully").

"Stop (…). Back inside, fellas (…), back inside."

If she knows their names she will use them (a small but crucial point).

"Bilal, Nazim, Craig, (…) back inside (…) now, thanks."

They whinge, naturally. "Gees – it's recess, come on!"

She re-directs. "I know it's recess," she partially agrees. "Back inside fellas (…), I won't keep you long."

Most students come back (certainly Day 1, Session 1, the students are generally more likely to comply not having worked through, fully, the teacher's leadership style). They come back in (grumbling and muttering). I've been in classes where they flop in their seats sulking and muttering ("Gees what kind of sh-t class is this!").

She stands at the front of the class, scans the group, *tactically* ignores the sulkers, and says, "When you're all settled, I'll explain (…)".

They quieten.

"This is *not* a detention folks. It's a minute past the bell. In a minute you're out of here." She smiles. "This is a class *reminder*. In our class we leave the place tidy, straighten the tables, chairs under the tables, litter off the floor. As I said earlier (…), let's do the next class a favour. Let's try it again. Thanks for all those who did make the effort two minutes ago. So; let's all try it again."

This time when the class leaves they are more subdued, more focused. This approach is preferable to saying, "Right!! If you're all going to waste my time, I'll waste your time!!"

She stands at the door giving a brief goodbye as the students leave. It has only taken a couple of minutes but she has *re-established* the class routine she had discussed earlier about a "thoughtful class exit" (p. 51).

If something very valuable has gone missing (lost, mislaid or stolen) the teacher will (where possible) finish the lesson earlier and have a class discussion about the missing item.

"I don't know if someone has taken item X by mistake, or accidentally put it in their bag, but item X has gone missing. It is very important to _____ (the person concerned), as I'm sure you can understand. I'll stand outside this classroom for three minutes and I expect the item to be back on my desk, no questions asked. I'll *then* dismiss the class."

Prior to this mini class meeting the teacher might send for a senior colleague to give some immediate assistance in finding the item.

Situations like these are always tricky especially when time is of the essence. Senior colleague support should always be involved if the item is important and is not returned.

Before you leave your working area

1. Put all materials away (lids on felt-tip pens, pencils in containers, work away).
2. Tidy your own work space; help others out too.
3. Chairs under tables. (ON tables at end of day.)
4. Litter in bin. Check.

THANKS! Mr Rogers

Notes

1. A mind-map is a visual representation of a core idea, issue, question or concept with its supporting and subsidiary ideas, concepts or questions. It can give focus and direction and help to hold several ideas or concepts together.
2. *Punch* was an English satirical magazine, which is not well known in Australia.
3. Some infant teachers affect a babyish voice when working with small children. This is unnecessary. Obviously we need to modify concepts in our language use, but we don't need to adopt the kind of tone or manner that Joyce Grenfell portrayed so skilfully in some of her comic monologues.

Chapter 3
The language of behaviour management

What do we live for, if it is not to
make life less difficult for each other.
George Eliot (1819–1880)

No formulas! The language of management, and of discipline, operates in a dynamic relation-ship. Developing skill in this area does not simply involve a series of words, phrases or sentences. If it is our *intention* to discipline with respect and confi-dence, that intention needs to come *through* the language. Only then will our language be relationally dynamic.

Being assertive (for example), when it is called for, requires some skill in communication and control over one's non-verbal behaviour but it is the *inten-tion to assert* one's needs, or rights, or to protect someone else's needs, feelings, and rights, that really signals assertive behaviour. Assertive behaviour also needs to be context appropriate. Assertion often means we communicate with a firm, resolute, unambiguous tone and manner, matched by confident (non-aggressive) body language. In this sense the *skill* of assertion is "conscious" and not simply the outcome of reactive feelings.

Two students were rearranging the furniture as I was seeking to establish class attention in a Year 9 English class. I asked them their names.

"What?" was the sulky reply.

"What is your name please," I asked again; pleasantly and indicating no threat. I was just getting a "name check".

One of the girls leaned back, languorously, sighed and said, "Crystal!" and tut-tutted loudly as if I'd asked her to do some great, onerous, task.

I added in a relaxed, but decisive, tone, "Crystal (…) I'm not speaking to you in a rude tone of voice and I don't expect you to speak rudely to me either." I then added, "You're moving the furniture and I'm ready to start the class. I want you to leave the furniture as it is and face this way now. Thank you."

She sighed (less demonstrably now) and I resumed the flow of the lesson.

Assertion is not about winning: it's about establishing and affirming fair rights and needs.

I was discussing the issue of corrective language (discipline) with a group of teachers once and someone raised the question "But that language isn't *me*". We were discussing reflective rephrasing of, for example, negatives: "When … then …" rather than "No you can't … because …", or "Hands up for questions …" rather than "Don't call out …". I think what my colleague meant (when she said "that language isn't *me*") was, "Should we have to *think* about what we say when we discipline?" Does "being me" simply mean I say the first thing that comes into my head?

I believe we have a responsibility, as professionals, to think about the way we typically, *characteristically*, communicate in management and discipline contexts. It can even help to plan a basic repertoire of language that can enable us to discipline more effectively and (hopefully) less stressfully.

The language framework developed in this section is not formulaic; it is meant to give some conscious focus, and some utility, about management and discipline language when developing a personal discipline plan.

It is pointless (for example) to use a potentially positive sentence – "Michael (…), Dean (…), you're talking; you need to be facing this way and listening, thanks" – if we say the *words* in a mean-spirited, sharp, petty, pleading or whining tone of voice.

Language is dynamic and context related and provides the basis for potential workable relationships.

Key principles and skills of the language of management and discipline

1. Keep the corrective interaction *unintrusive* wherever possible. For example, we can manage such behaviours and issues as calling out, lateness, leaning chairs, uniform misdemeanours and students without equipment with "low" intrusion (a brief non-verbal cue, an incidental direction, a rule reminder). By keeping most correction "low" intrusion, we keep a pleasant, positive tone to classroom life so that when we need to be *more* intrusive (as context may demand) such intrusions will be seen to be significant. These are times when our first response to a student's behaviour needs to be highly intrusive, but that is the exception (reserved for hostile or aggressive student behaviour).

2. Avoid *unnecessary* confrontation (this includes embarrassment, *any* sarcasm, any sense of continued hostility or looking threatened). Humour (repartee, the *bon mot*, the witty Pythonesque turn of phrase …) can defuse and reframe tension and lift the spirits of teacher and student alike. Sarcasm invokes hostility and resentment – why wouldn't it?

3. Keep a respectful, positive tone of voice wherever possible.

4. Keep the language itself positive where possible:
   • "*when – then*' is more invitational than "*no*, you can't, *because* …";
   • avoid *overuse* of "shouldn't", "mustn't", "can't", "won't" and interrogatives such as "why?" or "are you?";
   • avoid pointing fingers or gesticulating when making a corrective or assertive point – use an 'open hand' when emphasising;
   • be brief where possible (avoid *long* directions or reminders about behaviour).

5. Re-establish working relationships with the student as quickly as possible. Even a brief return to a student's desk to ask how their work is going is enough. Often a pleasant manner and a brief encouraging word will help.

6. If you need to communicate appropriate frustration – even anger – do so assertively rather than aggressively:
   • keep the assertive statement brief;
   • focus on the primary behaviour or issue;
   • avoid servicing "secondary behaviours";
   • de-escalate any residual tension (p. 134).

   I have worked with teachers who create unnecessary tension and confrontation by their overly vigilant tone, manner and language. A teacher has just explained the rule for asking questions and a little later a student calls out. The teacher "says", "Is that using the rule, is it?!" Does the teacher really want an answer? "Didn't I just say to you *all* to put you're hands up *without* calling out? Didn't I?!" Others add innuendo or sarcasm: "Are you deaf or what …?"; "Don't they teach you manners at home?" Such *characteristic* teacher behaviour only creates palpable tension in a room, it creates (in some students) anxious and resentful learners. It is unprofessional, unnecessary and wrong.

If we need to communicate annoyance or even anger (where necessary and appropriate), we can do so in a professional manner consistent with our feelings (p. 133f.).

7. Follow up on issues that matter *beyond* the classroom context. This emphasises that you, the teacher, care enough to make clear and sort out the issue of concern with the student (p. 71f.).

A framework for management and discipline language skills

Many of these skills are detailed in examples used throughout this book. They are set out here (in summary form) to highlight the "least-to-most intrusive …" nature of management and discipline language.

Tactical ignoring

The teacher selectively attends to student when on-task, tactically ignoring aspects of secondary behaviour (p. 66f.).

Tactical pausing

The teacher briefly pauses in a spoken direction or reminder to emphasise attention, and focus (p. 3).

Non-verbal cueing

The teacher supplies a cue that carries a clear (unspoken) message, reminder, or direction.

Incidental language

The teacher directs or reminds the student without directly *telling* them: e.g. "There's some litter on the floor and the bell is going to go soon …" (i.e. you know that I know that I'm encouraging you to pick it up). In this approach the teacher describes reality and allows the student to process the "obvious" expectation: e.g. "This is quiet reading time" to students who are whispering to each other. Sometimes it will be appropriate to combine the description of reality with a behavioural direction: e.g "This is quiet reading time now (the incidental). Read quietly inside your heads. Thanks" (the behavioural direction: teacher taps own head). It is very effective from upper primary level onwards.

Take-up time

This refers to the teacher refocusing eye contact and proximity after having given a direction or reminder.

Behavioural direction

The teacher directs a group or individual by referring, directly, to the expected or required behaviour: e.g. "Jason (…), Dean (…), facing this way, thanks". Behavioural directions are appropriate for communicating the *required* behaviour, as when students are talking while the teacher is talking and the students need to be facing the front and listening.

- Focus on the expected or required behaviour.
- Use verbs/participles (rather than negative clauses): e.g. "facing this way and

listening …" rather than "Don't talk while I'm talking please", which only tells the student what we don't want them to do.

- Finish with "thanks", or "now" if the student/s vacillates and prompt attention is necessary.
- Keep the direction or instruction brief: "Michael (…), Troy (…), sitting up and hands in laps – now" to infants. In this example, "now" is said firmly but not sharply.

Rule reminder

The teacher briefly reminds the class group, or individual(s), what the rule is: "We have a rule for asking questions"; "Remember our rule for safe scissors …". The teacher does not need to *spell out* the rule each time. Rule reminders can also be given through a question: "What's our rule for …?"

Prefacing

The teacher focuses on a positive issue before engaging discipline. For example, the teacher sees students being a bit silly at their table. Walking over, he has a chat about the painting they are working on. As he turns to leave he adds, very quietly, yet firmly, as he scans the group, "Remember to use the paints thoughtfully". This approach is effective when one has a positive working relationship with the class. It sets the discipline within a *relational focus*. It is obviously more effective in the on-task phase of the lesson and in non-class settings. I have also found it helpful, sometimes, to direct a student aside (from his immediate peers) to then have a brief disciplinary chat. The distraction, early enough, may stop a subsequent disruptive pattern of behaviour.

Distraction/diversion

The example in "Prefacing" is a typical "distraction".

The teacher notices that a student is folding a worksheet during the instructional phase of the lesson, and says, "Damien (…), the worksheet will be easier to read *un*folded. You'll need it later". Calm, *not* sarcastic, the teacher then gives take-up time (p. 68).

One of my colleagues notes some typical distractions/diversions in her infant classes. They can prevent a scenario from getting out of hand by not focusing on the negative behaviour but on the positive.

"I can see that most of you want to help in getting the plasticine but I did say that I need one helper so what do you think we should do?" Then I thank the children for waiting and being patient. Or before saying that, I could say, "Tom has his hand up and he is also sitting quietly with his legs crossed. Tom would you like to get the plasticine?"

Ryan is playing with a pencil. "Ryan, can I see your picture please? What would you like to tell me about your picture?"

Mary is crying for her mother. "Mary, I have a picture for you to colour in and take home to show your mother. What colour are you going to use for the bow?"

Joshua is wandering around the room. "Joshua when you finish counting with the blocks would you like to paint the big picture of Humpty Dumpty?"

Joshua throws the tambourine into the box after the teacher explains to put them away carefully.

"Joshua what did you do?"

"I threw the tambourine in the box."

"What were you supposed to do? Show me the way you were meant to do it. Why do you think we need to be more careful?"

Direct questions

The teacher uses an imperative form of question rather than an "open" form: e.g. "what", "when" or "how" rather than "why" or "are you".

"What are you doing?"

"What should you be doing?"

"What is our rule for …?"

These sorts of questions direct responsibility to the student rather than asking for reasons. Direct imperatives focus on a student responding to their *present* responsibility rather than looking for reasons *why* they are not behaving considerately or responsibly.

"We need you to do your work in a way that doesn't create a problem for … How are you going to do that …?" to a Year 10 student engaged in time wasting and noisy off-task behaviour.

I asked a Year 8 student what she was doing. I had noticed her doing some maths homework instead of the set classwork.

"Jacinta (…), what are you doing …?"

She said, "Nothing …" and covered her work.

I gave some brief feedback, "Actually it looks like you're doing your maths homework. What should you be doing?" (the direct imperative).

She answered quickly, "This shit … I mean, sorry, this sheet …" We both grinned. "Sounds like you know what to do …"

Directed choices

A "choice" is given by the teacher within the known rules or routine: "Yes you can work on the drawing when you've finished the diary writing" ("when … then" ; "after … then"). In this sense, the choice is expressed as a *conditional* direction: "We'll organise a toilet break when I've finished this part of the lesson". All choices given to a student are, in a sense, conditional. They refer back (one way or another) to the rights and rules and responsibilities.

"Choice"/deferred consequences

Here the teacher makes the consequences of *continued* disruptive behaviour clear within a choice: "If you cannot work quietly here … I'll have to ask you to work separately …" (to two noisy students).

"If you choose not to put the personal stereo away I'll have to ask you to stay back after class [or …] to discuss your behaviour" (p. 103).

This assumes that, earlier, the teacher would have reminded the student about the rule and (if necessary) given the student a choice to "… put the personal stereo in his bag or on the teacher's desk".

Blocking, partial agreement, refocusing

Blocking is a strategy whereby a teacher blocks out a student's procrastinating argument.

A teacher directs two students to face the front and listen (during instructional time). They whinge, "We're not the only ones talking …!" The teacher blocks their avoidance whingeing by gesturing with an open hand, palm facing out, towards them and *repeats* the direction. In effect she is saying, "I'm not interested in *why* you were talking, or who else was talking. Hear the direction and face the front and listen". In this she is redirecting to the main issue (at *this* point in the lesson) and avoids over-servicing the secondary behaviour. It is normally helpful, having blocked the procrastination, to give take-up-time and reclaim group attention (p. 68).

There are occasions when students whine and whinge, for example when infants try to explain who took whose toy. The teacher firmly, kindly but firmly, blocks: "Michael (…), Troy (…). Stop" (hand gesture). "I'll listen when you use reasonable voices ." It can help to then tune in to how they are feeling and then focus: "What is our rule for …?", or "How can we sort this out so that …?".

Partial agreement

The teacher deals with the student's procrastination or avoidance by *partially* agreeing with the student (where appropriate) and refocusing back to the rule or required task.

A teacher reminds a student (who is chewing gum) of the rule. The student challenges by saying, "But Mr Scroggin lets us chew gum in his class".

Instead of arguing, the teacher *partially* agrees, "Maybe he does". The teacher *then* redirects, "In this class the rule is clear. The bin is over there, thanks" (the incidental direction). At this point it is often helpful to give the student some take-up time.

Assertive comment/direction/command

There are degrees of assertion in one's language and voice. Fundamentally when we assert we are making our rights (or others' rights) clear in a decisive, firm, non-aggressive way: "That language is *unacceptable* here. We have a rule for respect. I expect you to use it". Firm, non-aggressive eye-contact, a clear, calm voice and directed, focused, language are at the heart of assertion. Our confident "calmness" also affects the other person's calmness and the audience, who feel the ambient tension.

It isn't easy. Our insides may be saying "I'd like to maim this sod!" But we're professionals. Assertion enables our professional skill to strongly emphasise expectations without getting into a heated argument or slanging match. If the student argues, block and refocus (p. 59).

Commands

When giving commands, keep them short, and establish direct eye contact: "Michael (…)!" The first word should be sharp and louder; to gain *attention*. "Michael (…)", bring the level of the voice *down* as eye contact is established, and cue the command in a firm, decisive, assertive voice: "get down off the table – *now*." In a fight situation, if the names of children aren't known, use the loud generic attentional command, "Oi (…)!, Oi (…)!" – then a firm assertive voice, "Move away *now*." Use non-verbal cues to indicate the students should separate. Direct the audience of peers away and immediately send for adult assistance. It is preferable to give commands only in those situations where unambiguous, *immediate* stopping of disruptive behaviour is warranted. We also need to be able to back-up our commands if a student refuses to obey. Our back-up should consist of a school-wide time-out plan, involving adult support, assistance that can be invoked as quickly as possible in a crisis.

Obviously, we cannot plan for every contingency. These key principles are the underlying framework of the way we communicate and relate in our teaching and management.

The key language skills are suggestions of the sorts of things one can say in typical management and teaching contexts. The language "forms" can serve as *aides-mémoire* to give some prepared focus.

Settling the class outside the classroom

As I approach 8D, in the corridor, I scan the students arriving. Some have US-style "baseball" caps on, some wear sunglasses, a few are still eating, a couple of students towards the back have mobile phones in their hands, a couple of students are listening to personal stereos, a couple of boys are "testosteronically bonding", and so on.

I've worked with colleagues who make no *conscious* management of this corridor restlessness. Opening the classroom door they let the students in with no consciously focused distinction made between the outside (playground) culture and the inside (teaching/learning) culture. Some teachers don't even greet the students as they form or line-up outside a classroom. There are sensible reasons for corridor settling and age-appropriate lining-up (p. 38): the brief settling signals (by the teacher); a change of pace, place, space and purpose in terms of group behaviour.

I find it helpful to comment briefly on hats, personal stereos and any testosteronic bonding or pushing *before* directing the class group inside.

Firstly a brief, group-settling direction as I scan the group or line.
"Settling down folks … (…). Thank you. Morning, everyone – just before we go in (…)! I notice several students with hats on …, Ben (…), Lucas (…), Marcus (…)."

This brief description of reality is often enough to make the issue of "hats-off" clear without directly *telling* the students. Sometimes it is enough just to give a non-verbal cue (hand-to-head) for caps off.

"Down the back, I can see mobile phones (…). We're going into a learning environment …" Giving a non-verbal cue to the lads listening to personal stereos, I add, "We're going into the classroom. Remember the rule about personal stereos. Thanks." Re-scanning the whole group, "Looks like we're ready folks. When you go in, remember to …"

It can help Day 1, Session 1 (and the next few sessions), to emphasise our expectations about seating and settling once inside the room. With infants I find it helpful to ask them, "What do we need to do when we go inside our class?" and then fill the gaps in their forgetfulness as necessary.

This corridor-settling does not take long but it *prefaces* the teacher/student expectation about purposeful behaviour on the other side of the classroom door. In time, the outside settling should become a habit so that all that is necessary is a *brief* line-up, or grouping, before moving into the classroom.

It is worth discussing with colleagues how they normally settle a group prior to classroom entry: what sorts of things they do and say, and why.

The first three minutes

The first three minutes are important in any lesson. The teacher has to both *initiate* and the *sustain* group attention.

Obviously the teacher needs to allow a little time for the students to take their seats (or sit on the carpet) during which time the teacher needs to convey that he or she is purposefully waiting for the class to be seated ("eyes, ears this way") and ready to begin.

It will help to have a brief discussion with each new class, in the establishment phase, concerning the basic expectations about classroom entry and settling at their work area or desk. Such settling varies with subject area, of course. In drama it may involve having shoes off, against the wall and sitting in a semi-circle; in an information technology (IT) room it may mean finding a seat, turning to face the front and sitting, waiting. The main thing is to have a workable routine that will enable 25–30 students to settle smoothly and consciously attend to group instruction/teaching time. Students also need to know that their attention (in the first three minutes) is expected ("eyes, ears at the front, thanks", "hands in lap" at infant level).

It can help (at upper primary and middle school) to establish and maintain a reasonable target time for group entry, settling, having relevant materials and being ready to engage in group learning. A reasonable target could be, say, 1–2 minutes. This target time is set as a class target, and encouraged and reviewed over the first half dozen lessons or so (Pearce 1997).

Cueing for attention in some classes may mean students go straight to an activity, as in English, where students file in, take their seats, quietly get out the class novel and read for, say, five minutes. Some schools still direct students to stand behind their seats quietly at the beginning and close of each lesson. Carried through positively, even this can be a useful cue. There are a range of non-verbal cues to establish group attention in the instructional phase of the lesson (see pp. 40–41).

Managing distracting and disruptive behaviour during the instructional phase of a lesson

The typical disruptions that can occur during the instruction phase of class lesson can range from rolling on the mat and hiding under tables (hopefully only at infants level – athough I did have a lad hide in a low cupboard once in Year 7!), through to those annoying pockets of private chats while the teacher is seeking to engage and teach the class.

The most common disruptions in this phase of the lesson tend to be: talking while the teacher is talking; cross-talking across the classroom; calling out to the teacher; lateness; leaning chairs and motoric restlessness; fiddling with stationery; and clowning (attention-seeking behaviours). Most of these behaviours tend to be exhibited in the establishment phase of the year as students test out their relationship with each other, with the group and with their teacher.

When exercising discipline in a whole-class, whole-group context it is important to be aware of what we do and say such that we avoid alienating the cooperative students. In this part of the lesson or activity, anything we do or say, in discipline terms, has an immediate audience effect beyond the individual (or small group) that we address. For example, if we are overly confrontational we create a tone, an emotionally palpable tone, that can hinder motivation and cooperation. While there are some occasions when a brief, unambiguous communication of frustration and anger is appropriate, most of the time, when we are dealing with the sort of disruptive behaviours noted earlier, it is important to be respectfully positive. Being positive, confident and *appropriately firm* are not antithetical concepts.

Several students are engaged in private conversations as the teacher is establishing initial class attention and focus. The teacher visually scans the room, standing relaxed (not slouching), and cues for group attention (p. 40). She briefly *describes* the behaviour of the disruptive students.

"A number of students across the room are talking while I'm trying to teach (…)."

Sometimes this description of reality is enough; it acts as an incidental direction. Sometimes we will need to add a behavioural direction.

"Facing this way and listening, thanks."

"Thanks" is to be preferred rather than please. "Thanks" carries an expectation of what is directed rather than a request (please).

Sometimes this private natter, or talking while the teacher is talking, is *unfocused* student behaviour rather than *disruptive* student behaviour. Either way the approach noted above keeps the discipline least intrusive (p. 56).

If the description and direction is focused on an individual (or several individuals) it is important to preface with the student's name(s): "Dean (…), you're fiddling with the window blinds" (the description of student behaviour). "*Facing* this way and *listening,* thanks." "Facing …" and "listening …" *behaviourally* direct the students to the expected behaviour.

Behavioural directions

When using behaviour directions it is helpful to focus on the required or expected behaviour, briefly and positively wherever possible (p. 57).

"Dean (…), you're calling out [the descriptive element]. *Hands up* and *waiting* thanks [the *behavioural* part]" is in preference to "Don't call out …" or "Why are you calling out …". Equally unhelpful is the question "Are you calling out?"

Students coming into class late

A student comes into class late. The teacher walks over to the door and asks, "Are you late?" It is surprising that the student doesn't answer, "Course I'm late!"

If the teacher asks, "*Why* are you late?" it sounds (particularly if the teacher is frustrated) as if the teacher is interrogating the student, when in fact the teacher may only want a reason. Does it matter, at that point in the lesson, *why* a student is late? Trying to get answers, and reasons, at the classroom door only feeds (in some students) incipient attention-seeking or even power provocation.

Teacher: Why are you late?
Student: People are late sometimes you know. *[If the student's tone is sulky, or hostile, the lateness issue can quickly become a scene where the student believes he must play to the gallery.]*
Teacher: Don't you speak to me like that!
Student: Yeah – well I'm only late, you don't have to hassle me. The girls are late sometimes – you don't hassle them do you?
Teacher: *[The extended index finger appears, in the air, in the space between them. The teacher's voice is rising]* Who do you think you are talking to?!
Student: Yeah well you're hassling me about being a few minutes late – Gees!
Teacher: Right! Go and sit over there. Now!! *[The teacher points to the few spare seats. The student doesn't want to sit there. He wants to sit in his normal seat, which is already occupied.]*
Student: I'm not sitting there. I sit down the back with Nathan and Travis …
Teacher: Look, I don't care where you sit. I said sit there!
Student: Nope. *[He sulkily folds his arms and looks away. The audience of his peers are having a "field day" on this one.]*
Teacher: Right! Get out – go on, get out! If you're not prepared to come to my class on time you can get out. Go on, see Mr Brown!
Student: Yeah, I'm going anyway, this is a sh-t class …! *[He turns and storms away.]*

Of course we need to address the issue of the student's lateness, but it is unnecessary to dwell on the lateness in front of the class like this. Some teachers get drawn in easily by the student's secondary behaviour (the tone of voice and the avoidance communication.

When students are late it is always helpful to welcome them, briefly and positively, especially in the first few lessons. We won't know, initially, if a student is late because he or she is lazy, disorganised or time-wasting, or if there are home-related issues (relevant to late arrival for Period 1).

Teacher: *[Welcomes student at the classroom door.]* Welcome (…). It's Tony, isn't it? *[Teacher is still learning names. He puts his hand out to shake hands with Tony. Tony frowns, looks a little tentative – not expecting this approach. The teacher, briefly and politely, acknowledges Tony's lateness.]* You're late. There's a spare seat over there – next to Carlos. *[The teacher doesn't tell Tony to sit there: he describes the obvious reality. He focuses on the important issue at this point in the lesson: direct the student to be seated and get on with the lesson.]*

Student: I don't sit there … I sit down the back with … *[He's less defensive with this teacher, but still procrastinates.]*

Teacher: Those seats are taken, Tony … *[The teacher could add, "And if you'd been here on time you would have had your bleedin seat!" … He resists the temptation!]* We can organise a seat change later. *[This adds a (future) choice, defusing any residual tension. At this point the teacher redirects his eye-contact away from Tony, turning to re-address the class; he scans his eyes across them.]* As I was saying folks … *[Resuming his lesson flow, as if Tony will (naturally) sit down where the teacher has incidentally directed. He does – he walks across to the seat in a slightly exaggerated, posturing, way and flops down. The teacher tactically ignores this residual secondary behaviour keeping his focus – and the class's attention – on the lesson.]*

He follows up with Tony later, at the end of the lesson, for a brief chat about the student's lateness. If the student is persistently late (three times over several consecutive days) he will take the lateness issue further with the year advisor to see if there is a pattern across other classes.

When students are late

- Welcome the student.
- Acknowledge (briefly) the lateness.
- Direct (incidentally where appropriate) student to a seat.
- Give take-up time (p. 68).
- Resume the flow of the lesson or activity.

Discipline in the establishment phase of the lesson

- Scan, focus, scan (avoid maintaining eye contact for too long with any one individual or small group).
- Keep language brief.
- Use positive language where possible.
- Focus on specific behaviour (when disciplining) or focus on the relevant rule.
- Avoid arguing with students – verbally block or partially agree and refocus back to the rule or main issue.
- *Tactically* ignore non-verbal secondary behaviours wherever possible and wherever appropriate. If a student's secondary behaviour is also inappropriate, or disruptive, address it briefly and refocus the student(s) back to the expected rule, or behaviour.

Description of reality (directing incidentally) in a civic setting

Have you ever had someone push in on you in a supermarket queue? It surprises me how many people let others, in effect, have more "right" to the front of the queue. On these occasions I often incidentally, politely and briefly *describe* our little bit of shared reality: "Excuse me (...), the queue starts there". An open hand rather than a pointing finger indicates the back of the queue.

A pleasant smile – no hint of sarcasm or "I'm threatened by you" or "I'm better, more important, than you". On some occasions I've had people say, "But I'm in a hurry". I find it helpful to briefly add (before turning away and giving some take-up time), "We're in a hurry too (referring to the others in the queue) the queue starts there. Thanks." Of course if the pushing-in person is 15 stone and has emblems of the Wermacht tattooed on his head, let him pass (or move to another queue)!

I was in the crowded underground station at London's Victoria Station one day last year. The commuters were going through the ticket barriers at rapid speed. There was a New Zealand couple (I could tell by the accent from a few yards away) trying vainly to get their crumpled ticket into the automatic barrier. They don't have underground railways in New Zealand. I was annoyed by the several pin-stripe-suited gentlemen huffing and puffing because the couple (replete with the fruits of their London shopping) were holding them up for 30–60 seconds of their life.

I walked over and said, in a firm voice, scanning the 20 or so in the queue, "Excuse me folks (...). These people are clearly struggling with the machine (...). There're several more over there. Thanks." I beckoned with my hand. They moved away, frowning and huffing, a few sighing – and several looked sympathetic. I think they thought I worked for London Underground. I don't – I'm a teacher, and I wanted to support my "Kiwi cousins".

I said to the older couple, "G'day – these machines aren't easy are they?" They looked relieved, more relaxed.

"You're Australian?"

"Yes ..."

We had a brief chat, sorted the ticket, and they went on their way.

Kyriacou has noted, "if one behaves as if one has authority, it is surprising how far this attitude exerts a momentum of its own leading pupils to behave accordingly" (1986: 132).

I would add that even in some civic settings adults can pick up the subtle cues and signals (as well as through language) and behave more considerately.

Non-verbal cue-ing

Many disruptive behaviours can be addressed – even nipped in the bud – by a non-verbal cue.

A couple of students are leaning back in their chairs as the lesson begins. The teacher pauses in her delivery and verbally cues the students, "David and Liam (...)". They look towards her. She cues non-verbally by extending her thumb and three fingers down to indicate a chair with four feet on the floor. When she initially established this class cue she communicated *both* the verbal and non-verbal aspects of the cue to associate the idea of chair legs "on the floor".

Non-verbal cues minimise the need for the teacher to verbalise the required behaviour every time. This is particularly helpful in early years classes.

Typical cues are:

- The teacher crosses his or her index fingers then beckons with the right hand to indicate facing the front to cue for "cross your legs and face the front".
- The teacher raises one hand, and and covers his or her mouth with the other to indicate "hands up without calling out" (to students who call out in class discussion time). Some calling out can be *tactically* ignored if the teacher is confident in such an approach but a non-verbal cue can act as a *brief* reminder without disturbing the flow of the activity too much.
- The teacher puts one hand over the other and pulls it in to the chest to indicate "keep hands and feet to yourself". This is an important cue for restless, touchy infants.
- The teacher touches one eye with a forefinger, then an ear, and uses a beckoning hand to the front of the room to indicate "eyes and ears this way now".
- The teacher holds up a thumb and forefinger a little distance apart to indicate "use your partner-voice, thanks". This is an effective reminder/direction during on-task learning time as the teacher is moving around the room. He or she may be working at one table and can remind a table group nearby by cueing across the room. I have used this reminder cue countless times in secondary classrooms.
- A similar cue I have used for years is the thumb and two fingers turning down, rotating an imaginary volume control (old-fashioned technology that one!).

As with any discipline strategy it is important to avoid any unnecessary tension. If the cue above were given with a jerky, thrusting hand and a glare and a big sigh from the teacher it would hardly be seen as a *simple* reminder!

When using a non-verbal cue for the first time it will be important to associate the meaning of the cue by giving both the non-verbal cue and the spoken reminder/direction.

Eye contact

Eye contact can engage attention, show interest and indicate intent. A stare, however, can create ambiguity if unaccompanied by verbal direction. Too long a stare may reciprocate, in some males, a perception of hostility or threat. Dodge (1981, 1985) has researched attributional bias in aggressive children, observing that aggressive boys *selectively* attend to the available cues in their environment, with a perceptual and attributional bias towards aggressive intent in the other party.

As teachers we can avoid unnecessary hostile attributions with such pupils by considering proximity, and following eye contact with a brief direction or reminder; avoiding unnecessarily extended eye contact; giving take-up time; and avoiding unnecessary win–lose perception by how we frame language – i.e. using appropriate choices (p. 59).

Tactical ignoring

Tactical ignoring is a difficult skill. It is a *conscious* decision not to attend to some student behaviours such as sulking, sighing, eyes to ceiling, the "hang-dog look", the wry mouth and frown when you direct students to do something really difficult like go back to their seats, or put their hands up without calling out, or put their pens down while you're talking to the class!

Tactical ignoring is also a form of non-verbal communication to all students (not just the student you are *tactically* ignoring). It demonstrates that the teacher is focused on the main issue and it further avoids overly reinforcing attentional secondary behaviours (p. 117): e.g. "Don't you raise your eyes to the ceiling like that …!" "Why can't you do something without sighing? What's wrong with you?"

We obviously should not ignore behaviours that the students know should not be ignored: any repeated and loud calling out, or butting-in that affects a teacher's right to teach; any verbally rude or defiant language; any hostile or aggressive behaviour.

In a class discussion, for example, it can be very effective to tactically ignore the few students who incidentally call out. It sends a message that the teacher will notice hands up *without* calling out or finger clicking. Of course, the teacher needs to do this in a way that does not appear anxious, tense or uncertain. Otherwise the ignoring adds confusion to what is happening. Students seem to know the difference.

Prefacing the tactical ignoring

The teacher is moving around the Year 3 classroom assisting, encouraging and clarifying. Bilal calls out across the classroom for "Miss" to help him. He has his hand up (he thinks as long as he has his hand up, even if he is calling out or clicking his fingers, he's within the rule and will get her attention). From a distance across the room the teacher gives a conditional direction and *then* tactically ignores Bilal's subsequent calling out: "Bilal (...), when you have your hand up without calling out then I'll come over to help". The *subsequent* ignoring now has a frame of understanding ("when … *then*").

A common example at kindergarten age occurs when an overly concerned, or anxious mother drops off her 4-year-old on Day 1, Week 1. The child cries, holds on to its mother and pleads. The mother assures the child, over and over again, "Yes I love you … my precious. I'll be back …I will. I promise … be a good boy … yes, I do love you". The child is really crying and may be anxious (although some children do learn to manufacture tears for attention). The mother naturally wants to reassure the child, but ends up reinforcing the child's attentional behaviour: the 45-minute goodbye. Most teachers quietly reassure the mother that if she goes, leaving the child with a confident, smiling assurance (once or twice) the child *will* settle down. ("Please ring later, in half an hour, Mrs Smith …") The teacher (after initial, warm assurance) will then tactically ignore the child's crying and firmly, pleasantly and kindly redirect the child without over-servicing the child's attention-seeking behaviour. In this example tactical ignoring involves selective attention reassuring, and refocusing as the child settles.

Take-up time

I was teaching a Year 10 class, as a mentor teacher, and as I scanned the room during on-task learning time I noticed that a student had what looked like a novel on top of his exercise book. I walked over.

"It's Damon, isn't it?" It was my first session with the class and I was still learning names.

He looked up (not attempting to close the book). "Yeah – it's Damon."

"I notice you've got a book there, a novel? What's it about?"

"It's about a serial killer," he said, looking up with a grin.

"Well, let's hope he's not after a teacher," I said (and meant it). This brief chat is a form of prefacing (p. 58) prior to some task refocusing. I thought it best to focus on the task.

"How's the work going?"

"It's boring," replied Damon.

"It may well be boring, Damon, but it's our work for today. Do you know what to do?"

My tone was pleasant, expectant of cooperation. He sighed, leaning back. "Yeah, sort of."

I gave a brief reminder of the task, pointing back to the board and adding, "By the way, the novel. I'd like you to put it in your bag or if you like you can leave it on my desk till the bell." He grinned back. "I'll come back and check on your work a little later, Damon." This was the discipline part of the brief engagement. The walking away, at that point, allowed some take-up time for the student and also gave a task refocus. With older children it only escalates unnecessary confrontation to take, or snatch, the distracting item. Similarly, if a directed choice is given to the student (as above) to stand there, waiting, until they put the item away also creates unnecessary tension.

Take-up time can also convey trust in the student that he or she will respond appropriately. It allows some face saving in potentially tense situations. It is important to go back to the student later to check if they are back on task and also to briefly re-establish the working relationship.

A student walks into a class late. Rather than make a big fuss the teacher welcomes the student, beckons to a spare seat and continues the flow of the lesson while the student is moving towards the seat. This gives the student take-up time, increasing expectation of cooperation. The teacher quickly resumes the flow of the lesson taking the spotlight away from the potential scene (p. 64). It will be important to follow-up the lateness beyond instructional time (during the on-task time), when a one-to-one chat can occur (p. 71).

With younger children the teacher may need to repeat a direction or reminder a few times until the child responds, and *then* give the take-up time as the child responds.

As children get older our management and discipline language should seek to engage the emergent adult within the young person by:
- not talking down to a student, or merely talking *at* them;
- seeking to engage the student in thinking about their behaviour: hence choices (p. 59), incidental language (p. 57) and thoughtful use of questions, particularly in front of a student's peers;
- not forcing students into a psychological corner (instead using deferred consequences (p. 103)).

An aside on uniform misdemeanours

Some schools still retain pettifogging application to rules about uniform and jewellery: only sleepers, but no pattern on the sleepers; studs, but only gold or silver, no pattern; socks must *always* be worn knee-high; no rings, or bangles, or friendship bands; hair must be a certain length; and so on. There may well be good reasons for some of the rules but is the application of the rules that ought to concern our *thoughtful* management.

A young girl is wearing a ring in class. A present from her father, it has a sentimental almost "Linus-like" psychological comfort for her. New to this school, she comes across a teacher who notices this major crime and asks her to hand it over. The girl is both upset and very frustrated.

"No. No way."

"Give it to me .... now."

The teacher repeats his command and puts his hand (palm out) to indicate he expects her unquestioning compliance.

"No!" the girl clenches her fist. She (quite naturally) doesn't know if she'll ever get it back. She mentions that the teachers in the other classes hadn't said anything.

"Right. You're on detention."

This may sound like a manufactured example, but it isn't. True, the teacher concerned may not have known the girl's psychological attachment to the ring. True, the teacher may be seeking to be vigilant about the uniform/dress code. The problem is he has not tuned into the girl's welfare as part of the discipline process and he lacks any skill in managing natural adolescent behaviour. He seems only concerned about the pettifogging application of the rule. He may also hold demanding, absolutist views about control and vigilant teacher discipline.

In another class at the same school a teacher comes up to a student wearing a ring during on-task time.

"Rachel, that's an attractive ring."

The girl has a brief chat with her teacher.

"You know the rule about rings?" (The teacher's voice is quiet. She is keeping it low key).

"But other teachers haven't said anything," the girl frowns.

"Maybe they haven't, Rachel, but the school rule is ...." The teacher partially agrees (p. 59) and refocuses to the school rule. The teacher gives a non-verbal signal to the student's pocket indicating for the girl to put it away in her pocket. The girl owns her behaviour. Relaxed vigilance.

End of story. If the girl refuses a fair directed choice like this, the teacher knows the issue is probably an incipient power struggle and will defer the matter to an out-of-class follow-up (p. 71). If the teacher catches her with the ring on again in a school like this the issue may occasion a stay-back session to emphasise the rule.

If you ever happen to teach in a school that promotes a confiscation policy on rule-breaking jewellery, at least give the dignity of assurance of returning it the same day. I've known "power-merchant" teachers to keep rings and non-dangerous *objets d'art* until the end of term! That is simply psychological harassment. It always staggers me that some students will easily hand such items over. In schools where students do not evidence unquestioning compliance to teacher control such an order ("Hand the ring over") would be laughed at.

More than personality

I have heard teachers observing some of their colleagues' behaviour management practice with the disclaimer, "Oh, it's just their personality. That's why they can get through to those students". While personality is important, if they observe more carefully, they will note that these colleagues are also aware of their own non-verbal communication and the impact of their global set of behaviours on others. They will note that these teachers are conscious of their management and discipline language.

There are skills that can enhance personality and aid positive communication: increasing positive congruence between what we communicate (content), how we communicate (non-verbal tone), timing (when we intervene) and why we choose to communicate this way at all (our values and our aims).

While some people are naturally effective communicators, most of us have to learn that our non-verbal behaviours have significant weight in our daily communication. These non-verbal behaviour cues can enable positive, workable relationships with our students (and colleagues). Even when we are frustrated and angry, some non-verbal cues will make the communication process less stressful and easier to repair and rebuild when the heat has died down (p. 134).

> A common belief is that group management skills are simply a natural gift. You either have it or you don't. Our evidence does not support this belief. Its most damaging feature is that teachers who have difficulty controlling classes tend to put this down to personal inadequacy rather than to a lack of particular skills that can be acquired through training or advice from colleagues.
>
> The most talented, "natural" teachers may need little training or advice because they learn so quickly from experience. At the other extreme, there are a few teachers for whom training and advice will not be properly effective because their personalities do not match the needs of the job. *It is clear, however, that the majority of teachers can become more effective classroom managers as a result of the right kinds of training, experience and support.*
>
> (Elton Report 1989: 69, rec. 13–16, emphasis added)

As in all reflective teaching we should, essentially, consider the *effect* of our behaviour on others and trust that they will do likewise (no new message this, just a difficult one).

Seen on a school notice board

I will not yell in class and I will not throw things & I will not pinch or even hit and I will not have a temper tantrum & I must always be a good example to all the kids ... because I am the teacher ... I am the teacher ... I am the teacher ... I am the teacher ... I am the teacher ...

Some wag had added at the bottom:

To be read each morning in case it will be one of those days.

(When is it not?)

Following up with students beyond the classroom setting

There are a number of reasons why we will need to follow-up with students beyond the classroom:

- To clarify an issue relating to class learning (homework or misunderstanding about class work or a student getting behind with their work). In this case the follow-up is normally to emphasise empathetic teacher support. There should not be any emphasis on punishment for students who are currently struggling with classroom learning, or work/task assignments.
- To initiate a discussion about a concern regarding the student's behaviour.
- To follow through with any *deferred* consequences (p. 103). A typical example is when a student has left a mess and has made no effort to clean up. At primary level teachers sometimes use deferred consequences for students who have made no effort to complete classwork.
- To initiate a process of mediation with students who have exhibited conflict behaviour in class time.
- To initiate detention or formal stay-back procedures (p. 106f.).

When following-up with students in an out-of-classroom setting:

- Consider whether a follow-up or follow-through session is merited in the first instance.

  At secondary level it is often difficult to follow-up issues between classes (especially during a six-period day!). Sometimes one can manage a *brief* word of follow-up after class and sometimes that may be enough. If the issue is important enough, though, it is worth directing the student to come to a later meeting (e.g. during the lunch break). In that brief moment after class we won't be able to go into the details; it will be enough to make the appointment.

  Ethical probity
  When conducting any one-to-one teacher–student stay-back session, it is crucial to be sensitive to ethical probity, particularly with a male teacher and female student or vice versa. It will help in any extended one-to-one sessions to have a colleague of the opposite sex present in the room (abstractedly working on their work programme) while conducting the follow-up.

- Whether the follow-up is a brief chat, a task based consequence (i.e. cleaning up mess left), an interview with a student or even a detention (p. 106f.) it is important that the teacher emphasise the certainty rather than the severity of the consequence (p. 99).

  I have seen teachers confront students after class with their pointed index finger a few inches from the student's face, exhorting their "pound of flesh" (emotional, psychological, pay-back). "Yes!! You're inside now, eh? Missing playtime. Well it serves you right. If you had done what I said you could be outside now wouldn't you?! Eh …! But no …, no …, you had to play the big man didn't you?!"

  I can understand how some teachers *feel* at this point. I can understand that they want to make the child *feel* bad, and even suffer, through this process. But it is counter-productive and unnecessary. The student, in this case, will hardly learn anything constructive about the consequential nature of his or her behaviour through such an exercise.

- Tune in briefly to how the student is (probably) feeling at this point – they probably want to be outside with their mates, and may be really annoyed, even angry, or possibly even anxious. By briefly tuning in we humanise the

follow-up while retaining consequential certainty. "You're probably feeling annoyed that I've asked you to stay back after class [or to have this meeting at lunchtime, or ...]". Our tone and manner here (as so often in discipline transactions) are really important. If we sound as if this follow-up session (however short in terms of time) is some kind of win for the teacher, the student will probably define the issue in those terms as well.

- Focus specifically on the student's behaviour, or the issue of concern you have as their teacher: "I'm concerned about what happened in class when ...".

  If it is a task-related consequence it is enough to direct the student(s) to the task-requirement: "Bradley when the work area is tidy (be brief and specific) then you'll be ready for recess ...". With task-focused consequences it can help to refer to the class routine/rule: "In our class we leave our work areas tidy ...".

  In helping to *specifically* focus on a student's disruptive behaviour it may be appropriate to mirror the student's behaviour (Rogers 1997). When mirroring the teacher briefly acts out the typical, characteristic, disruptive behaviour of the student (i.e. calling out, frequent seat leaving, loudness or talking while the teacher is talking) and even their 'secondary' behaviours (pp. 10–12).

  When mirroring behaviour in this one-to-one context:
  - ask permission of the student: "I'd like to show you what I mean when I'm referring to you calling out ..."; "Do you mind if I give you a brief demo of how loud you often speak in class ...?"; "Let me show you what I see you do when you push and pinch others when you're sitting on the mat in carpet time [this to an infant student]";
  - keep the actual mirroring brief;
  - avoid the impression you're getting some Machiavellian satisfaction out of showing the student how annoying, or stupid they are;
  - having mirrored the student's typical classroom behaviour, physically step back (as it were) from the kinaesthetic re-creation;
  - refer back to the mirrored behaviour to further clarify the issue of concern: "So *that's* what it looks like when you ...";
  - with older students it can help to invite a response: "So how many times do you think you call out like that?"

Mirroring is an attempt to illustrate and clarify a student's characteristic disruptive behaviour and to enable teacher–student dialogue. It is used in the context of teacher support, to help the student own and change their pattern of behaviour.

- Where appropriate, invite the student's right of reply. This can be verbal or written. Ask questions that will enable the student to focus on their behaviour in the light of what happened (to occasion the staying back) and refer back to the basic rights and responsibilities in the student behaviour agreement (p. 27f.). In this the teacher is making the important point that, in some way, the student's behaviour has affected someone else's rights.

  The basic questions we can ask are: "What happened …?"; "What rule or right was affected by your behaviour …?"; "How do you see what happened, and how do you feel about it?"; "What can you do to change things … fix things up … sort things out … make things better …?". These can even be presented as a written proforma. We could call this proforma the "4W" form, after the four questions prefaced "What …?".

  Some supplementary questions when involving a student in a longer follow-up session can include:
  - "What do you want to happen – for you?"
  - "What do you think will happen if you …[keep reacting in class like …; be specific]?"
  - "What can you do so that others can get on with their work without …[make reference, briefly, to the student's current behaviour]?" 'What can you do so that others can feel safe?"
  - "How can I, and your other teachers, help you to …[be specific about the key behaviours necessary to change for the student to get some success back into his classroom learning and social engagement]?"

  The spirit and tone in which these questions are asked are crucial. If they are asked in a provocative, confrontational way they will (obviously) create the very resentment and resistance the teacher is seeking to refocus with the student.

  The emphasis with all extended follow-up on issues of behaviour is to enable the student to become more self-aware (with regard to their behaviour).

  The outcome of these questions should be some understanding, even some plan, that will increase the student's sense of self-monitoring and regulating behaviour (see also p. 122f.).

  If the student does not respond to *supportive* questioning, or even refuses to cooperate, the teacher can still make the following points clear so the student is as aware as possible of what needs to change:
  - "This is what I see, and note, about your behaviour …[be specific]."
  - "It isn't helping you when you …[be specific]."
  - "This is what you'll need to do if you want to change your behaviour so that you can …[be specific]."

  Allow take-up time for the student to respond to *each* issue raised, and assure the student of your willingness to support them in making a behaviour plan.

- Another approach when working with students who present with resistant patterns of behaviour is to explore, with them, their likely goals behind their behaviour in terms of attention and power (see Ch. 6, p. 118).

  Some students will frequently use the line (even whine) that "I can't …": "I can't do the work …". A firm, supportive, focusing can often help:

"Perhaps you can't do the work:
- *because* you're not facing the front and listening during the teaching time …;
- *because* you haven't got your pen, ruler and pencil ready to start …;
- *because* you haven't read through the task [assuming their reading skills are proficient – if they're not we should always find creative ways to adjust the task as well as extend their thinking] …;
- *because* you're easily distracted by sitting near Dean …

So let's make a plan to … [address the cant's]".

A plan can then be developed that will incrementally build up academic survival skills and behaviours to enhance the student's learning (p. 122f.).

As with all communication with students in situations where there is natural, ambient, tension:
- calm yourself before trying to calm the student;
- avoid rushing the dialogue (allow some time for student response);
- be aware of your open, non-confrontational, body language;
- avoid crowding their personal space;
- keep the focus on the primary behaviour or primary issue of concern (avoid pointless arguing);
- refer to the student behaviour agreement (p. 27f.);
- keep a supportive, invitational, tone wherever possible.

• With task-based consequences it is enough to direct the student to the task, give them some take-up time and check for task completion.

• Separate amicably. I've heard teachers raise the strained-relationship stakes by having the unnecessary last word: "… and if you pull that stunt again I'll …!!"

• Track the student in terms of ongoing disruptive behaviour. If the follow-up session sees no discernible change in the student's behaviour or attitude it will be worth checking with other colleagues (through the team leader/year advisor) to see if this behaviour is *typical*, *frequent*, or *characteristic* across the year level and across classes. If there is typical, frequent disruptive behaviour in such cases it is wiser to have a year-level, whole-staff approach to working with the student (p. 121).

A colleague recently told me:

"I followed up all my rude students, all the difficult ones, and the ones with learning problems. I even withdrew students from colleagues' classes where necessary, to follow up. I used the 4W form (p. 73) (they didn't like that; they said 'Why don't you gives us lines like the other teachers. We have to think with these questions!') Well, by the end of first term I was buggered! But second term was a breeze."

He wasn't being smart, or clever. This colleague is a good, kind and patient teacher. What he was saying was that early follow-up and follow-through in the establishment phase of the year paid off.

Chapter 4
Effective teaching: fundamental understandings and skills

A teacher should have maximal authority
and minimal power.
Thomas Szasz

Effective teaching: some fundamental considerations

The term "effective" needs a little reflective thought. Effective at what? For whom? At what cost? In what way?

If "effective" is pursued merely or only in utilitarian terms then intentional humiliation, manipulation, sarcasm, public shaming and embarrassment can all be utilised by a teacher as long as such behaviour "effectively" shuts a student up, quietens down a class, creates anxious compliance or gets the work done. Hopefully none of us would want that. Many of us grew up with teachers who made us stand when we got less than 5 marks out of 10 in a spelling test (or whatever), or made us do a maths problem on the board (and we couldn't) or said we were "stupid" or "thick" because we didn't understand something the first time. Thankfully, there are few teachers like that in schools now.

"Effective", in any meaningful sense, also needs to include the *values* that underlie what we aspire to in "effective teaching". Core values such as respecting all students (even basic civic respect) and equality of treatment (fairness) are universally accepted by students of any age as redolent of "effective" teaching.

There are a number of characteristics of effective teaching that are present across every age of student and teaching situation.[1]

• The teacher appears to be self-confident, patient and good-humoured (bad days notwithstanding; p. 4). The teacher also displays a genuine interest in the topic and makes a genuine attempt to be actively involved in and concerned with each student's progress. Even a basic commitment to acknowledge and affirm a student's effort in their work, in their progress, will affect student motivation in a positive way. Of course, our acknowledgment, affirmation and encouragement need to be genuine if they are going to be accepted and valued by students (p. 22).

  Even a positive greeting to the whole class (as well as individuals as they enter) can assist in engaging a sense of basic *belonging* here in *this* place – our classroom.

• The teacher's explanations and instructions are clear and pitched at a level likely to "connect" in terms of student understanding, needs and comprehension. One of the most basic aspects of effective (and competent) teaching is that the teacher explains the purpose and relevance of what they are teaching and the particular learning tasks that flow from them. When we set up learning tasks and experiences (that flow from shared dialogue in the instructional phase) we need to make the aims of the task clear and outline the basic expectations (even steps) about how the learning can progress.

It is also crucially important that teachers make an effort to *engage* students and sustain reasonable attention to the topic. Such engagement also involves conveying some enthusiasm for the topic at hand.

> Teaching is an affective process as well as a cognitive one. It is essential therefore that one conveys positive attitudes not only towards one's subject but also towards pupils ... it is never advisable to devalue what one is about to teach ... better to present the subject to the best of one's ability and let the pupils decide whether it has any intrinsic merit
>
> (Robertson 1997: 70)

Mr Smith sees his class lining up haphazardly, in the corridor outside Room 15. As he walks towards them he doesn't greet them: not even a basic "Hi". He opens the door and walks in, and the students file in noisily.

He doesn't greet them, or welcome them, or calm the class down. He really hasn't made an effort to learn their names yet (it's Week 4).

He does not introduce the topic or integrate it into any prior learning.

He starts to write algorithms on the board (Year 8 mathematics), with little or no enthusiasm. There is no apparent consideration that some students who struggle with some of the more abstract aspects of mathematics may benefit from some *visual* connectedness.

Yes, he may be tired *today*. He may be bored. But if he *characteristically* teaches like this is there any wonder that there is a correlation between:
- student inattention and his approach to the topic that day;
- his lack of enthusiasm, or even *basic* engagement, and student disinterest and lack of motivation;
- student learning outcomes and teaching style?

A lack of basic commitment to the fact that children learn in different ways will affect student learning; not all students are auditory learners.

- The teacher is aware that his or her characteristic voice and actions can significantly facilitate students' attention, interest, motivation and cooperation. Although we are *not* actors we do have to project some visible presence, and pay some conscious attention to voice usage, manner, attitude and approach so as to *engage* students in our teaching presentation and communication. This means much more than the ability to talk, to "tell", and "direct".

As Robertson notes:

> Perhaps with the exception of the first few meetings with a class, a warm and relaxed greeting before the lesson begins will often make all concerned feel better and no matter how many times a lesson has to be repeated, nor how tired one feels, one's interest with the material must be kept alive or the class will soon share the lack of interest.
>
> (1997: 69).

- The teacher makes both a positive and *varied* use of questioning to motivate and monitor students' understanding and raise the level *and* quality of students' thinking. This issue is discussed at some length later (pp. 85–6).

- The teacher monitors the progress of a given lesson *and* monitors general and individual behaviour as it affects teaching and learning. Such monitoring enables the teacher to make appropriate adjustments to the flow and development of a given lesson as well as addressing any inattentive or disruptive behaviour with a focus back to the central business of teaching and learning. This monitoring is conducted as unintrusively as possible.

- The teacher makes a conscious and willing effort to encourage students in *their* effort and progress and gives thoughtful praise and encouragement:
  - keep the encouragement *descriptive* rather than global (i.e. "That was a moving and thoughtful description of ... in your poem about ..." rather than simply noting "good work", "brilliant work" or "9 out of 10 great work ...");
  - use private rather than public praise (which can create unnecessary embarrassment with older students);
  - focus on the students' effort and progress as well as errors and mistake; use errors and mistakes as opportunities for the student to learn and gain.

  The topic of encouragement is discussed later in this chapter (p. 88f.).

A colleague, Bill Kemp, outlines how he encouraged a reluctant learner in a Year 10 mathematics class. It is Thursday afternoon, last period, in Year 10 mathematics. Students are tired and it has been a hot week. Just around the corner looms the end-of-year mathematics exam. The kids have started revision lessons with me but they are still a bit unsure about exactly which topics are in the exam and which are not.

Michelle listens as I list the topics and chapter reference and exclaims, "No, not lighthouses. I hate lighthouses!" when I mention that Chapter 7 (trigonometry) is on the list.

I continued the session with my students, building them up and encouraging them in the strange, "language other than English" subject called mathematics, and genuinely looked forward to teaching the group again first period on Friday (in 18 hours' time). Michelle's comments triggered in me an automatic response to stop the standard "how high above sea-level is the lighthouse" problem being a stumbling block to her mathematical progression, and make it a springboard into a whole ocean of mathematical wonder (or at least give her the chance to pass this type of question in the exam!).

I created a hand-out sheet with three or four revision questions for the Friday morning class. The most important question on the sheet, of course, had a stick figure diagram of Michelle firing a shot from a cannon towards a lighthouse with the appropriate trigonometric detail on the diagram to help the students find out how far the shot travels to destroy the lighthouse (an old lighthouse under demolition).

The result the next day was very satisfying and fruitful. The class saw the stick figure named Michelle and the class tom-toms soon got the message around the room to check out question 3 on the sheet. Michelle read the question and asked me, "Did you make up this question because of what I said yesterday?". I acknowledged it and was pleased to read on her face a look of "I'm important. Mr Kemp has gone to all this trouble just for me. I'd better have a red hot go at these lighthouse questions". Michelle now owns that trigonometry question and, through her efforts to do her best to learn mathematics skills, has overcome the fear of the lighthouse question.

It is my joy to be teaching in a lighthouse to shine out light to students to guide them away, around and past the dangerous rocks of doubt and "I can't do it" attitudes and "I hate maths because I don't understand it".

- Any management of distracting and disruptive behaviour is minimised by keeping attention on the central business: teaching and learning.

"Relaxed vigilance" is a useful descriptor when addressing typical disruptions such as lateness, calling-out, butting-in, talking while the teacher is talking, inattentive motoric restlessnessm and so on.

"Relaxed vigilance" describes the teacher's confident, assured, firm expectations about cooperative compliance when engaged in behaviour management. Group monitoring, through periodic scanning and eye contact (of the class as a whole as well as individuals), is a way of saying "I know that you know that I know".

Circulating (during the on-task phase of the lesson) and proximity can even divert some potentially off-task and poor attentional behaviour. Circulating also allows teachers to monitor task engagement and to give feedback and encouragement. I've seen some teachers characteristically sit at their desk for the whole lesson and never circulate among their students.

When addressing disruptive behaviour:
  - keep the level and degree of intrusiveness low. Recall the principle of *least to most intrusive* (p. 56);
  - keep the engagement of disruptive behaviour brief and keep the language positive (where possible);
  - remember that tone of voice and manner are as important as the words themselves when communicating respectful discipline;
  - focus on the primary behaviour, or primary issue, wherever possible – avoid getting easily distracted by secondary issues and secondary behaviours (pp. 10–14);
  - where possible, conduct any criticism of a student privately, or if it has to be given publicly do so in a least-intrusive, *brief* and respectful manner;
  - give take-up time (where possible) following corrective discipline (p. 57);
  - use choices instead of threats (p. 59);
  - refer back to the class agreement on core rights, responsibilities and rules (p. 27f.);
  - have a well-planned time-out policy at the classroom and exit-from-the-classroom levels. No teacher should have to cope with a situation where a student effectively holds a class to ransom. Collegial back-up and follow-through is essential in the time-out process (p. 100f.);
  - always follow-up and follow-through with a student on issues that count. Avoid easily passing-on discipline/behaviour/management concerns to other colleagues. Utilise their skills, their relational good-will and their expertise to *help with* the follow-up or follow-through (p. 71).

- There are many (and varied) *potential* disruptions to a lesson from lateness, calling out, noise levels, not having equipment and seat-rocking through to play punching, testosteronic bonding and (rarely one hopes) hostile or aggressive behaviours. Effective teachers, and effective teaching, address potential (and likely) disruptions to learning by thinking through classroom management issues preventatively. Things to consider are:
  - organisational issues (from lining up and seating plans through to students who "haven't got a pen ...") (p. 45);
  - lesson materials and their distribution and use at appropriate times (so they don't distract particularly during instructional time);
  - thinking through how we'll *engage* students' interest within a given lesson or topic and how we'll stimulate some marginal motivation through examples, current issues, use of questioning, concrete examples or illustrations, and so on;

I noticed this young lad (Year 8 class) not doing his work. I also noticed that he was engaging his hormonal-bridge-building-possibility eyes on his amour. I asked him (quietly – an aside),
   "What are you doing?"
He replied, wistfully,
   "I'm thinking love thoughts".

W. Rogers.

- thinking through how time will be managed in a lesson;
- planning how we will deal with typical disruptions in the establishment phase of the lesson itself (such as lateness, noise level, settling a class, initiating and sustaining class or group attention, dealing with students who call out, butt in, or seek to derail a lesson). Such planning has to include what sorts of things we'll say to address these typical, or likely, issues (Ch. 3).
- how we will deal with typical disruptions during the on-task phase of the lesson (p. 43f.).

The key question we ask is: "How can I *prevent*, or *minimise*, unnecessary hassles or problems ...?"

Most of this preventative aspect of teaching and management occurs in the establishment phase of the year. This is where we develop, then *teach* and monitor the rules and routines to students about lining up or hats off; rules about toilet provision, going for a drink or chewing gum; routines for noise level, seating and how to get reasonable teacher assistance, through to how to pack up, leaving the room tidy and how we leave and exit the classroom (Ch. 2).

In establishing these fundamental routines and rules it is essential to discuss *with* students *why* we have such routines (basically, fair for all) and try to increase some commonality of *core* routines across classes (Ch. 2).

Most of all, the preventative questions are best explored within the context of colleague support. Colleague support can give assurance that we're basically on the right track (or the best track at the moment!). Colleague support can give the moral back-up that we're all in the same boat, facing common issues, concerns and problems and have common responsibilities. Colleague support can also give us the long-term professional support we need to reflect, evaluate, assess and appraise our day-to-day teaching. Such appraisal, of course, needs to be based in professional trust and professional goodwill. Teaching can, at times, be a lonely profession. Colleague support has the potential to meet the basic need we have to belong and work as a team of professionals.

I was sitting in a very large lecture theatre listening to an international lecturer. I was at the back, in tiered seating, and could see the few hundred below. The lecturer was introduced. He had an hour, presenting a keynote address. Within ten minutes he had lost a significant group of adults. He was hesitant and looked flustered, and his overhead sheets were complex and unreadable. His examples seemed obtuse and unrelated. His voice was often vocally monotonic and he rarely smiled or scanned the eyes of the group (scanning, of course, would have given him some feedback from sections of his audience). He frequently looked down at his notes. There were no lifting moments, or defusing moments of light humour (I'm not talking about jokes either); in effect he didn't connect with us. We never really heard what he *felt* as well as what he *knew* about the topic in question, or what impact his subject and topic had on him and his world. I'm sure his research was more than adequate. He just wasn't communicating; he wasn't making his world more common to, and with, us.

In front of me sat two colleagues (psychologists) who had started to write notes to each other, and giggle and whisper (quite loudly). They were completely ignoring this lecturer.

I leaned over and whispered, "He's trying to communicate to us."

They replied, "But he's so bloody boring!"

I thought (yet again) how fragile one's hold is on others' attention as a teacher. I felt for this man – he was clearly nervous and probably anxious – yet I also understood why my colleagues behaved as they did.

Effective teaching *behaviours* are not mere technique; it is not a matter of "a bundle of skills equals an effective teacher". The skills of effective teaching can be learned, but those skills need to be engaged within a desire to teach. The behaviours of effective teaching are not inconsistent with the appropriate sharing of our humanity and feelings.

Effective teaching is our normative, *professional*, responsibility.

Humour, warmth and rapport

William Glasser has said that one of our basic needs is the need for fun (1992). By this he means that the classroom teacher needs to recognise the importance of feeling both emotionally and intellectualy positive.

Children of all ages value and enjoy working with teachers who have a sense of humour, which can range from the funny turn of phrase to facial expressions, Pythonesque irony, appropriate farce and self-humour (as with *faux pas*). One doesn't have to tell jokes (my memory for jokes is weak). The *bon mot*, repartee, and an apt turn of phrase can all defuse tension, refocus jaded students and lift their spirits (even transitionally).

I have seen classrooms where there is no laughter, warmth or basic *joi de vivre*. The are depressing places to work and learn in. Of course learning cannot always be fun. It is a bit of a grind, actually. That's the point. In the "gristle" of it all, the humour gives the enabling sense that "we're all in the same boat, going in roughly the same direction". Shared humour affirms something basic about our humanity.

A note on teacher status and authority

When teachers seek to establish both appropriate moral authority and role authority it is important to realise that such authority is established, and earned, within the context of relationships built by the teacher. The fundamental nature of such relationships is dependent on conveying respect, knowledge and enthusiasm for what one teaches. Authority is also communicated through a relaxed confidence in one's management and teaching and a healthy acceptance of fallibility in self (and others). As Robertson (1997) notes:

> Teachers who wish to establish their authority should behave as if they are already *in* authority. This is not as simple as it sounds. A teacher by virtue of (a certain) "status" has certain rights to behave in ways denied to pupils, and in exercising those rights he reinforces his authority. This does not mean that he should be repressive or authoritarian but rather that his behaviour should be consistent with his status.
>
> Pupils are less likely to question a teacher's authority if, by his behaviour, he defines the situation as one in which his authority is legitimate. It is particularly important for a teacher to do this in the first meeting with a new class. (1997: 10, 11)

Some key aspects in conveying appropriate authority

- Moral authority superintends role authority. The power associated with one's authority needs to be understood as more than power over others.

  Do we use our leadership, experience and legitimate role authority to lead and guide young people towards increasing self-discipline and respect for others' rights? Our leadership, management, teaching and discipline are not aimed merely at controlling others but at helping them to control themselves and manage themselves and their learning.

  "Relational power", rather than the utility of "controlling power", is a crucial factor when establishing and maintaining one's moral authority with students. Relational power is in part established in the first meetings with our students and developed, and sustained, through demonstration of mutual respect and mutual regard.

- When establishing and maintaining such authority the teacher:
  - creates a positive tone of purposefulness in "why we are here together in school ..." and "why we are here today in *this* lesson and doing *this* activity ...";
  - sustains students' attention and motivation; this is a crucial factor in effective teaching. Without the ability to both initiate, engage and sustain attention and show some enthusiasm for one's subject or lesson, students are unlikely to either involve themselves in any workable (or meaningful) learning let alone behave in ways that consider classmates and teacher alike (see Rogers 1997);
  - ensures the appropriateness of the learning activity and task. This (obviously) ranges from catering for students' ability range, through consciously considering visual (as well as auditory) learning styles, to thoughtful seating plans, and how resources can be best utilised with individual or group learning.

  Basically, a teacher's authority needs to be based in effective teaching rather than a status position based on coercion or displays of authoritarian management (which ultimately fail in the longer term).

Well prepared lessons, the ability to present and communicate clearly and to communicate knowledge, information and skills with some energy and clarity, together with the ability to engage student attention and interest and develop shared dialogue and to clarify learning tasks and activities are crucial to any effective, overall management.

If, for example, a teacher typically stands in front of the class looking uninterested, or even bored with what he or she is about to teach; if he or she has not prepared some clear lesson focus and some key learning aims and tasks; if he or she does not use any visual learning cues and does not tie the learning focus into some fundamental shared experience; if his or her voice carries little engaging motivation, tone or perceptible interest (from known to less known) it will take a very patient class to sit through the lesson without some disruptive, off-task behaviours.

- A teacher's authority is quickly assessed by students through his or her overall behaviour. His or her *characteristic* tone of voice, facial expressions, eye contact, scanning and posture can all signal emotional state, and can convey how confident, assured or anxious the teacher is. The teacher's characteristic global set of behaviours (verbal and non-verbal) are typically assessed by students in the early stages of their relationship with a class.

  Pupils are typically reported as liking teachers who can keep order (without being too strict); are fair (i.e. are consistent and have no favourites); can explain clearly and give help; give interesting lessons, and are friendly and patient.[2]   (Kyriacou 1986: 139)

- When exercising our *rights* of leadership and authority we need to recognised that such rights depend on cognate responsibilities. There is a sense in which a teacher's authority is acknowledged and accepted by the *reciprocity* occurring in the leadership role.

  For example, when a teacher walks across to a student's desk and comments about a toy on their desk and then gives a directed choice (p. 59), "David, I want you to put that toy in your bag or on my desk, thanks ...", and the student puts the toy in his bag, the student, in effect, gives the teacher *the authority that the teacher confidently exercises at that point*. This is the nature of the "reciprocity" occurring within relational authority. For one teacher the words used earlier (in the choice about the toy) could sound like a directed choice; in the mouth of another teacher they could well sound like a challenge or threat; yet another teacher may make it appear as even a plea.

  When a teacher says to a class group, "Eyes and ears this way now (...), thanks" (or another of the many variations in the "gaining class attention" theme), the fact that most students do face the front and actually listen indicates a notable feature about this relational reciprocity; the authority to lead, guide, remind, direct, make choices clear, give consequences (etc.), and teach, depends on students acknowledging such authority *by their reciprocal action(s)*. This is the natural, even creative, tension in teacher authority.

  Authority exists in a relationship and is to a large extent granted by the students. It is in everyone's interest that there should be a context in which teaching and learning can take place and teachers must be granted the authority required to perform this role. For their part they will have to earn this authority by the quality of their teaching but it is also helpful from the outset to behave as if they already have it, in a more formal manner consistent with their rank.

When a person behaves in a confident and efficient manner we are inclined to believe that such behaviour reflects knowledge and experience. In the school situation the reality is that teachers *are* in positions of authority in relation to students but their behaviour must be consistent with this and hence imply knowledge and experience; thus the teacher can "claim" authority. (Robertson 1997: 75)

- Always be prepared to follow-up and follow-through with a student on issues that count, such as concerns about a student's learning or work, concerns about behaviour or the need to carry through with appropriate consequences (p. 71). As with all follow-up beyond the classroom setting, a teacher needs to communicate care and concern as well as the authority to address behaviour issues or apply consequences. Alongside any follow-up one should also be willing to repair and rebuild.

In any one school, there can be significant differences in the authority granted to teachers by the students. Those differences transcend age and gender. According to Robertson (1997), Kyriacou (1986) and Rogers (2000) it is one's personal qualities, demonstrated in effective teaching and management, rather than mere *role*, that determines relational authority.

While this may sound obvious in print I've seen many teachers, in practice, merely expect to have their authority accepted when they clearly are ill-prepared, do not find workable interest and entry points into student understanding, teach in a boring uninteresting way with little enthusiasm and give infrequent encouragement and feedback to their students.

It should also be expected of teachers that they are of such a personality and character that they are able to command the respect of their pupils, not only by their knowledge of what they teach and their ability to make it interesting but by the respect which they show for their pupils, their genuine interest and curiosity about what pupils say and think and the quality of their professional concern for individuals. It is only where this two-way passage of liking and respect between good teachers and pupils exists, that the educational development of pupils can genuinely flourish. (Kyriacou 1986: 139)

Dialects and accents – an issue to be considered

There are some distinct dialects across the UK. I still struggle, sometimes, to understand *every* word in some UK accents. No offence – I'm sure it's the same with understanding some Aussies, although *Neighbours* has been on your TV screens for a long time now! There are teachers whose dialect (or language other than English) is sometimes an occasion for children to tease them or have a bit of fun. I've worked with teachers who have sometimes been demoralised by calculatingly snide comments where several students collude by laughing loudly at the teacher's turn of phrase or use of words.

Communicating clearly and speaking clearly are crucial aspects of day-to-day teaching. Where teachers are aware that their accent, typical voice usage or English pronunciation may, potentially, affect their teaching and classroom management, the following will help.

- Plan ahead by discussing with colleagues what they might, or could, do should the issue arise. This could include typical responses to student comments.
- It can help to explain, briefly and confidently to students at the beginning of each of their first classes, that, "you will, quickly, notice that my accent, in

English, is a bit different. Sometimes I might mispronounce words from time to time. I work hard on my English. Thanks in advance for your understanding and support". *Prepare* a brief "explanation" beforehand. I've seen colleagues from Vietnam, Italy, Greece and Lebanon communicate this initial shared understanding, skilfully, with tact and even humour. It may be helpful to invite questions from the students. My own view is that the explanation should suffice. If our subsequent teaching is effective, the accent shouldn't matter (p. 75f.).

- If a student is rude or derogatory about one's accent or use of English, it will be enough to briefly, firmly, without any hostility, make the brief assertive point, "I don't make unfair (or put-down) comments about your speech; I don't expect you to make unfair comments about mine". The tone of such a statement needs to be confidently firm and calm. It is not a threat, it is an assertion – avoid any argument. In such cases it is enough to assert and then to move on with the lesson or activity. Sometimes even brief repartee may be appropriate.
- If some students persist in being disruptive by snide comments, "I can't understand you, Miss. You're not saying it clear. What do yer mean?" (or worse), use the time-out provision in the short term (p. 100f.).
- Always follow-up *any* abusive comments made by students (p. 71f.). If necessary ask a senior colleague (early in the first week) to call a meeting with the students concerned and conduct an "accountability conference" (p. 148f.).

Inviting and sustaining engagement

Students need to know that their *participation* in the lesson will be expected by the teacher. At the beginning of each lesson students will need to be reminded that their contribution to their learning process will be *supportively* monitored, and their involvement expected. For example, in an English lesson on Shakespeare's Hamlet, students know that later in the class time they will be asked to think about the main character in terms of "his relationship with his father", or "his mother", or "Ophelia" or "his moods" (adolescent hormones!). Having been given a set time students are then asked to share: "We should be ready, now, to hear what you think about how Hamlet coped with ...". In sharing, publicly, students will need to be given time to develop and construct their public contribution:

- relate this topic (issue or question) to your own experiences;
- give an example of, or analogy of ...;
- explain "this" (a given concept) in *your own words*;
- give a summary of ...;
- explain this ... as if to someone who had never seen, or heard, of ....

Teachers will often preface their teaching time with a statement: "You will need to be listening carefully – you might be asked to contribute to someone else's answer ..."; "Listen up, here folks – you'll need to know this ..."; "I wonder if anyone will have heard of this?"; "This is going to be a little tricky so ...".

When inviting student engagement teachers can use a wide variety of approaches beyond simple public questions and answers:

- Ask all students to write their answers on a card and hold it up (this "old-fashioned" approach can work well for simple check and scan checking by a teacher at primary level);
- Students can answer questions in an answer notebook; they then share their answers in a paired discussion or be ready to contribute to class discussion.
- The questions asked can be answered in a daily journal.

- Students can be directed to write a brief summary in response to a teacher's questions to a whole class. This increases task focus and avoids easy distractability.

Questions and effective teaching

The purpose of questioning is to *engage* thinking, *extend* thinking, *share* thinking or *clarify* and *confirm* thinking. There are many ways questioning can be used in whole-class and small group teaching. Questions also allow the teacher to check for understanding and clarify meaning. They provide a form of feedback for the teacher. Even rhetorical questions can be used in that way.

- It is important the teacher does not do most of the talking in class dialogue. Avoid piling topic upon topic with several multiple questions that can often sidetrack and even confuse student understanding of the key issue, topic or focus. I've see teachers talk for up to 20 minutes without any genuine student involvement. Getting students task-directed (even through whole-class discussion) is a crucial feature of effective teaching and learning.

  Making the task(s) explicit (and visible) and stating the desired and positive outcomes of a lesson are basic, but crucial, in most learning tasks. It is then important (generally speaking) to stick to the aims and the task focus through any spoken, or written, questions.
- Some key questions are best written up on the board or a worksheet to *keep the focus.*
- Short extending and refocusing questions, can also keep the students focused. During a vigorous series of answers from students, or during a class discussion, a teacher, in responding to an individual student, can extend their thinking through short refocusing and reframing questions: "So, you're saying … Is that right?" Even a brief, and positive, "So?" can cue the student to more fully form their answer and ideas.
- Questions, where possible, should also link back to what students already know to extend their natural curiosity.
- After a general cue to the class, "I want you to think about the main (issue, character, point …)", the teacher directs the class to share privately, or in pairs, then invites students' responses: "Alright (…), *we* should be ready to hear what you think about … Hands up, folks, so I can see who is ready to share …".
- Avoid discussing any *one* student's answer at length.
- If the teacher *invites* students to work on the board, in front of the class, at least direct other students to work on the solution at the same time. Answers can then be compared. Any such approach requires a cohesive class environment and no student should be forced to display knowledge in front of the class.
- Avoid embarrassing a student by picking on them (as a discipline device): "What do you think, Mark? Eh?!"

At primary age level many teachers now include a unit on active listening skills to enhance student attention in shared class discussion (see McGrath and Francey 1993).

Thoughtful questioning can also increase the active *cognitive* participation of all students. When using directed questions the teacher is also directing student effort into sharing their *thinking*; not in a simplistic right or wrong way, but rather supporting the process of learning.

Overuse of questions that require only one, right, answer or require a single word response can limit useful development in student thinking and expression:

e.g. "Who can …?"; "What is …?"; "Who is your favourite character in *Harry Potter* …?"; "Who can read *this* word?". Such questioning tends to limit extension to a student's thinking.

Contrast these questions:

- "Share with the person next to you about who was your favourite character … and *why* …". The "why" extends the sharing and allows the student to develop their thinking.
- "Think of your own example of hope or courage in … Write the key points down … When you have several, look up, here, to the front, so I know you're ready and we'll share as a group … *Thinking hats on folks …*"

"Wait-time" when asking questions

Rowe (1978 in Cummings 1989) develops an interesting case for what he calls "wait-time", where teachers allow some time ("wait-time") after asking a general question to the class or an individual.

Rather than a simple "What is the …?" (expecting a right or wrong answer), the teacher frames the question more thoughtfully: "Think about the difference between … Raise your hand when you are ready with the answer. Take a moment to imagine …". The teacher then scans the group allowing some "wait-time" *after* asking the question and *after* the student's response.

According to Rowe creative use of wait-time can:

- increase the length of a student's response;
- elicit a wider response rate from students;
- increase confidence in answering;
- increase the contributions of "slower" students;
- have a generally more positive effect on class behaviour.

According to Cummings (1989), teachers smile more often and nod their heads more if they perceive a student to be "bright", giving the student more encouraging non-verbal feedback and more opportunity to respond. Obversely when teachers respond to "low-achieving" students their perception of low-achieving affects the way they interact with those students.

Using encouragement

In a Year 9 graphics class a few years ago my colleague and I were teaching calligraphy using large Gothic script with flourishes, and miniature illustrations and motifs within and around the large capital letters. Using an ink wash, fine felt-tipped pens and gold and silver pens the students were in the final stages of some demanding, well developed and very attractive work.

I was talking with one of the lads about the shape and colours of his letters. "So, how did you get that neat scroll effect there, with the bronze and pale blue background?" I was genuinely interested.

He shared, with some enthusiasm, the drafting and planning process that had led to this final product. I hadn't once said his work was "great", "wonderful" or "brilliant'", but we did talk about his penmanship, the design, the final effect. In short, I was letting him know that I had noticed his effort, his journey (here) as a learner; an artist.

As I walked away one of the lads (who must have been listening) beckoned me over and said, "Hey, Mr Rogers, can you look at my work too?"

Students value encouragement and feedback. They benefit from the assurance that you have acknowledged their work; the effort and the direction of their work. Feedback can also clarify students' thinking and direction of their work. It can help fill in gaps, extend ideas or even just make the students aware of *their own* work.

It is important that children experience some success in their ongoing learning. Encouragement is a major way that we, as teachers, can let the students know how they are doing and where their strengths and areas of further development lie.

Positive teaching style

The most basic expression or form of encouragement is the teacher's positive body language: the encouraging and approachable manner, tone of voice and smile that say: "You can do it"; "Hang in there"; "You're trying hard"; "You handled that well"; "That's hard work, but …"; "Give it your best shot"; "I'm sure you'll make a responsible decision".

Even basics like how we enter a student's personal space and ask to see their work, remembering to use their first name, specifically noting what they are doing and giving short-term feedback on their work and effort applied, empathising when they struggle with difficult concepts; re-explaining (several times if necessary) are all expressions of encouragement.

I have worked with teachers who will come into a student's working space (also their *personal* space), pick up a student's workbook (without asking permission) and start making comments about the work: "Is *that* what I asked you to do … is it?" I have seen teachers walk over to a student's work and tap (with an overly motoric index finger) on their book: " … and *where's* the margin, hmm?!"

I have had teachers say, "Well, am I supposed to ask permission to see a student's work?" The answer is, of course, "Yes". It is *their* work. "Do you mind if I have a look at your work?" When a teacher says this (in a positive tone) she is modelling basic courtesy; it is not a matter of asking permission.

A positive, encouraging, manner engages a more positive learning atmosphere and can help in the maintenance of long-term positive behaviour.

When students frequently hear "You *never* …", "You *always* …, "*Can't* you get it by now?" and "Are you thick or what …?" one can understand that they would probably have low motivation and feel discouraged. While it seems unbelievable that teachers would ever talk like this to students, some do. One hopes it is *never* intentional. Contrast this with teachers who will explain a difficult mathematical process many times (if necessary), assuring students that, "Yes, it can take time to come to terms with this concept. It isn't easy, but we'll get there. I struggled with positive and negative integers too …!"

Both *en*couragement and *dis*couragement contain the word *courage*. Giving a child some fundamental courage, as a learner, is in part how we relate to the student, and in part the language we use. As an ongoing, adult learner I've noticed it was always the way I was treated *along with* non-judgemental feedback that enabled my learning, my motivation and even my assurance that mistakes and misunderstandings did not mean that I was a failure.

When I was a full-time teacher I started (and finished) some postgraduate study. It was long and arduous and I wondered (at times) if it was all worth it. During the course of the research I was undertaking I was required to do some statistics units. My first university teacher was offhand in his manner. He treated us (students in our late 20s or 30s, and some in their 40s) as if we were a group of high school students rather than adults. He seemed unaware that we had all had busy days teaching and had trudged off, in the evening traffic, to the university to further our careers. His teaching style was high on expectation (that we all knew quadratic equations, orthogonal contrasts and so on) and low on tolerance of struggle, confusion and "where the hell does all this fit in". His non-verbal sighs, eyes to the ceiling and tut-tutting frustration at our "obvious" and "simplistic" questions contributed to us feeling inadequate learners. It all came back to me; I was a student again, at high school, with a teacher I didn't like who was seemingly unconcerned about us.

My second "teacher" (another stats unit) was a professor (still is). The first day we entered the university classroom (as adult learners) Brian welcomed us personally and when we were sitting down as a group said, "Hello and welcome, everyone. Look, I know you're probably all feeling bushed after a long day with your Grade 5s or Year 8s .... You can see I've got some tea/coffee, hot water and cups over there. I'd like you to grab a cuppa, regroup, settle down, and I'll explain the course, the way in which we can work together in this unit and the sorts of projects we'll tackle together". We, all, immediately felt better (the cuppa helped). We felt we could probably do this none-too-easy subject.

Brian never failed to explain the statistics concepts carefully; in several different ways where necessary. He used visual examples and examples that would relate to our work. He encouraged us to engage in small-group work to support each other. He never failed to address and answer what we thought (at times) were simplistic or stupid questions. He was always willing to chat after class, to fine tune or qualify misunderstandings. He always gave *descriptive* feedback on our work (rather than "18 out of 20. Well done"). I enjoyed going to Brian's classes (although maths has never been my high-comfort-zone *forte*). I even passed – quite well. He wrote a personal note to me (to everyone) on the completion of the exam.

I learned a lot more than statistics from Brian. I was reminded about how to be an effective and supportive teacher.

It is easy, as teachers, to become conditioned to negative behaviour; to easily notice and over-attend to the range of disruptive behaviours that occur from shuffling and whispering while the teacher is talking; to addressing lateness and calling out. While we have to correct disruptive behaviour we also need to balance correction with encouragement. I've heard some teachers come out with the ludicrous comment (about encouraging positive behaviour and effort in work): "Well, they *are supposed* to be doing that anyway".

It is also very important to balance any correction with encouragement. This can be as basic as moving around the room and acknowledging the students' presence (smile, nod, OK sign) when they *are* working, *are* on-task; or encouragement can be as focused as specific attention to task and giving descriptive feedback and praise.

Sometimes all that is required are just a few apposite words, as when a student, answering a question in front of his or her peers, hears the teacher say, "That was a thoughtful question and an interesting way of looking at ..." rather than saying, "No, that's not the right answer". If the student is wrong in his or her work or in answer to a question, a brief noting that, "... was incorrect ... but you tried ..." is enough. We do not need to communicate that the student is inept, stupid or can't learn.

When encouraging students

• Be conscious of the small as well as more involved expressions of encouragement: the affirming smile that basically humanises; brief task-checks such as "How's it going?"; "Where are you up to?"; "How's it coming together here?"; "Have you considered?"; "Can I suggest?"; "It might help if ..."

The teacher notices a student's page without the margin and date. Instead of asking why there's no margin, the teacher asks if she can have a look at the work, gives some feedback and as she turns the book around to face the student she runs her finger non-verbally down the left-hand side of the page to indicate to the student to remember the margin, and points to the top right of the page as if to say remember the date. She winks. He smiles back. Done. Small acts – but important small acts.

- When giving verbal or written encouragement and feedback focus on descriptive comment rather than merely global praise or negation.

  For example, if we say a child *is* bad because he displays anger we easily associate that *he* is bad *because* (or when) he gets angry. We all get angry and it is our angry behaviour that is "good" or "bad", "right" or "wrong". When we focus on a child's *behaviour* we're on safer ground.

  The same principle can be applied to a range of behaviours: "That desk looks tidy and well organised, Stephen … books on one side, writing materials on the other. It'll be easier to find things now, eh?" Here the teacher focuses on the child's effort (his behaviour). The teacher describes what the student has done. Rather than telling a student that she was good because she shared her play lunch we can say, "That was a kind thing to do … [or a thoughtful act, or cooperative, or considerate]". Descriptive feedback takes a little longer but it *acknowledges* – it demonstrates you know – and it *affirms* the student's effort and the direction of that effort.

  This approach can be applied to the student's academic work as well. To write "Well done", "Great work", "Marvellous" or "Excellent work (9/10)" on a student's work can, of course, encourage a child but it doesn't say *what* is "great" or "marvellous" or "excellent" (or why). Compare those remarks with comments like "The words you've used to describe the loneliness and isolation of the moors … I could feel how the main character must have felt when …". Here the teacher is adding a few words to *describe* what was "good work"; the teacher is also affirming the student's effort. The student can also see where their strengths are demonstrated.

  Errors and deficiencies can also be acknowledged: "remember to check your work for spelling and layout …". It can help to use pre-arranged symbols to highlight (on their work) where margin, paragraphs, spelling and even grammar need to be checked. This avoids too much red marking, which can sometimes make a visible mess of a student's work. Avoid judgemental reminders: "Don't forget the date … [the margin, the paras]"; or "You should know how to spell 'because' by now". "Remember to …" is a more cooperative reminder to read on one's work.

- When encouraging a student it can also help to acknowledge the effort and struggle in their progress (particularly when the student whinges that "It's too hard …"): "Yes, it can be difficult to roll clay into a flat shape …"; "It took me ages to understand algebra, David. It's not an easy concept to get your head around …"

  Conversely it doesn't help if we easily, and frequently, do for the student that which he can do for himself: "Here, give me the scissors … I'll show you". It would be more helpful to say, "That's a difficult shape to cut. Can I show you how to make it easier?"

  Yes, there will be students who seemingly reject even the most supportive and well-intentioned encouragement. If a child appears to reject our feedback it is enough to meet such rejection with a brief assurance that it was well meant and leave it at that.

When using feedback to assist a student with frequent errors or unhelpful patterns of behaviour it can help to begin a one-to-one feedback session with comments like: "Have you noticed …?"; "Are you aware that …?"; "Do you hear yourself say …?"; "Are you conscious of …?"; and "How do you feel when …?" These openers can lead to specific, supportive, feedback comments about students' work or behaviour. One of my primary teacher colleagues uses the student home–school diary to give encouragement:

(22 March 2000) Congratulations on your spelling, David. This word list was not easy and I can see you are really trying; 7 out of 10 shows improvement and application. (Do you know I found spelling a bit hard when I was your age!).
Mr Smith

This brief comment shows that the teacher identifies with the student as well as giving some descriptive feedback and encouragement. What often happens is that these comments are also read by the parent who (often) gives secondary encouragement. Here's another example:

Karl, I noticed you shared your colouring pencils with Taylor during art time. That was a considerate thing to do. Taylor felt you cared about him (and it saved me trying to find some spare pencils – thanks for the cooperation).   Ms Joyce

As with any comments home to parents (diary, notes, letter, certificates), their value, as encouragement, depends on the quality of the relationship between the giver (as teacher) and the receiver (the student).

- Avoid qualifying – even discounting – the encouragement or feedback. If you notice a student putting litter in the bin thoughtfully, without a reminder, it is enough to say, "That's thoughtful, David – makes the cleaner's job easier". We don't need to add, "and if you did that more often we'd have a much tidier classroom, wouldn't we?"

  If a student demonstrates neat writing (uncharacteristically? – who knows he may be on the cusp of a change), what he doesn't need to hear is, "Now – why can't you do that all the time?" Comments that begin, or include, "never" or "always", as in "You *never* finish your work" and "You *always* call out in class", are also discouraging.

  Also, when marking a student's work be sensitive to the fact it is *their* work (and avoid scribbling comments or feedback all over the pages). Unobtrusive marking can demonstrate that you care about the finished product (p. 89).

- With older students (upper primary onwards) there is a tendency to feel uncomfortable about the more public expressions of praise. A brief, positive word to a student aside from his or her peers is often well received.

Working with a Year 8 student in an EBD school (a few years ago) I was trying to encourage one young lad to use a quieter voice in class time. I made an individual behaviour plan with him to focus on partner-voice in class. I drew a cartoon picture of him using a quiet voice while he was writing at his desk. I gave him a copy of this postcard-sized reminder of our plan and I had a copy for myself, and his regular teacher.

On a number of occasions during class time I noticed him making an effort to remember to use his partner-voice. I quietly beckoned him to come over to the front desk area. Here, away from his classmates, I quietly gave him some feedback. "Ahmed, I noticed you were consciously using your partner-voice. It makes it so much easier for everyone … your teacher and me. You're remembering your plan, old chum."

I put a tick on my copy of the plan (and, later, on his copy). Sometimes I just caught his eye and gave a small OK sign. When he forgot his plan I gave a private cue to remind him of partner voice : thumb and forefinger a little apart to show a small distance (as it were); the distance of partner voice (p. 66).

Many teachers also use incentives such as stickers, stamps, charts, free activities, certificates and even vouchers (such as those used in primary playgrounds where good behaviour is 'caught' and a voucher given that can be traded for an ice-cream, and so on).

Whatever incentives teachers use it is essential that our characteristic teaching practice includes the principles of supportive and descriptive feedback and encouragement to our students regarding their effort, their goodwill, their contribution, and their thoughtful and cooperative behaviour, even if they are supposed to be doing that anyway! Like us, students benefit from and even look for acknowledgment and affirmation.

Case study

He had been told that it was a very difficult class; a Year 9 low-stream English class (predominantly boys). The teacher's personal preference was for mixed ability teaching but ability streaming was the school's current policy. He was determined to help these students go beyond their label and not let his personal views on mixed-ability teaching affect his desire to positively engage this new class.

It had taken him a couple of lessons to establish the beginnings of a positive working relationship (pp. 25–7).

Most of the disruptions to class learning are minor – annoying and frustrating at times, but minor. For example, as the students entered the classroom there was some general chatter and restlessness. Having greeted them in the corridor, he directed a sense of group calmness and settling (pp. 38, 61). He now stands by the door to greet them as they come in. He doesn't, however, engage in chit-chat, or have mini discussions about homework or issues that can be addressed later (if necessary) during the on-task phase of the lesson. He smiles as he briefly greets and acknowledges the students and beckons them to their seats.

He stands at the front of the classroom, purposefully waiting, scanning the room. As they settle he cues for class attention. Sometimes he needs to raise his voice a little, then steps the voice down as the group settles. He thanks them, greets them *as a group*, and begins a fresh lesson. He never shouts at them to get quiet. They like that. (I know, they told me.)

Today he is developing a unit on punctuation – a revision unit. He is aware that the students may think this is old hat or even kindergarten stuff, but it is part of the revision requirement. He begins by engaging a class discussion about bicycles, punctures and repair kits.

He uses the analogy of a puncture repair kit to associate "puncture" and "punctuation". Having welcomed the class he steams ahead.

"How many of you still ride bikes?" Hands go up. "What sort of bikes do you ride?"

As the sharing proceeds, one of the students comments that, "Gavin's bike is a shit bike".

It's just audible. The snigger goes around the room. The teacher looks in the direction of the comment (he's not sure who said it) and says, "That's not a helpful comment (even if it's true)." His tone is pleasant, matter-of-fact – and he moves on.

"How many of you have ever got a puncture?" Several hands go up. They're interested, they still like their bikes. A few students call out. The teacher reminds them (briefly) of the rule. Scanning the faces he says, "Remember our class rule for questions ...., thanks."

"Jacinta (…)," he nods and smiles toward her, "tell us about the worst puncture you remember." Several students laugh. She recounts her story. As others contribute he is aware of not over-engaging on any one answer or contribution, and he continues to *periodically* scan even as he listens to each individual contribution. A student walks in late, posturing a little. The teacher welcomes him, acknowledges that he's late and directs him to a seat (p. 63). He continues, not making a big deal of the lateness.

He develops the analogy from a puncture (a hole, or several holes, like Jacinta's punctured tyre) to punctuation in a mass of words (commas, full stops, question marks, "talking marks" to show where direct speech is being used, exclamation marks and even capital letters). He puts up a large poster with a dozen sentences. The written vignette is an account about "my first bike", written in the first person without punctuation, so it is quite confusing to read; a mass of words. He invites a few students to read it. They find it, naturally, difficult. There's good humoured laughter as one idea runs into another giving confusing messages. He is clearly enjoying himself, although he must have taught punctuation many, many times. He is aware that each lesson is a fresh lesson. He does his best (bad day notwithstanding). He doesn't overdramatise, he is not overly ebullient, but he has a relaxed, positive, good humoured rapport that is able to engage interest and sustain motivation – he can even enthuse on most days.

He notices Jason leaning back a bit heavily and noisily on his seat. He's aware that this is probably just unconscious restlessness.

"Jason (…) four on the floor, thanks."

He adds a non-verbal cue with his hand (pp. 65, 66). He moves on. He notices a few students chewing gum. He tactically ignores this *now*; the chewing isn't affecting the flow of teaching and learning. He'll address it later, in the on-task phase of the lesson.

Krista has her hand up. He acknowledges her question, and she asks to go to the toilet. He suspects she might be wanting just to get out for a few minutes. He says, "When I've finished this part of the lesson, Krista, we'll organise a toilet break". She frowns and leans back, satisfied. (If she had appeared desperate he would have given her the benefit of the doubt and addressed the issue later if repeated requests were made in subsequent lessons.) He moves on.

"So, folks," he scans the group, "what can we do to this mass of print to make it meaningful?" He discusses the role of punctuation; these holes and marks (punctuation) help us to clarify meaning in written expression. "How? We puncture the text – all these words." He taps the text on the board.

As the answers come he sometimes extends or develops them. "So, what you're saying, Matt, is … is that right?" If a student is on a helpful track with their answer or contribution he extends by simply adding "So …?", or "and …?", or "keep going …?" with a smile and eye contact that say, "Keep going, you're on the right track".

"So, what does punctuation do then …?"

"What purpose does it serve?"

"Think about the tyre on the bike that's punctured. Remember when Jacinta and Rob shared how they learned to fix punctures themselves using a puncture kit?"

"I have a punctuation kit here, which is a kind of reverse of what a bike repair kit does ." He holds up a poster of an open tin. "Right, what do we need in this kit? This little kit, folks, will help us repair our writing, put it in some ordered form so it makes reasonable sense, eh?" The poster illustrates the tin and its contents: capitals, full stops, commas, speech marks, question marks. He then takes suggestions from the class on how to repair the text.

The rest of the lesson (and the next) is involved with focused activities to apply the punctuation repair-kit to differing texts (on worksheets).

Before they move on to the on-task phase of the lesson he reminds them of the task; the need for "partner-voice, thanks" (p. 46); "and you know what to do if you need my assistance – check the set task, read through, check with your immediate classmate first, ask for my help, go on with the class novel while you're waiting for me to assist …".

If students talk at any time when he is engaged in group teaching or discussion he will not talk over them. He knows how easy it is to reinforce the tacit acceptance (in students) that it is OK to chat and natter quietly *while* the teacher is talking. Sometime he just *tactically* pauses, sometimes he just gives an incidental reminder to the group (or individuals): "A number of students are talking (…)"; or "You're talking and I'm trying to teach". His primary focus is not the disruptive behaviour itself; it is always the teaching and learning process for that class session. Any discipline is a means to enable the protection of fundamental rights (p. 29) and the engagement of focused learning. Many times in a lesson he will periodically scan the group, and call on students at random to check for understanding – most of all to *engage* and extend their thinking.

As he moves around the room later, in the on-task phase of the lesson, chatting, encouraging, refocusing and clarifying, he asks questions that assist, probe and encourage: "Anything still unclear?"; "What questions do you have about …?"; "Is it easy or difficult – why?"; "What do you need to know to help it connect?"

At the close of the lesson (a double period) he has a "round-Robin" of class questions, calling on students at random to invite responses about the lesson topic and asking questions such as: "What do *you* think the purpose of today's activity was?"; "Is there anything that still isn't clear …?"; "Does anyone have any questions …?"; "Would you be able to use what you've learned today?, How?"; "How can you recall, remember, the key ideas from today?"; "Would anybody like to share *how* they could punctuate more easily, clearly, now?"; "What's made the difference?"

He finishes the lesson early enough to briefly summarise, collect work, cue for projects or homework and remind the students to leave the room tidy and leave the room in a non-Darwinian-survival-of-the-fittest-way (pp. 51–2). Most of all, he tries to end each lesson in a positive way (even if it has not been the best lesson).

Those students who do not really apply themselves, or are calculatedly lazy, he speaks to away from their peers (one-to-one; p. 71) He doesn't berate them, or make them feel guilty or punish them for poorly developed and poorly applied work. He does point out (privately) that he knows they can do better, that the choices we make about learning now affect what we do later and that he'll always be available to help.

He knows that building a cohesive class group takes time but plans thoughtfully towards that end, not leaving cohesion to mere chance.

The lessons do not always go this well. There are some difficult days (from time to time) but he has built up the general confidence of the students in this class to believe they can communicate more thoughtfully, more substantially and more interestingly (even) in their written expression.

When he's had a particularly good session – a lesson that has gone well – he spends some time reflecting on what happened to contribute to the relative success. Was it the lesson content? Was it the engagement and the way he taught that day? Could it have been the timetable slot at that point in the week? Was he feeling particularly well?

When he's had a particularly difficult session with the class he similarly reflects. How did he deal with the students who were late? Was the learning task clear? Was he trying to cover too much? Did he give enough feedback?

He is a reflective practitioner. I know; I've worked with him.

Skill development takes time

Working as a mentor teacher I have noticed colleagues struggle with new skills; notably new ways of communicating when managing, disciplining or even encouraging students. As with any new skill it is important to remember that it takes time to develop the comfort zone wherein the language comes easily and naturally, without too much conscious thought.

I've played golf only several times (by invitation – it's not my game). As I watch others play, as I watch their fluidity of stroke and eye, and follow through, it *looks* easy. When I try to play I *feel* wooden. My legs don't seem to connect with my arms and head. I hit the ground several times with the club, then I hit the ball too hard. I can't even see where it is going. It skews off a long way from the green I aimed at. I *over* concentrate.

But I can still swim quite well, and dive, ride a bike (although infrequently), draw reasonable pictures (there're some in this book), and juggle three balls in the air quite well. Why? Because I *practised* these skills many times; I had felt a need; I was motivated and I kept at it until there was a kind of second nature about the skill.

To get to that habituation level one has to go through the discomfort zone, as it were. That is normal. Knowing about skills (through reading or in-service education and training (INSET)) and being able to use them in an integrated way, as a teacher, are two different things. Initially the new skill *feels* uncomfortable; the words, the tone, the manner, may not seem "me". As P. G. Wodehouse once put it, "My tongue seems to get entangled with my brain". However, if we see a need and value in the skills, and if we see how those skills can be integrated into our *overall* teaching and management, we will succeed (with effort, time, normative failure and some colleague encouragement).

In time we won't need to think, "Am I avoiding unnecessary focus on the secondary behaviour by *tactically* ignoring the residual secondary behaviour; and refocusing the procrastinating and reframing to the core issue?" We'll just do it.

Home truths

My daughter once said to me, " Dad, why do some teachers bother to get into teaching when they hate kids?" By "hate" she meant dislike expressed, at its worst, in mean-spirited, churlish, petty, unthinking behaviour; a lack of fundamental humanity expressed in a sense of caring, positive support and mutual regard. Having worked with some teachers who seem to present a characteristically miserable-soddish attitude to teaching and to their students, I know what she meant.

Whenever I've discussed the issue of effective teaching and effective teachers with students they always emphasise several key aspects of teacher behaviour. The comments below in brackets are directly drawn from high school students I have taught. (Some of the positive behaviours are expressed in negative terms.)

Effective teachers:
- teach clearly and with interest in the subject and the students' needs ("the work is interesting"; "they try to help you connect to what they're talking about"; "they help us with the work"; "they don't moan if you ask them to re-explain things"; "they give us a chance to talk and explain too");
- build a sense of class cohesion as it relates to learning together and being together here in "this place" – the classroom ("They let you all know why we're doing this subject or lesson"; "they give choices"; "they have manners"; "they trust you"; "they have a sense of humour" [this is a very frequent descriptor]; "they're not chauvinistic or sexist"; as one student said with a wry smile, "If we're stuck here together ... and we're all human beings ... we have to do it with less pain!") (I knew what he meant);

- discipline fairly ("they discuss/explain the rules"; "they don't take sides"; "they don't shame you in front of the class"; "you get a fair chance"; "they give you fair warning even non-verbal (*sic*)"; "you make mistakes but they don't hold it against you"; "because they have a good relationship with the class the correction is accepted better"; "they're fair"; "there's give and take").

The kind of relationship a teacher builds, and sustains, is central to effective teaching and learning. It also increases the likelihood the students will cooperate with us when we exercise necessary discipline.

My own children have said, about their teachers, that they often enjoyed a *particular* subject because of the particular teacher who taught it that semester or that year.

One of the most powerful and influential aspects of a teacher's relationship with individuals and groups of students is the teacher's willingness to empathise. Perspective-taking means the ability to see a student's struggle with work or behaviour or their relationships in a school; to tune-in to a student's frustration or anxiety; to give feedback on learning and behaviour, and always to give a right-of-reply. As Branwhite reported, a teacher's capacity to empathise was the most valued teacher quality cited by pupils (Branwhite 1988, cited in Kyriacou 1991: 57).

Teaching is not for everyone

Teaching in schools is clearly not for everyone. It is a profession that is naturally, inherently, even normatively, stressful. Its daily demands are multi-task and simultaneously require one to not only have planned well on the one hand, but also to be flexible and able to think on one's feet.

The ability to relate well to others and to communicate clearly and effectively, the ability and skill to enthuse and motivate, and the ability to cope with multi-task, group-oriented activities, as well as individual activities, are not merely desirable; they are essential attributes and skills.

There are teachers who present with poor or ineffective teaching and management practice. Supporting teachers who struggle because they, themselves, are a key factor in a hard-to-manage-class setting is not easy, in part because you need to see the colleague's failure and struggle without seeing them *as* a failure (p. 19, 20).

If such teacher behaviour can be addressed within a school-wide perspective of shared values, aims and practices about managing classroom behaviour the task is made somewhat clearer, although not necessarily easier.

If a struggling teacher does not request or invite colleague support it will be important to approach that colleague to informally share, at the very least, concerns about their welfare. If you have walked past a really loud class on enough occasions to know that the behaviour in that class (even briefly observed) is more than bad-day syndrome, it is professionally irresponsible not to meet with the colleague in question and offer support. In providing such support we will need to consider the following.

- Wherever possible any offered support should be "early-intervention"; before a spiral of discouragement, or defeat, sets in.
- Senior teacher involvement can often set up further colleague networking (even mentoring) and address more serious concerns such as harassment (p. 147f.).
- The offer of support should be made discretely and confidentially (wherever possible).

- The emphasis in the first meeting allows the colleague to share their concerns, needs and problems with honesty and balance. Emphasise the positive areas of their teaching and management as well as the areas of concern.
- Set up a plan of support, developed with other colleagues (perhaps even a mentor; p. 152) to enable ongoing support. Early features of the plan may need to include time-out options (see p. 100f.).

Where there is *characteristic* laziness, indifference, lack of commitment, poor teaching, inappropriate management and discipline, insensitivity and even active dissent in some teachers' behaviour this will need to be supportively confronted within the school's shared values and practices as they relate to a teacher's professional rights and responsibilities.

Teachers who *characteristically* present as ineffective in their teaching practice (global descriptors such as ineffective and poor need careful and thoughtful delineation) are best advised and counselled out of the profession.

A cooperative and supportive school based appraisal system working with a more consciously supportive Office for Standards in Education (OFSTED) could help such teachers to reassess their professional choices, obligations and responsibilities earlier in their teaching journey.

Notes

1. These are drawn principally from Kyriacou (1986), Robertson (1997) and Rogers (2000).
2. While this sounds like a tall order, it is not inconsistent at all the bad day syndrome. Children fully understand and respect bad-day syndrome in adults, and if the teacher communicates, briefly and respectfully, why they are having a bad day, children are normally quite forgiving. Of course, if our frustration or anger have been disrespectful, we should apologise.

This drawing shows an infant class (5-year-olds). The teacher on the right, Joy, is comforting a young boy who is upset. I am supervising play-lunch. (In Australian schools, children eat packed lunches in the classroom with their class teacher.) Infants have morning play at 11:00a.m., but play lunch needs to start aeons before then. They take a long, long time!

I'm also singing to the group. "I can see some sandwiches, some sandwiches … I can see yummy sandwiches in your play lunch today." As I sing a student comes to my chair with a pencil. I hadn't asked her. I am thinking of a cup of tea (meagre pleasure!). I ask myself, "Why does is seem so really long til morning tea time?" – Teaching infants is different.

Chapter 5

Management beyond the classroom: behaviour consequences

When I do good no one remembers,
when I do bad no one forgets.
Anon

Behaviour consequences (punishment?)

During most of my teaching career teachers used the word "punishment" to describe what happened when a student had to face the consequences of inappropriate or wrong behaviour. The verb "to punish" was often used, uncritically, to mean anything we did *to* a child such as detention, giving lines, withdrawing a privilege (such as missing out on a valued activity), wearing the dreaded dunce's cap (a conical hat with 'D' for dunce[1] written on it and worn by the student while standing in the corner) or, of course, the cane (whoosh! ouch!). I had that a number of times.

I put the word *punish* in parenthesis in the heading (adding a question mark) because I wanted to question the easy facility with which we use the word. Whether we use the word "punishment" or "consequences" may mean little to the child. It is what happens to the child through the process of consequential outcome that matters.

The degree to which a child will see the teacher's action as fair "punishment" depends on:

- what we do when we "punish";
- the intent we convey through the "consequential process";
- whether we use the "consequential process" as an end in itself (mere punishment) or as a means to an end – the end being some understanding, some learning (in the student) about their behaviour.

For example, a fair consequence can easily be applied punitively by a teacher whose intent is to make the child *feel* punished by the way he or she speaks to and treats the child through the consequential process.

Behaviour consequences, as a feature of thoughtful discipline, are an attempt by the teacher to link the disruptive or wrong behaviour of the student to an outcome that, hopefully, will emphasise fairness and justice, and may even teach the child something about accountability and responsibility.

When we apply a consequence, even a simple consequence of directing students to stay back after class and "clean up their mess", we are organising outcomes so the students experience the consequences of their own behaviour. Through *behaviour consequences* teachers seek to emphasise that as students "choose" to be disruptive they also "choose" to face the consequences of their behaviour; they are not *simply* pawns or victims when they do the wrong thing. We treat the students as if they are volitional.

One of my colleagues has introduced her Year 5 class to the term "reparation":

Sometimes we let classmates and teachers down by choosing not to be responsible towards people or property. Sometimes we're irresponsible because we do not care enough. Sometimes we do the wrong thing by mistake; we don't mean to.

When that happens we work to fix things, or sort things out through an apology or paying back that person in a helpful, positive way. We call this making "reparation".

When we do the unfair and wrong thing our reparations help earn our class's and our school community's trust back again.

All our behaviour has consequences and we are responsible for the consequences of our behaviour.

In this sense the teacher is emphasising a consequence as something the child is involved in as well as something organised by the teacher.

In working through consequences with children we need to make clear that all behaviour has consequences. Some consequences are naturally occurring: when we stay out too long in the sun without a hat, sunglasses and sun-cream, we risk sunburn; unbrushed teeth, in time, will need dental work, and may lead to halitosis (phew!); if you don't plan the progress of a long assignment the due date comes quickly. Children can see the reality of situational consequences like these and, hopefully, learn from them. *Behavioural* consequences are also an attempt to teach responsibility and accountability. The teacher links a consequential outcome to a behaviour: "If you choose to leave the mess like that you'll need to stay back at play-time and ..."; "If the work is not completed now ... then ..."; "If the assignment is in on a due date ... then ..."; "If you continue to make it difficult for others to work you'll have to work away from others ...".

Managing consequences

- *All* consequences are referred back to the student behaviour agreement, which outlines the rights, responsibilities, rules and consequences (p. 27f.). It is within the emphases of the classroom agreement that the student needs to see his or her inappropriate behaviour, while also being encouraged to accept the support offered to face the consequences of irresponsible and wrong behaviour.

- Consequences are both "non-negotiable" and "negotiable":
  - Non-negotiable consequences should be known in advance, clearly stated in the school policy and applied decisively. Non-negotiable consequences are applied for such behaviours as: repeated disruptive behaviour in the classroom (this would occasion time-out, see p. 100f.); swearing at a teacher; any possession (or use) of drugs or weapons; violent behaviours; harassment and bullying. Non-negotiable consequences normally occasion some form of time-out, detention, or suspension procedures. They may also include withdrawal of privileges, as when a repeatedly aggressive student is denied (excluded) from a school camp after due process.
  - Negotiable consequences normally refer to consequences worked through with the teacher who is witness to the inappropriate or disruptive behaviour (p. 71). Teachers often use a stay-back session (or even a detention, p. 106) to discuss with the student questions such as: "What happened?"; "What rule (or right) was affected by your behaviour?"; "What's your side

of the story?"; "How do you see what happened ...?; What can you do to fix things up [sort things out, make things right] ...? Teachers will ask "How can I help ... (pp. 73–4)?"

Most students actually come up with a tougher consequential outcome, through such negotiation, than their teacher. We often have to help them trim their consequential suggestions back to reality.

- A consequence is more than mere punishment, in that we seek to address the reality of the inappropriate or disruptive behaviour by applying a consequence that tries to gain some *relationship* between the behaviour and its consequential outcome.

  For example, when a student is caught smoking at school, the rule, and consequence, is clear: a detention. In this case though, the smoker's detention occasions a "Quit" video (a positive educational video addressing the habit of smoking and how to break the habit).

  If a student has damaged school property, or another individual's property, he is required to make "reparation" (p. 98). This normally occurs after some cool-off time and discussion or mediation.

  An infant child uses the class waste-paper bin as a urinal (he knows the difference). It was attention-seeking behaviour. In his own time, later, he washes the bin out with detergent. Another infant washes out a boy's jumper that he has thrown mud on. Many reparative, and "task-related", consequences can be applied in this way.

  The emphasis is one where the students experiences the consequences of their own behaviour and (hopefully) see some relevance in the applied consequence and are encouraged to be more responsible next time in similar situations.

- Concentrate on the *present* and the future change flowing from the consequence. Avoid over-focusing on the child's past misdemeanours.

- Keep the respect intact when working through a consequence with a student. I have seen (too many times) a teacher keep a student back after class for a talk, or a detention, only to berate the student and harp on at the student about why he or she is a rotten, unthinking, uncaring, nasty "piece of work".

  Keeping the respect intact means that even when we have to apply severe consequences we do so without the easy temptation to engage in some kind of psychological payback. The *certainty* of the consequence has a more powerful teaching effect than intentionally applied severity: "You could be outside playing now couldn't you?! But you're not, you're in here with me! What did I say to you before in class? Didn't I say that if you kept wasting my time, and your time, you would have to stay back at recess? Didn't I – um?! Well? You've lost your playtime now – serves you right doesn't it?"

- Consequences should also be applied within a framework that has "degrees of seriousness". We wouldn't, for example, give detention for not completing homework, whereas we might give detention for *continued* refusal to cooperate with reasonable teacher requests in class time. We would, then, probably use the detention process to sort out the problem behaviour with the student (pp. 71–2).

The key questions to ask when framing and applying a behaviour consequence include:
- is the consequence *related*, in some way, to the disruptive behaviour?
- is the consequence *reasonable* in terms of 'degrees of seriousness'?
- do we keep the *respect* intact?
- what does the student *learn* from the consequence?

The messages of *consequential* discipline – whether an after-class chat or a detention – are that:

- our school has fair rights and rules expressed in the behaviour agreement (p. 27f.);
- your behaviour is effectively your choice (even if others were involved);
- when teachers apply consequences to irresponsible and wrong behaviour they do so because people's rights are affected and individuals ought to be fairly held accountable for their behaviour and face their responsibilities.

We also need to balance consequential aspects of discipline with appropriate *support* such as mediation, restitution, counselling and (when appropriate) individual behaviour plans (p. 122f.).

Time-out I can recall my primary school years at Harlesden in London. It was a drab, brick school with a few scraggly trees and narrow stairs to the head teacher's office (a place of fear!), the pointed iron railings giving a prison-like appearance to the enclosed asphalt, concrete and brick. I recall standing in the corner of the classroom with a dunce's cap on: it was that school's version of time-out![1]

Time-out is a consequential step or process that seeks to link separation from the classroom group with, serious, infringement or abuse of rights behaviour.

Reading a story to a Year 1 class, I saw a boy at the back of the group (sitting on the carpet) pinch the lad in front of him a few times. I gave Patrick the rule reminder: "Patrick (…), hands and feet to yourself". He stopped. A little later he started again

– pushing the boy this time in the small of his back – and the other lad fell forward. This time I directed him to take time-out (cool-off time).

"Patrick (...), Patrick (...), cool-off time. Over there – now."

I pointed to an area at the back of the room, with a chair, a small table, an egg-timer (5 minutes) and a sign on the wall simply saying "cool-off time" (the term in the infant classrooms for time-out).

He whined back at me, "No, I'll be alright, Mr Rogers, I will!"

I repeated, "Patrick (...), Cool-off time. Over there – now."

On such occasions our voice needs to be calm but firm – decisive – and there should be no plea-bargaining ("Are you sure you'll be good now, Patrick, will you promise me?"); forget that. Once you have decided on a consequence like time-out it is the certainty of the consequence that will carry the message that "If you keep annoying others, or hurt them or make it difficult for them to learn you will have to have cool-off time (time-out)". In-class time-out like this is quite effective at infant and even middle primary level.

There are some important considerations when using this style of time-out.

- Time-out is a short-term consequence; not an end in itself. As a means to an end, it can help and support disruptive students by giving them a chance to calm themselves (away from their immediate audience) and give them a chance to think about their behaviour. It is also fair for the other students in that they, too, have a chance to refocus beyond the disruption to their basic rights.
- Time-out, as a school-wide consequence, needs to be utilised as a least- to most-intrusive option in managing disruptive and unsafe behaviour. At the least intrusive level, *in-class* time-out may be an option; at the most intrusive level of application students may need to be escorted from the classroom to a time-out place where they can calm down and, if necessary, parents or care-givers may be notified.

When applying time-out as a consequence it is important that the teacher exhibits calmness *and* firmness. If the teacher starts shouting and grabbing the student, not only will many students become uncooperative and resistant, but the students watching will become unnecessarily anxious or give unhelpful attention to the disruptive student. There are some (rare) occasions when a teacher will need to physically restrain a student. The school should have a policy on this aspect of crisis management.

There may be occasions when a student's behaviour is too disruptive for in-class time-out.

- Direct the student to leave the classroom and go to a nominated teacher or place in the school. The nominated place will often be a classroom next door, or nearby. Some schools have "time-out rooms" set aside where students can be directed for time-out. Here they are supervised for the class period during which the disruptive behaviour occurs. Infant age children will need to be escorted from their classroom, by an adult, to a time-out place (p. 102).
- In directing students to take time-out it is important that the initiating teacher makes clear to the student what is happening. William Glasser (1992) makes the point that in using time-out (in the short-term) the teacher needs to communicate that it is the student's behaviour that is being addressed; we are not rejecting the student: "Troy, I've asked you several times to work in your

seat and not wander and annoy the other students. If you're not willing to settle down here you'll have to leave our classroom and take time-out. You know the class rules. I will get together with you later to help you sort things out."

- If a student refuses to leave the classroom to take time-out, or we suspect that in directing the student to leave he will become even more disruptive, the initiating teacher should have the back-up of colleague-assisted time-out. All teachers have a cue card in their classroom – a poster-sized card with a symbolic colour (e.g. red) and the classroom number on it. This cue card can be sent, with a trusted student, to a colleague teaching nearby (maybe even next-door). In a more disturbing discipline situation the card will be sent to a senior colleague (team leader, year head, deputy) who will come speedily to escort the student from the classroom (and their audience) to a "time-out place".

  There are occasions when even senior teachers (yes, even senior teachers) cannot make, or get, a disruptive student to leave a classroom or playground where they are engaged in repeatedly disruptive, or dangerous, behaviour. In these rare situations it is wiser for the senior, support colleague to stay *in* the classroom with the disrupting student while the host teacher calmly escorts the rest of the class away from the classroom (in effect escorts the "audience" away). The supervising teacher then stays with the student until he or she has calmed down and is ready to leave the classroom.

- With infant and middle primary aged children any directed exit from the room for time-out should be accompanied by an adult. In many schools, teachers utilise the support of a teaching colleague next door. The cue-card (mentioned earlier) is sent to the support colleague, who briefly leaves her class (door open for line of sight) and escorts the disruptive student to the next door classroom to calm down.

- Teachers should always follow-up with any student later that day (or later that week at secondary level) to work through the concerns or issues that occasioned time-out. This is especially important at secondary level where a teacher may not see a student for a day or two. If there is no follow-up the old animosities may still be there and brought back in the classroom later that week.

- During the time-out period it is important that the student is not unhelpfully reinforced, or over-attended to, by counselling, or special activities or jobs for the teacher. Time-out is not primarily a punishment; it is a decisive consequence where we send the clear message that "*if* you continue to make it

difficult for others in our class to work, feel safe or be treated with respect *then* you will have to take time-out away from your classmates until you have calmed down and are prepared to work by the fair rights and rules here". Counselling can occur later. If students associate time-out with counselling, or special jobs (or activities), some students may use disruptive patterns of behaviour to gain what they perceive to be special privileges, or time away from class-work, during time-out.

No student should be allowed to hold a classroom to ransom by *repeatedly* disruptive behaviour in the course of a lesson or activity. Nor should we ever convey the message to students that we will ever tolerate repeatedly disruptive, unsafe, threatening, dangerous or aggressive behaviours.

Students should be made aware of what time-out is, and what it means. This awareness-raising can be occasioned when teachers are developing their student behaviour agreements in the first week of Term 1 (p. 32).

If a student has been in time-out on several occasions, in close succession, they will probably benefit from an individual behaviour plan to help them with the behaviours or learning issues that have necessitated time-out (p. 122f.).

Deferred consequences

While consequences for disruptive behaviour can be applied immediately, or close to the occurrence of disruptive behaviour, there are occasions when behavioural consequences need to be deferred to a later stage.

It is pointless to force a consequence in the immediate emotional moment if a student is too upset or angry. The student (and sometimes the teacher) needs time to calm and settle before the consequences of their disruptive behaviour can be worked through.

Nathan (Year 2) had left his work area messy (pencils on the floor, bits of screwed up paper). I had reminded him, prior to lunch play, that he needed to clean-up. He didn't; he groaned and moaned and complained that other students hadn't cleaned up yet, although they were actually doing it.

He prevaricated. I gave him a choice, with a deferred consequence: "If the workspace is not tidied before big play (I beckoned him non-verbally to the mess) you will need to stay back to clean up".

He moaned. "I don't care!"

I replied, "But I care, Nathan. We always clean up our work area." (It can help with reminders about classroom routines to use inclusive language: "our", "us", "we" p. 31.)

When I directed him to stay back, at the close of the lesson, he did so, but sulkily. I reminded him of our class agreement and directed him to clean up (the deferred consequence). The message that I was trying to convey, *through the consequence,* was that if the mess is left it will need to be cleaned up later and that an individual's responsibility will be called in, eventually.

I had been teaching a social studies class and I was moving towards lesson closure. I noticed Anne get up out of her seat in the last few minutes, walk from the back of the room and stand with her bag in the doorway. I saw the class watch her as she moved towards the denouement of this potential little *contretemps*. It was my first lesson with this Year 10 class and I had been warned that it was a difficult class. I looked across to Anne standing there (as did the class).

"Anne". She looked back at me from the door. "You're out of your seat – we haven't finished yet and the bell hasn't gone yet."

The class was watching. I could feel that ambient tension – the students wondering what was going to happen and what I was going to do.

With hand on hip she said, "If the bell's about to go I might as well stay here then, mightn't I?" The voice carried (it was meant to) a clear tone of "What yer going to do then?" Anne's little power play with the new teacher. It's wearisome at times, isn't it? A few minutes to go and I'm thinking of a well-earned cuppa and also saying to myself (at nano-second speed), "Well, what do you do next, old chum?"

In the language of *deferred* consequence I said, "Anne, if you stay there and choose not to leave with the rest of us I'll have to ask you to stay back after class."

"I don't care!" How many times have I heard this? The hands on the hips said it all. I can understand teachers who, at this point, want to rush over, wag a finger, and say, "You will care!! I'll make you care!! I've got the power to ...!" The power to what? To yell? To threaten? To play the game of "I have more power than you have? Who is the adult here? I cannot (in reality) make this young girl do anything. I cannot control her or force her to go back to her seat.

When Anne said, "I don't care!" I replied that I did care.

"Do you?" was the sarcastic reply.

At that point, with the bell about to go, I turned my attention back to the class group, some of whom had possibly been disappointed that I hadn't given Anne a chance to over-react and storm away.

"Alright, folks, time to pack up. I'll see you again on Thursday. Remember there's another class coming in next period. Let's do them a favour ..." (the cue for straightening the furniture, picking up any litter and leaving quietly in an orderly fashion). Anne was still standing there, arms crossed now. I imagined she was waiting for her friends. The bell went. As her friends met up with her at the door, she walked away. I called her back.

"Anne (...), Anne (...), I need to talk with you now thanks."

"Naa! – gees, it's recess." I could sense she was winding herself up.

"I know it's recess. I still need to speak to you ... for a minute or so."

"Nope, I'm going ...," she whined.

"If you leave now it will get messy. I'll have to involve the coordinator." Another deferred consequence – not a threat. I walked back into the classroom leaving the choice (in effect) with her. Less than a minute later she came into the classroom.

"Well – what do you want!!"

We had a calmer chat, her audience having gone. I briefly recounted her behaviour and how I felt it affected the class, and also me as a teacher. I then asked her how she saw the whole thing. She complained that she didn't like social studies. This is not untypical of the secondary behaviour noted earlier (p. 10–14). I explained that she didn't have to like social studies, but the issue I was wanting to focus on was "getting out of your seat, throwing your bag in the doorway and refusing to go back to your seat before the class was dismissed ...". We also briefly discussed her tone and manner. She grinned through this, a grin that said that she "knew that I knew she knew I knew" and I gave a wry smile back.

The chat was brief, by the open door (for ethical probity). We parted amicably and I noticed that Anne was far less abrasive during the next lesson. We were on that (sometimes slow) road to a "workable relationship".

- Deferred consequences can often be linked to a choice statement or reminder: "If the work is not completed now, you will need to …". This assumes, of course, that the student is able to do the work but has been task-avoiding. No student should ever be forced to do a set amount of work that he or she is unable to realistically manage.
- Deferred consequences can carry the message of certainty: "If … then"; "When … then". If the language is framed as a threat, or carries a *tone* of threat, the deferred consequence loses the message of it's certainty. It is not about winning; the process of deferring consequences is to create a management context of fairness, and justice, through certainty.
- Deferred consequences allow there to be a calmness between the initial disruptive event and the consequence applied, enabling the parties to more effectively address the behaviour and appropriate recovery or restitution. For example, it is unhelpful to force a student to apologise in the heat of the moment (to an adult or a child). I have seen some teachers make an already difficult situation significantly more difficult by forcing the student to "apologise *now* or else …". Even adults would find that difficult.
- Deferred consequences need to be established fairly, with appropriate certainty, rather than any *intentional* severity.

Students who don't/won't stay back after class

It was Period 6 and my colleague, Frank, and I had been team teaching a Year 7 mathematics class. Nazim and Halid had thrown pencil cases at each other. From a brief glance, as it happened, it looked as though Nazim had started it. I quickly redirected them to work separately. Nazim picked up his pencil case and walked over to another desk muttering "oaths and incantations". He sulked and did no work during the last 15 minutes of class.

Just before lesson closure (and the bell for freedom) I reminded the class about "doing the cleaner a favour" (chairs up, litter in the bin, etc.). Taking my notebook from my top pocket I directed my gaze at Nazim and Halid and said, briefly, "I'll need to see you both *briefly* after class."

I always carry a notebook with me in (and out) of class to record names of students I need to follow-up with for a chat about either work-related issues or behaviour concerns. It acts as an *aide-mémoire* for me and acts as a quasi-legal reminder to the student that I'll need to follow-through an issue of concern with them.

When I gave Halid and Nazim the direction about the brief stay-back (to make a further appointment for some follow-up about pencil case throwing) Nazim got really agitated.

"I'm not staying back for you!! I gotta get a bus!!" He nearly shouted the words.

I said, "It'll only be for a few minutes, Nazim".

Halid's body language indicated he was ready (maybe not willing but ready) to stay back. But Nazim was adamant.

"Nahh!! I gotta get a bus!!"

He dropped a few, muttered, f—ings *en route*. I noticed my colleague, Frank, tense up as Nazim started to bad-mouth me. I knew that Frank (a beginning teacher) had had a number of earlier run-ins with Nazim. I tactically ignored the outburst and finalised the class dismissal (as positively as I could).

The bell went; as the class filed out Halid stood to the side of the room and leaned against the wall. In a flash the other student, Nazim, raced for the door like a jack rabbit! I managed a quick command.

"Nazim, back inside – c'mon."

"I'm f—ing going – I gotta get a bus!!" were the last words as he raced away.

My colleague started to chase after him into the now-busy corridor; students from all directions were all leaving classes near us. I called him back.

"Frank! Frank (...) Leave it." He came back into the room, very tense, fists clenched and forgetting Halid was there, and said, "Just once Bill, just once I'd like to get that bastard!" I could see he was really tensed up so I said I'd go through the chat with Halid and suggested he get a coffee and I'd catch up with him a bit later.

Ten minutes later we were having a coffee in the English staff room. He was noticeably calmer.

I asked him, "Frank, if you had *actually caught* Nazim, as he ran down the corridor, what would you have done and said? Presumably you would have had to restrain him. Just calling 'Halt' or 'Running is verboten!' would probably have had little effect."

He gave a weary, frustrated, laugh and said: "*I don't know* what I'd have done!"
And that's the real issue – *he didn't know what he'd do.*

"Neither of us are fit enough to chase a student like Nazim – no offence, Frank. If you had caught him in the *mêlée* of the Year 7 and 8 scrum, and restrained him, can you imagine his mum within 24 hours, at the newspaper or on the TV: 'Teacher maims boy on way to get bus!' Frank, it's not worth it mate. The *Pyrrhic* victory is not worth it ... Your career ..."

In the larger scheme of things whether we win in the immediate moment at 3:40p.m. today is not important. Even the concept of "I must win", in this context, is inappropriate.

We discussed the *certainty* of the consequence as distinct from the *severity* of the consequence.

"We can catch up with him tomorrow ..." and we did – after the heat had died down. Nazim was a lot more reasonable (next day); we used the lunch detention time to work through some of the issues about his disruptive classroom behaviour (pp. 106–107).

I remember viewing a short BBC television series, a drama, that set out to show how a newly qualified teacher had coped in his first school. It was pretty black at times, illustrating the pressures of one's first year, and first school. The struggle for class management as it interfaced with the struggle for teaching and learning was the dominant theme.

At one point in this bleak picture of modern schooling, an older teacher (my age – early 50s) is seen chasing a Year 8 lad down a busy corridor. The boy has refused to stay back after class and has bad-mouthed the teacher. The teacher finally grabs the boy, pulls him into a vacant room and knocks him over and is seen reigning frustrated blows on him. The newly qualified teacher is half a minute behind his colleague. He pulls his older colleague off with some difficulty. Standing between the puffing, angry adult, and the student on the lino he tries to calm him. The older man says words to the effect that, "There (puff, puff!) wouldn't be a teacher here (puff!) who hasn't wanted (puff) to do that to him".

I can understand how such a teacher in real life (convincingly played by this actor) would have felt. But it's just not worth it.

Detention

Most schools utilise detentions of some kind, even if they do not use the term as such (the other terms I've seen used are stay-backs and time-in). Essentially, the consequence of detention emphasises detaining a student (during the day or at the end of the day) because of disruptive behaviour. Theoretically the purpose of detention is to link the withdrawal of time privilege (or right) with some attempt at helping the student to reflect on his or her behaviour.

Detention is a significant behaviour consequence. It's effective currency can be devalued, or even abused when teachers:

- merely use detention as a *stand-alone* punishment;
- use detentions for minor behaviour management issues such as homework not completed or uniform misdemeanours. These issues can be addressed more thoughtfully by the teacher following up the issue with the student in a supportive discussion. In such cases it is important to assure the student that this "is not a detention but an opportunity to work through the issue or concern";
- keep whole classes back for (say) a lunch-time detention. This strategy is sometimes used by teachers in the mistaken belief that they can set in motion peer-pressure from the more responsible students. That does not work (of course); it does lead to resentment from the more responsible, and cooperative, students.

  I've worked with teachers who have used whole-class detentions as threats and pay-backs ("I'll make you suffer"). When I've explained to such teachers that they are losing their class I've had some say, "I don't care – they've *got to learn*", as if this indefatigable exercise will eventually turn the tide on the disruptive element; it doesn't. We have to care; if there are several students who are disruptive we use the detention system for them, and not for the whole class. If the disruptive behaviour is low level but disparate *across* the class (talking/chatting while the teacher is talking, calling out, general noisiness) it will be more effective to have a classroom meeting to assess and refocus *group* behaviour (see p. 143).
- use detention merely to punish the student by making them sit and do nothing for half an hour.

It is important to clarify what we are seeking to achieve through detention. Is it *just* a punishment or is it a means to assess *what* happened, and seek some further reparation? Many schools use the following general approach for detentions.

When a student enters a detention room (sounds a bit like a prison doesn't it?) they are welcomed by the supervisory teacher. They are given a proforma that has four or five questions on it:

- "What happened …?" (i.e. "that caused you to be in detention")
- "What is your side of the story …?" (a right of reply question)
- "What rule or right was affected by your behaviour?"
- "What can you do to fix things up/make things better [p. 73]?"

A supplementary question can be added:
- "What can your teacher do to help you fix things up … [p. 73]?"

A copy of this completed proforma goes back to the tutor/form teacher, a copy stays with the initiating teacher (who supervises the detention) and a copy may be sent to the administration (with date, name, form group, etc.). In some schools, students keep a copy.

It is pointless getting the student merely to write lines during detention ("I must not …", "I must …") or copy out the school rules. If we are going to use writing as a consequence, at least get the student to write *about their behaviour*. In some schools each detention session begins with a brief referral by the supervising teacher to the rights/responsibilities code (p. 27f.) as a context for why the student's behaviour has occasioned detention.

As with any consequence we need to try to link the disruptive behaviour to the detaining (time) experience. Getting students to use detention time to clean up will be less effective if the reason for their detention was repeated calling out in class, or being rude to a teacher. In this last instance the student should use the detention time to work through an appropriate apology and reparation. The supervising teacher's role is to enable that process. In this sense detention is *part* of a more involved consequential chain.

Hopefully your school will have a thoughtful detention policy that addresses questions and issues such as:

- What sorts of behaviours or issues do we detain students for?
- What are we primarily seeking to teach the student through detention (time)?
- How should we run a detention session? What sorts of things do we typically seek to do (and say) in managing the detention session? What should the student, normally, be directed to do? What are the preferred options? (i.e. the protocols for after-school or lunch time detention.)

and:

- the role of supervising teacher;
- the use of incident report sheets and the 4W proforma noted earlier (pp. 73, 107);
- the link between detention as a "primary" consequence and the secondary consequences that may need to be developed from detention such as apologies, some restitutional process or some behaviour agreement for the future.

One of my colleagues was supervising the school buses at the end of the day (bus duty). One of the boys on the bus was teasing a student walking by. His response to the teasing was to kick the bus in a fit of frustration and pique. The bus duty teacher called the boy over but he ran away, shouting. Rather than chasing him (unwise) the teacher followed it up the next day with a lunch-time detention. During detention she discussed what happened, how the student had felt about being teased and the fact that he had run home ignoring the teacher. She communicated her care and understanding but spoke about the kicking-the-bus incident. She asked how the bus driver might have felt. She further asked, "What can you do to help fix things up, or sort things out?"

Through the teacher's mediation the student agreed that even if he was angry he shouldn't have kicked the bus and he should explain to the driver what had happened.

He wrote a letter to the bus driver apologising that he had kicked the bus but he was angry because of the teasing from the boy in the bus. He assured the driver he wouldn't kick the bus again.

The teacher took the young lad to the bus driver - early (before the Period 6 bell) and the lad nervously gave his written apology to the bus driver and said, "I'm sorry for ...". The bus driver read it and said, "It's not easy to apologise, is it?" tuning in to the lad's probable feelings. "Especially to an adult, but you did. I can see a little scuff mark on the bus. Next time you get angry with another student let your teacher know rather than the bus, eh? " and he shook the lad's hand.

The bus driver's goodwill and the teacher's mediation skill enabled a useful outcome *from* the detention. In this sense the detention was used as a *primary* consequence with the apology/restitution acting as a *secondary* consequence.

In some schools detentions are conducted by senior staff on referral from their colleagues. In other schools, each teacher conducts his or her own (subject or class based) detentions. Some schools use a combination of both systems. If a teacher initiates a detention carried through by another colleague it will be important for the initiating teacher to effect some repairing and rebuilding with the student concerned rather than seeing the incident as handled, and somehow finished, by the colleague conducting the detention. If the initiating colleague does not make an effort to be involved in some checking and re-establishing with the student, the detention process may adversely affect the teacher–student relationship.

Detentions can also to be used to track which students, classes and teachers are experiencing difficulties. They are an early warning, from which senior colleagues can (and should) offer moral and practical support.

Notes

1. "Dunce" is a word introduced into the English language by the disciples of St Thomas Aquinas (in the 13th century) to ridicule those who followed John *Duns* Scotus. It has come to mean someone who is slow-witted, a dullard; in other words, stupid.

Chapter 6
Challenging children and emotional and behavioural difficulties

> We cannot really separate individual
> endeavours from social endeavours.
> **Oliver Sacks, *Awakenings* (1990: 268)**

Argumentative and challenging behaviour in students

Argumentative and challenging student behaviours are far more common in classrooms these days. I've worked with a number of private (independent) schools and teachers there, too, have noted a perceptible increase in more challenging behaviours.

In one such school where I had worked as a consultant, a beginning teacher recounted how she had asked a Year 10 student "Why" she was out of her seat during work time. The young girl turned, faced the teacher with a firm "I've-got-you-sorted look" and said, "Why? If you must know I was just talking to my friend about borrowing a pen [sigh]". Here she ticked off the first point on her finger. "Secondly, I really don't think it's any of your business, Miss, and thirdly we pay your wages here … and I was *just* going back to my seat. OK?" The student had said all this in a quietly confident, "street-lawyer" way. I asked my colleague what she did in response and she said she was just lost for words! "I felt stymied!"

When I've shared this account with other colleagues, more than a few have said how they feel they'd like to "maim" the student. I can understand both the feeling of loss of authority and control that some teachers might feel and the possible temptation to "maim".

How would you deal with this minor out-of-seat behaviour (for it is minor disruptive behaviour)? What is more annoying here is the secondary behaviour; the attitude, manner and words used by the student in response to the teacher's questions (pp. 10–16).

It is worth pointing out, again, that an interrogative question about behaviour ("Why are you …?"), especially in front of the student's peers, is an invitation to a "slanging match".

I've never had a student say to me "… we pay your wages here". If I ever did, my response would be an exclaimed and satisfying "Eureka!! So you're the one … You've been paying my wages, eh? I've been looking for you for a *long, long* time …!" However, a brief "I" statement with a redirection to the task at hand is, normally, more than enough to deal with this little piece of "cock-sparrow" behaviour: "I'm not speaking to you rudely (or disrespectfully). I don't expect you to speak to me rudely". Then the teacher could refocus from the student's avoidance behaviour ("I was just getting a pen") to the task at hand.

Sometime the imperative question can help: "What are you supposed to be doing now?" Of course, a pleasant, business-like and respectful tone is important.

In response to the question, "What are you doing?", I've had students say, "I don't know what I'm supposed to be doing, do I?" In this case it is enough to simply, briefly and firmly point out what they should be doing and give them some take-up time. It will be important to come back, later, to check for time on-task and (also) to re-establish a working relationship with the student.

Is there a "distribution" of challenging students in any one class?

In any classroom group, there is often a basic distribution of challenging students in proportion to those students who are more cooperative and considerate:

- 70–80 per cent of the students are probably reasonable, considerate, naturally respectful, cooperative and display basic civil behaviours, *given the chance;*
- 10–15 per cent are argumentative (at times), or can be challenging in their behaviour. Sometimes such students are exercising attention-seeking goals, in effect saying: " Hey (…) *notice me*. I'm being funny, stupid, 'cool' …"; "My calling-out, my seat-leaning, my late entrance with a body language flourish … is inviting you to *notice me, attend to me*!!" And, of course, if a 5-year-old boy is rolling under a table and barking like a dog, it is difficult *not* to notice and attend simply in order to discipline him and protect the learning, and safety, rights of the other students.

   Sometimes students challenge others, particularly the teacher, through expressions of inappropriate power – a kind of game where the student, in effect, says, "I can do or say – basically – what I like and how I like and you can't stop me …"; "I'm the boss here …";
- 1–5 per cent display *frequent*, and often intense, patterns of disruptive behaviour. They may also present with emotional or behavioural difficulties (EBD), or behaviour disorders such as attention deficit or attention deficit hyperactive disorder (ADD/ADHD).

Caveat

It is very important that in using terms like EBD, ADD or ADHD we do not easily *label* the child as an *ADD child*. The negative effect of labelling is well known in education literature. Children often conform to the expectations that adults have about them and may also view themselves as inadequate, ineffective, useless or a troublemaker *within* these labels and expectations. The term EBD, as used here, is descriptive of children's typical behaviour in a given context.

Attention deficit disorder is an increasingly diagnosed disorder in children in the UK (as in Australia and the USA). Children diagnosed with ADD are often prescribed Ritalin or Dexamphetamine, medication that can assist with aspects of concentration, focus and impulsivity. Like any behaviour disorder, however, the positive assistance offered by medication will need support from behaviour therapy to give some direction and guidance to a child's increased concentration or decreased impulsivity.

Corey (aged 13) had been diagnosed as ADHD and was on four tablets of Ritalin a day. I discussed his behaviour with him and asked him if his tablets had *taught him to enter the classroom without "grandstanding"*. He returned my smile with a knowing grin. I then asked if the tablets had taught him to sit in his seat without serious rocking backwards, or had taught him to put his hand up without calling out or clicking his fingers (I mirrored these behaviours to him; p. 72). He grinned again.

"Nahh …!"

"Well – do the tablets teach you to stay in your seat, focus on the learning task and give it your best shot for – say – ten minutes or so without getting up and wandering …?"

"Course not – no." He realised the track I was leading him on to. We discussed other aspects of behaviour such as a quieter voice in class time and supporting other students by not annoying them.

I asked him who was "in charge of Corey". Who really drives Corey along in the minutes and hours of a day? I used the analogy of a car and a driver. It seemed to connect. We then discussed how a driver has to be focussed, has to select his gears, speed, indicator, has to decide where to go and why and how. We then discussed *how* he, Corey, could better (more helpfully, more thoughtfully, more cooperatively) drive his own behaviour. From this came a behaviour plan as both map and guide. This analogy of driver/car/behaviour is one that my colleagues and I have found quite helpful in developing behaviour plans with older students.

Corey still kept on the Ritalin (although the dosage was reduced) but the behaviour plan (p. 122f.) gave him added confidence and specific focus to work on aspects of his behaviour, and the special attention he received from key teachers assisted in building his self-esteem. It was a bit "three steps forward and one, even two, steps back" on some days but the colleague support – across all the teachers who taught Corey – helped to give some consistency and supportive encouragement to both the teachers and Corey.

Supporting students diagnosed with ADD

When working with, and supporting, children diagnosed with ADD (or ADHD) it can help to:

- seat them near a classmate who is both supportive and a positive role model. If table group seating is used, be sure these children sit with the quieter, less distractable children (even if they promise they will be fine if they sit next to overly motoric Craig!);
- use visual cueing to significantly assist student focus and attention. Seating near the front of the room (near to where the teacher engages instructional learning and class dialogue) can also help. Small picture cues for work tasks (on their table) can also act as a *aides-mémoire;*
- have work schedules for key learning tasks, with set structure for work development. It can help to have a daily progress sheet with goal based targets (even small, incremental, targets – breaking up the total requirement into time-manageable tasks). This gives a sense of time sequencing. Structure is important for children diagnosed with ADD; avoid giving too many choices;
- check for understanding when giving task instructions by asking the student to repeat back;
- make normal learning *routines* clear, even how to utilise workspace, set out workbook(s) and analyse tasks (read twice, check "do I understand?", "do I know what is asked of me here?", "how do I get help ?"). Give older students a table pencil case (p. 124) instead of a huge pencil case, full if interesting distractions. An uncluttered desk will help;

- allow time for reasonable movement in class time if only to quietly come and check the incremental progress (every five minutes). The teacher then gives a brief, positive feedback;
- avoid keeping such children in for extended lengths of time at recess – they, particularly, need physical activity at playtime.
(See Geffner and Brians 1993; Green and Chee 1995; Rogers 1997.)

Attention-seeking behaviours

Chris, a Year 8 student, was repeatedly calling out in one of my English classes; 8, 10 or even 15 times a lesson. His calling out was sometimes masqueraded as asking a question; sometimes it was a silly comment; mostly it was "attentional-behaviour". When I believed his behaviour was affecting my right to teach *or* other students' rights to learn and participate I would firmly and briefly remind him of the rule: "Chris, we've got a rule for asking questions. Use it thank you".

He would often use such a rule reminder as an occasion to further seek attention, "But I was *only* asking a question! Gees – is it a crime to ask a question in this class?"

I could easily see why other teachers found Chris' behaviour so frustrating at times.

It also doesn't help when a head teacher, who having interviewed and chatted with a child (presenting with significant attentional behaviours), then says to the teacher, "He's no problem with me – I get on with him very well". Of course! With an audience of one he's fine, but back in a classroom or playground setting the child's behaviour is affected by his belief that he can only belong when others are giving him lots of attention – even for disruptive behaviours.

- Some attention-seeking behaviour can, in the short term, be *tactically* ignored. Infant teachers know that by not giving any verbal or non-verbal recognition we can sometimes avoid unnecessary reinforcement of the behaviour; I say *sometimes*. As with all teacher discipline and management there is no guarantee – no simplistic formula in any management or discipline approach.

  It can help to *preface* the tactical ignoring when a student is calling out. Prefaced tactical ignoring involves the teacher giving a conditional direction, *then tactically ignoring* subsequent calling out behaviour: "Craig, *when* you've got your hand up without calling out [the prefacing, conditional direction] *then* I'll answer your question". It can help to briefly add, "Remember our class rule". The teacher then turns their eyes and attention away from the student to focus on students with their hands up ... tactically ignoring any subsequent calling out.

  As noted earlier (pp. 66–7), *tactical* ignoring is a teacher behaviour that is context dependent. We should never ignore any behaviour that sees a child hurting others (even pinching, or so-called low-level testosteronic bonding) or *persistently* disrupting other students' right to learn (by repeated, loud calling out; touching others' work; annoying them).

  The test of any efficacy regarding tactical ignoring is the degree to which the student reduces, or stops, his disruptive behaviour. Tactical ignoring is only effective if the rest of the class takes their lead from the teacher and also ignores the disrupting student.

- If the disruptive student gains any significant *kudos* from others in the class it will be important to briefly and firmly describe what the student is doing (in their attentional behaviour) and direct them to the appropriate behaviour

(p. 57):"Chris (...), you're calling out. Remember the class rule. Hands up without calling out". If the student challenges, argues or tries other diversionary tactics, keep the focus on the primary issue.

Avoid the temptation to be sarcastic and score points. While repartee, and even a workable *bon mot*, can defuse and refocus some attentional behaviours (from upper primary age upwards) sarcasm only feeds attention-seeking and power-seeking behaviours. If the student makes silly, rude comments the teacher needs to make *that* point clear:

> "That's not a helpful comment, Craig. You know that."
> "That comment is rude [or ...] and not acceptable here."
> "We have a rule for respect. I expect you to use it."

In such cases a firm, assertive, tone will carry the meaning.

On some occasions an immediate in-class consequence will be appropriate. If a student continues to be disruptive by, say, talking to or annoying students next to (or near) them, we can often use a choice/consequence statement: "If you continue to ... I'll have to ask you to work somewhere else in our classroom". If they continue with the disruptive behaviour and we then direct them to move and work somewhere else (the consequence) some students prevaricate or argue: "But I'll be alright now! I will Miss, I'll be good ...!!" If you have raised the consequential stakes it is important to carry the consequence through with certainty (p. 115).

If the student refuses to move to another place (I've had this a few times) rather than end up in a win/lose situation it may be preferable to give a deferred consequence: "If you choose not to move now and work over there I'll have to follow this up with you at recess" (p. 71f). An alternative is to use the colleague-support exit/time-out plan (p. 102).

- In some case where the attention seeking behaviour is significantly affecting the teacher's right to teach and the students' right to learn we will need to exercise the time-out consequence immediately. When directing a student from the classroom to take time-out, a calm exit is important. Avoid any last minute grandstanding by using a loud voice or threats ("and you're going to be in detention *as well*!!").

- If attention-seeking behaviour has occurred several times, over a few classes, some early and thoughtful follow-up will be imperative. It is often in these longer-term sessions that teachers can (more consistently) make clear to the student what he or she is doing in class and even *why*, and engage the student's understanding and cooperation (p. 71f.). Such a process needs to be seen as helping the student to understand and take responsibility for his or her behaviour rather than using such follow-up time for yet another punishment.

  In such one-to-one settings it is important that the teacher assures the student that their main concern is about the student's behaviour, and the effect it is having on other students' learning, and (of course) the teacher's right (and ability) to teach.

  If you are uncertain or uncomfortable about pursuing a semi-counselling approach like this, invite another colleague to work with you. The key focus areas in such a follow-up will address the following.
  - Is the student aware of their behaviour? "Are you aware of what you do in class when you call out ...?" Be *specific* about the student's typical, characteristic behaviour. In response to such questions, students often shrug their shoulders, and some laugh (nervously, or because they think their behaviour *is* actually funny).

- Describe the student's disruptive behaviour, specifically and briefly (some mirroring may be helpful; p. 72). Ask the student *what* they need to do to change the way they currently (and characteristically) behave. Point out that this behaviour is affecting others in the class and describe *how* it affects others.
- A simple, achievable agreement may help the student have a *focus* for *personal* behaviour management. I have found that a simple, printed agreement can often help such a focus by concentrating on three things that the student needs to *stop* doing (so that others can get on with their work without having to put up with X, Y and Z behaviour), and three things they need to *start* doing to gain some success in their learning and so others can get on with their learning without having to put up with X, Y and Z.

     The three things are specific, achievable behaviours. For infant age children the thing may be one behaviour such as "sitting on the mat (without rolling around or touching others, and facing the front and listening, and joining in with hands up …)".

Earlier this year I was asked to work with a difficult class of 11–12-year-olds (Year 5–6). There were several students who had been described to me as attention-seeking and power-seeking. One was described to me as "oppositionally defiant". These early, brief descriptions proved all too true.

On the way into my first lesson with the class, Kelly (I didn't know her name at that stage) started to ask me who I was in a repetitive way, in a voice that seemed to say, "Look at me – look at how I'm hassling this new teacher who is going to work with us …".

Later in the first class period, she called out frequently, sometimes with her hand up, sometimes without. One feature of her calling out was the sing-song tone of voice she used. Initially, when I *tactically* ignored such behaviour she would say things like, "I'm talking to you … can't you see me?" She would sigh and turn to a classmate adding …, "I'm talking to him, and he's not listening …". I could hear all this as I tactically ignored her.

Sometimes I would *preface* the tactical ignoring (p. 67); sometimes I'd give a rule reminder at the onset of her calling out.

This student's behaviour irritated her teacher and I can understand why. As I worked with my colleague my struggle with her students – in a sense – ratified, and supported, their struggle.

In their research on classroom behaviour and dynamics, Rudolf Dreikurs *et al* (1982) discuss such behaviour in terms of the child's purpose in a given context. According to Dreikurs, behaviour is directed towards particular goals. The general goal is to belong to the social group (in this case the classroom peers, or a small group of peers). In pursuing that goal some students (like Kelly) pursue their belonging *through* attentional behaviours. In this sense the *frequent* calling out, the silly comments, nuisance behaviours, the non-verbal sighing, rolling of eyes, and so on are not only the cause of the behaviour, but are also its purpose. The goal (to gain attention or power ...) is itself the cause, the active force, as it were, behind the behaviour, even if the child is unaware of what they are doing. As children get older their "private logic" may well embrace such thinking as, "I only really 'belong' when people pay lots of attention to me; when they notice me a lot".

Being aware of that purpose helps to explain the child's behaviour in its peer context. It is understandable that when we give undue attention to such behaviour (partly from our own frustration and partly because we are seeking to manage classroom dynamics) we also reinforce, or sometimes *over* reinforce, the student's goal.

I have worked with children who use frequent expressions of charm, cuteness or powerlessness ("I can't do the work") to gain significant and frequent adult recognition (attention). This, too, can be seen as a child trying to gain both excessive assurance and a sense of "belonging".

In the same classroom, on the same day, I noticed (how could I not) Liam making frequent hand gestures across the room, to a classmate, while I was talking to the whole class. Several students laughed and giggled. I directed them to "face the front and listen, ... Liam (...), Liam (...)!" He turned and faced me, sighing.

"You're making hand signals to your classmate." I briefly looked at his classmate. "You need to be facing this way and listening, thank you." He raised his eyes to the ceiling and folded his arms – and settled for a while. He repeated the same behaviour a little later. This time I called his name, "Liam (...) ...", and non-verbally cued him to face the front. He was getting, if briefly, the attention he was after. I was doing my short-term best to keep attentional focus on teaching and learning while giving minimal attention to the secondary behaviours (pp. 10–16).

Later, in the on-task phase of the lesson, I noticed he wasn't working; he was chatting to his classmate, but not working. When I encouraged him back on-task he became resistant. "NO ... I don't want to do this. I hate this kind of work ...", he muttered. I helped him refocus and gave him some take-up time, but he still refused to do the work. At times he refused to listen, or look at me when I spoke to him, or walked away while I was talking to him. This was more than attention-seeking.

It is eminently understandable that teachers feel threatened, even some-what defeated by such behaviour. I can understand how some teachers feel they need to show the child who is boss here. The child's displays of power may be active and vocal, or expressed in passive displays of power through non-verbal resistance. The child's private logic here, focuses on beliefs such as: "I can do what I want and others can't stop me ..."; "I am going to be the boss here ..."; or "*I count* only when I can do what I want; when I call the shots ...".

When I got to know these students a little better, I decided that I would pursue an approach that Dreikurs describes as "goal-disclosure".

Disclosing a student's behavioural goal

Dreikurs *et al.* (1982) propose an approach designed to supportively help the student understand "why" they are behaving the way they do. This approach involves particular questions being asked to raise the student's awareness about the possible goal of their behaviours. The tone of these questions needs to be supportive and non-judgemental if they are to help the student understand their "purposeful" behaviour. This approach needs to take place in a supportive, one-to-one, context.

- The first question raises the child's awareness about their specific behaviour through an open question: "Do you know why you ...?". Be specific about the, actual, disruptive behaviour: "Do you know why you call out many times in class ...?" ;"Do you know why you make frequent comments like [here the teacher recounts typical clownish, and silly, comments]?" Most students respond to such a question with a non-verbal response (a shoulder shrug, a wry frown or smile); sometimes a muttered, "Nope". Allow some brief reflection even if the silence is a little uncomfortable. It can also help to increase the specific shared awareness about the student's behaviour by some brief mirroring (p. 72).

- The teacher then *suggests* what they think about *why* the student typically behaves the way they do: "I'd like to tell you what I think ..." or "Can I suggest why you call out a lot [or butt in, and so on]?" I've never had a student say "no" to this propositional question. The teacher then moves the question towards a reason (goal) as to why the student typically behaves this way *in class*.

- Some suggested goal disclosures might be:
  - "Could it be that when you call out a lot you want the class to look at you and notice you?"
  - Or, if the issue is clownish behaviour, "Could it be that when you say things like ... [be specific] you want the class to look at you and laugh?"
  The disclosure of the child's goal is meant to sound strongly hypothetical rather than a judgement ("*Could* it be ...?", "I'd like to *suggest* ...").
  If the student's goal is some sort of power exchange (refusal to comply with teacher requests/directions; frequent answering back in front of peers; walking away while the teacher is talking; harassing others, including the teacher), the disclosure would focus on this aspect of the student's behaviour:
  - "Could it be that when you refuse to do the work you're wanting to 'show' me that you can do what you want and that I can't stop you ...?"
  This assumes that the student *can* do the work and that their behaviour, regarding task refusal, is a display of attentional power. It further assumes that the teacher knows the student well enough and has a positive working relationship with them for them to engage in dialogue in this way.
  - "Could it be that you want to do what you want, when you want – and that you believe no one can really stop you ...?"
  - "Could it be that you want to be the boss, call the shots ...?"

- Most students respond to a disclosure of their goal is non-verbal ways: raised eyes, a slight grin, a shoulder shrug. This recognition reflex (as Dreikurs terms it) is often the student's assent; their acknowledgment that the teacher is on to something.

  If the student says "no" (in response to the disclosure – "*Could it be that …?*") it can help to ask, "If that's not the reason, can you suggest why you call out lots of times [or refuse to do the work when I know you can do it …]?"

  It will also help to point out to the student that they have *learned* to behave like this at school. Somewhere, sometime, they *chose* to behave this way. They *choose* to behave like this now. As the teacher has suggested, the student has *learned* that certain ways of behaving get them the kinds of attention, or the kinds of attentional-power they seek. We might well admit to the student that we cannot *make* them learn, or (in fact) do anything. Only they can *make* themself *do* things. They do not, however, have the right to do what they want. They will have to face the consequences. The teacher is seeking – through this process – to work on a cooperative plan. The student can also learn to *change* their behaviour – and for good, worthwhile, co-operative reasons.

  Teachers can work with the student to refocus attentional, power-seeking behaviours into more cooperative opportunities so that the student can gain a sense of social belonging in purposeful ways, such as positions of responsibility (monitor roles, peer-monitoring, cross-age tutoring – this positive role is often taken up with some enthusiasm).

- In light of the disclosure, invite the student to work on a plan. A key feature of this plan will involve the teacher consciously noticing, and giving descriptive recognition, for cooperative attentional behaviour (see p. 122f.).

- An approach that involves the wider class group – through a whole class discussion – can highlight (for the student) what their peers think of behaviours such as frequent interruption and clowning (and why).

  In conducting such meetings it is important that we do not *name* an individual student (although no doubt particular names will be uppermost in most students' thinking!)

  I have run such meetings with children as young as early years. The basic rules for such meetings are: "One at a time"; "We're here to discuss issues that affect us all"; "We do not put anyone (or anyone's ideas) down"; "We listen to everyone's contribution"; "If we make any decisions as a result of our meeting those decisions have to fit with our classroom behaviour agreement" (p. 27f.).

  For example, there may be a decision, from the group, that students who persistently disrupt learning should have to work away from others or even face time-out (if they do not respond to a teacher reminder or warning).

  Consequences like those noted above would need to be consistent with the classroom behaviour agreement, would need to relate to the behaviour in question and be respectful in their application.

Working with challenging children and children with EBD

The concept of challenging children varies across schools and across a teacher's perception and experience. For one teacher, in one context, a student coming late to class is a major discipline incident. For another teacher the incident is a minor irritant and only *potentially* a discipline issue (pp. 63, 64). Children with EBD present with far more serious concerns for the teacher.

There are many aspects of a child's life, temperament, home and background circumstances and environment that we have little or no control over and that contribute to and affect behaviour in a school context. The way some children are treated at home – dysfunctionality in the home environment, structural poverty and parental long-term unemployment, lack of positive guidance, discipline, values and role models, the amount and kind of television that even very young children watch, poor nutrition – are all aspects of a child's life that have an impact on the child's behaviour at school. We cannot *control* those influences, structural factors and impacting relationships in a child's home environment. It took me a while as a younger teacher to really appreciate this frustrating truth. It is also of little help to keep whingeing about these factors: "If only …".

Our emphasis and energy is better placed supporting the student, in their ongoing welfare and learning at school. Where, and when, we can support their welfare out of school we will (particularly if the child is at risk). This does not mean we are unsympathetic to those factors noted earlier. (Indeed, there are occasions when we can hardly imagine how some of our students cope, how they stay as sane as they do.) It means we avoid:

- *blaming* home environments for the child's disruptive behaviour at school;
- too easily *excusing* the child's disruptive behaviour because "he comes from a difficult home";
- too easily making the child the victim of what we may believe are causative pathologies; i.e. "he is this way because he comes from a difficult home and has a dysfunctional parent, and dysfunctional siblings and … therefore he can't really help his behaviour or can't really change".

It is important to recognise that while disruptive patterns of behaviour clearly have a contribution from family dynamics, structural poverty and abuse (how could they not?) a student's disruptive behaviour at school is also learned in context. Negative behaviour is also reinforced when parents and teachers easily over-service or reinforce it. It is hard not to get very impatient with such students or even get angry and shout at such students. In a kind of reinforcing, socially cybernetic loop, adult behaviour can reinforce the child's attentional and power-seeking behaviour.

Yes it is understandable that teachers will shout or yell at students who frequently roll around on the mat make animal noises while scratching their "nether regions", or who walk away while the teacher is talking to them, or call out all the time, or hide under tables and refuse to join in, or task-avoid and task-refuse ("It's rubbish!!"; "I hate it!!"; "Can't make me!!"; "It's shit!!"), or swear and yell at their teachers, or push and shove and hassle other children in order to get adult attention, and so on.

It is hard, as a busy teacher with 25 *other* students, to take time to reflect on what we do currently when managing some children, or what we can do to help such children *learn* to behave more thoughtfully, positively and cooperatively. Any reflection and any workable plan for such students needs to be developed on a team basis, or even a whole-school basis.

The key elements of any team approach to working with students who present with EBD include the following.

- There should be a well established time-out plan (p. 100f.). There are students who can easily, even quickly, hold a class to ransom. When a significant pattern of behaviour is affecting fundamental rights in the classroom a teacher needs *immediate* time-out support (as does the rest of the class). While we often think of the disruptive child as taking time-out, the teacher (and class) also need cool-off time, and calming time, from such behaviour.

- *Teacher time-out,* in a crisis, can also include a senior colleague withdrawing several disruptive students from the classroom to calm and settle the rest of the students (see p. 145).
- With very disruptive students we have found it helpful to relocate the child in another class for one or two periods a week to give the class teacher a breather. This relocation involves the child having a set time period, with work, in another teacher's room. It is to be distinguished from time-out.
- Develop a case-supervision approach with the student. A "case-supervisor" is a teacher who works with the child one-to-one on their behaviour by developing an individual behaviour plan. This plan is then communicated to and utilised by all the colleagues who teach (or support) that student.

  At primary level such case-supervision is normally conducted by the class teacher. At secondary level case-supervisions are normally senior teachers who have responsibility for working with students who present with EBD behaviours. Such teachers will be selected for their ability and skill in rapport building, communication and behaviour therapy. They also need to be colleagues who are well respected by staff and students alike.

  It is also important to consider the ethical probity of one-to-one settings where a teacher spends some time "alone" with a student. If the student concerned is a female it is wise to appoint a female as the ongoing case-supervisor, and a male case-supervisor for a male student.

Case supervision   In working with students described as EBD (students who come to school every bleedin' day, as some of my colleagues describe), it is unhelpful to leave each teacher to come up with their own strategies and approaches. It is more effective to take a collegial approach, not blaming any one teacher that they can't cope with or manage Jason, or Troy, or Melissa.

It also won't help to blame the parents. We need their understanding and support. While this does not mean that we do not communicate an honest appraisal of a child's disruptive behaviour, it does mean that such appraisal needs a cooperative approach and not a blame profile (Rogers 1997).

- A behaviour profile needs to include how *frequently* a child calls out, butts in, wanders, pushes in line, and so on; how *intensively* he calls out, butts in, wanders ...; and how *generally* he exhibits such frequently disruptive behaviour across all teachers and all classes. It is also important to determine if the behaviour is *durable* (all lessons, every day) or is it more a bad-day syndrome pattern, occurring *some* days more than others?
- In working with such students early intervention is crucial. As soon as a "pattern" of disruptive behaviour is clearly present (in terms of *frequency, intensity, generality* and *durability*) the senior staff will need to support teachers in developing a collegial plan. This plan will involve both structural colleague support and case-supervision. *Structural support* involves time-out plans, classroom rotation (see "relocation" above) and timetabling meetings for case-supervisors and teachers.

  Case-supervision involves a key teacher working with the child, one-to-one, on a long-term basis. The case-supervisor's role involves, in the main, developing a personal, individual, behaviour plan with the student. The case-supervisor also communicates that plan to all teachers in the team, explaining the purpose and elements of the plan, and discussing discipline, encouragement and time-out options within the plan. The case-supervisor also liaises with parents to explain how this plan will support their child's learning at school, and invite parental understanding, cooperation and support.

This individual plan emphasises key behaviours that will enable the child to improve their social interaction (and acceptance by their peers), and their on-task learning.

The plan further involves teaching and reinforcing those behaviours with the child through modelling, rehearsal and encouragement. The case-supervisor *teaches* the child behaviours such as:

– how to enter the room thoughtfully (without loudness, pushing, shoving, or "grand-standing");
– going to their seat, or sitting on the carpet space (infants), without hassling others' personal space;
– how to put their hand up without calling out during instructional and on-task time;
– using partner-voice in on-task time.

It is the teaching of these specific expressions of positive behaviour that are, in effect, the plan. The case-supervisor's role is to discuss the child's present disruptive behaviours in light of their expected behaviour and then *teach* the student – through the plan – to be self-aware and self-monitoring within the new and required behaviours.

Key elements in developing individual behaviour management plans

Case supervision involves a one-to-one approach with the student over time. The key elements are set out in Figure 6.1.

- *Picture cues* are often used in individual plans at early years and middle primary level, and with older students on a case-by-case basis. To help the dialogue with the student about their behaviour the case-supervisor prepares

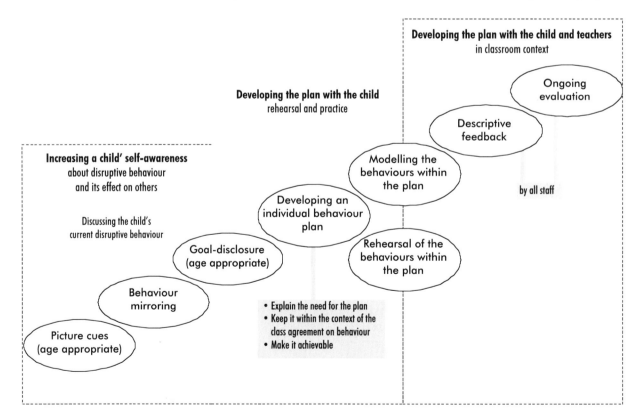

Figure 6.1 Key entry points in behaviour recovery: developing an individual behaviour management plan (© William Rogers 2000).

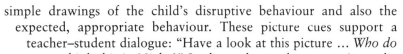

simple drawings of the child's disruptive behaviour and also the expected, appropriate behaviour. These picture cues support a teacher–student dialogue: "Have a look at this picture ... *Who do you think this is, Nicky?*" Students almost always nominate the picture of the student (rolling on the mat or calling out or being loud ...) as themselves.

The teacher then asks the child what they (the child in question) are *doing* in the picture. The teacher avoids asking the child, at this point, why they are calling out, or rolling on the carpet, and so on. In the background of this picture the teacher will have drawn (in smaller figures) other children with sad, or concerned faces and also an adult's face (the teacher) with similarly sad or concerned face to indicate social concern and disapproval.

These drawings of students being disruptive (in such plans) can be simple stick figures. The student will still nominate themselves as the disrupting student.

The teacher can then refer to the social disapproval displayed in the picture cue (the sad or concerned faces), and discuss, briefly, the effect of such behaviour on other students and the teacher.

- *Mirroring* has been discussed earlier (p. 72). The teacher invites the student to see what their *behaviour* looks like when they call out, or push and shove or are talking loudly, or are leaning their seats and so on.

My colleagues and I have used mirroring with every age group. It is important to use such a technique with the child's permission ("Do you mind if I ...?", or "I'd like to show you what it looks like when you ...", or – with older students – "Can I give you a demo? - It will be clearer if I do"). If children refuse (which happens very rarely) use the picture as the focus for discussion.

As noted earlier, keep any mirroring *brief*, physically *step away* (having shown the student what the disruptive behaviour looks like) and *refer back* to the behaviour: "*That's* what it looks like when you ...". Many boys, particularly, will laugh when teachers mirror the student's typically disruptive behaviour; that is normal.

There are, I believe, some limits to mirroring. I, personally, never mirror back to a student hostile and aggressive swearing, or throwing furniture. In these cases it is enough to pick up a chair, pretend to throw and put it down. That is ample. A simulated "f___", without the full word, is enough.

It is also helpful to briefly refer to the class behaviour agreement (or specific rule) and ask, "What are you supposed to be doing when ...?" This question can lead into the plan (see below).

- With older children (upper primary age on) *goal-disclosure* can help raise self-awareness; discuss the student's disruptive behaviour in terms of their attentional or power-seeking goals (pp. 118–19).

- Develop the plan itself. The second picture (see over) illustrates the expected, desired, appropriate behaviour (as contrasted to the first picture).

The teacher discusses what is different in this picture. For infant and middle primary age, simple pictures keep the attentional focus in the discussion. "So, Nicky, what are you doing in *this* picture?" or "What's *different*, here, in this picture? What are you *doing* here?" The teacher then draws the discussion around to the appropriate behaviour.

Pictures (as an *aide-mémoire*) can be used with older children, too, where appropriate to the child and context.

Above is a plan I developed with a Year 8 student who was frequently loud, and restless with his hands. He had a habit of clicking his knuckles, in part to get attention and, probably, in part because he was struggling with the work – an avoidance behaviour.

I had drawn a simple drawing and we discussed his behaviour in terms of possible attention. He rather liked the drawing and asked me if he could have a copy. The actual plan for behaviour change involved:
- keeping his hands quiet and using them to work with writing;
- a modified work-task – he struggled with particular subjects and we were able to negotiate some goal based learning tasks with the teachers concerned (and the heads of department);
- a small *table pencil-case*, which helped him have a less cluttered desk. Instead of a large pencil case full of bits and pieces as well as defunct pens we gave him a smaller pencil case to house a blue pen, a red pen, a pencil – no sharpener – and an eraser;
- the drawing as his *aide-mémoire*, as well as a record of his plan. He kept a copy in his school diary. Each teacher who taught him also had a copy of his plan and were encouraged to give him descriptive feedback (privately) during the lesson, and at the end of the lesson wherever possible.
- a twice weekly meeting between the case-supervisor and the student to talk about his progress with *his* plan – we always emphasise the plan as the *student's* plan.

The teacher's role is to support and encourage the child's ownership of his responsible behaviour *within the plan*.

• It is also important that the case-supervisor *models* the behaviour expressed in the plan. I have sat on the floor and modelled how to have eyes and ears to the front, I have modelled partner-voice, personal space awarenes, how to say sorry, how to put your hand up without calling out, and even how to manage feelings of frustration and anger when they come.

- The case-supervisor encourages the student to *practise* the behaviour (the plan); this involves rehearsing the behaviours several times (one-to-one).

   During such rehearsal the teacher can fine-tune aspects of behaviour such as "personal space", "hands in lap", "keep hands and feet to yourself when sitting on the mat", "partner-voice", "how to line up", "how to move through the room without annoying others" and "how to get teacher help during on-task time".

- Each teacher in the year team who teaches the student needs to be made aware of the student's plan and any special cueing, or disciplinary approaches. For example, for a student who is particularly loud, in helping the child to focus on partner-voice the case-supervisor will rehearse a reminder cue – perhaps the teacher simulating the turning down of volume (pp. 65–6). This minimises teachers having to over-use *verbal* disciplinary reminders.

   Each subject or specialist teacher also has the same copy of the plan as the student (the visual *aide-mémoire*). If the student is disruptive in class time, teachers are simply asked to remind the student (particularly during on-task learning time) about their plan: "Remember your plan", or even "What's your plan? What should you be doing now in your plan?" It can help as a disciplinary focus.

- The student's behaviour is monitored, and tracked, within the plan, across the year level.

   All teachers working with the student are encouraged to give the student descriptive feedback at some point in the lesson. This encourages the student when they are behaving within their plan.

   Such encouragement is best given privately where possible (i.e. out of direct hearing of others): "You remembered your plan; you used your partner-voice …". The *descriptive* feedback briefly focuses on what the child did (in terms of their behaviour, "their plan") that made a difference. Avoid global praise like "fantastic", "brilliant", "great", "wonderful".

   Sometimes a brief, non-verbal cue will encourage a child back on-task: a smile when the child is working within the plan; a thumbs-up; an OK sign. Such non-verbal encouragers are even appropriate in the more public, whole-class setting.

- Once (even twice) a week the case-supervisor will meet with the student to go over the plan (or any new plans) particularly focusing on: "What part of the plan is easiest for the student and *why*?"; "What part is hardest and *why*?" The *why* question, in this case, helps the child to be more self-reflective and increase their self-monitoring behaviour.

   Plans can be adapted, developed and fine-tuned in these meetings.

- Any plan is a means to an end: the end being to help the child become more responsible, more self-regulating in respect of their behaviour *as it affects others around them* (including the teacher).

   In *evaluating* the plan case-supervisors work with their collegial peers to determine if there is any positive change in frequency and intensity of disruptive behaviour; whether the student is still needing time-out; and if there is any stability and generalising of the expected behaviours.

   There are some students for whom no amount of one-to-one time, or behaviour therapy seems to help or affect changes in their disruptive behaviour at the school. In these cases we will have to work at alternatives outside a mainstream school setting. No student can be allowed to continually,

persistently, disrupt the learning and safety of others in a school. Alternatives to mainstream schooling in such cases are not only important for the welfare of the other children in the school; they are also important for the welfare of staff.

Inappropriate or "bad" language and swearing

Not all "bad" language or swearing is the same. Even adults sometimes (sometimes?) swear out of frustration. Even teachers (teachers?) swear in staff rooms, in the photocopy room or after the hostile parent has finally left. Whether we like it or not, swearing, as it has been traditionally understood (or sometimes, "bad" language), is more common today than in times past.

For some people swearing is even *passé*. Certainly in many films, books and television shows it has become the norm in descriptive dialogue as well as in expressions of frustration and anger.

I was discussing issues of playground behaviour with some dinner ladies (mid-day supervisors) one day and the issue of swearing cropped up, as it often does.

"What kind of swearing?", I asked.

"What do you mean?", they said, initially puzzled.

"Do the students swear at you or each other?"

"Sometimes at each other – rarely at us," they noted.

"So, what is the most frequent kind of swearing?"

It turned out that students were using swearing ("shit", "f__ing") mainly in conversations or frustration outbursts in game playing.

Should we then distinguish between "kinds" of swearing? If so, why and how?

Thoughtful teachers distinguish between a child who mutters, "Shit" (*sotto voce*) out of frustration and a student who swears *at* a fellow student or teacher. Some swearing is also muttered, in passing, when the student walks past, or away from the teacher ("wanker", "a__hole", "dick-head", "bastard").

Swearing as hostile intent directed at another person (student or teacher) needs to be dealt with immediately by the teacher – firmly, without aggression (this only feeds the latent hostility or anger): "That language is totally unacceptable here. When you've calmed down we'll sort this issue out"; or "Michael (…), We don't swear *at anyone* here. Full stop." Block any argumentative appeals as to why they swore at so and so (or even why they swore at you!). Avoid pointing, gesticulating and hand movements. An open, blocking hand movement helps to assert the firm voice without aggressive intent. Direct the student to take informal, or formal, cool-off time (p. 100f.). It is pointless asking (or demanding from) the student reasons why they swore (at you the teacher, or at a fellow student).

I have known teachers appeal to a swearing student: "Why are you swearing at me? I'm not nasty to you am I? What have I done to hurt you?" This non-assertive stance, expressed in a "please be nice to me" voice, is totally counter-productive and often feeds latent student power.

In the immediate emotional arousal, when hostile swearing is present, it is important to keep the assertive statement brief, focus on the issue or rule (about language or respect), direct the student to take some cool-off time and follow the issue up later with a third party (a colleague) for support if necessary.

Younger children will need a direct, immediate rule reminder: "We don't swear like that in our class." Follow this by immediate time-out in the room, where possible, or out of the room if the child is physically hostile or aggressive.

In the immediate emotional moment avoid long explanations about *why* the language is unacceptable and resist the moral lecture, "Is that the kind of language you use at home?!" I've actually heard teachers say that *and* I've heard students reply in the affirmative.

If a student swears *sotto voce* (on the run as it were), such swearing can sometimes be tactically ignored in the immediate, emotional, moment and followed-up later when the student has calmed down. In depends in part on how *sotto* the *voce* was (did we really hear a frustrated, loud, whispered "wanker"?) and in part on the audience reaction. It is often enough to say something like: "Paul," – use the child's first name because it gains some attentional focus, and personalises the adult–child discipline role – "I heard what you said. I don't speak to you like that. I don't expect you to speak to me like that." Then direct the child back to the task or to what he should be doing now or to cool-off time if necessary.

If we can direct the student aside for a brief chat (using similar language to above), even better. If other students have heard the muttered swearing they need to see us do something.

We can sometimes add, in the one-to-one aside, "David, I heard you swear at Paul earlier ...". I've had students look puzzled here (because they don't always think what they say is swearing). I sometimes add in the swear word they used, or write it down. "Look, I know you were uptight with Craig before (this briefly tunes in to how the student was probably feeling) but we have a class rule about respectful language ...".

In a particularly "hard" high school in the western suburbs of Melbourne I was teaching an English class. As I was moving around the room (in the on-task phase of the lesson) I overheard one of the more vocal (and time-wasting) lads call a girl near him a "f__ing bitch", just above *sotto voce*. I knew they were friends but I could hear the frustration in his voice. I went over and said something like, "Look, Adam, I heard what you said to Belinda ..." I pushed the piece of paper on which I had written down his swearing language across to him.

"I didn't say that!" He sounded annoyed.

I added, "I heard you Adam ..."

He explained, "I tell you I didn't say that! I said f__ off, you bitch. I didn't say f__ing bitch. Gees!" He was upset that I'd got the words wrong *not* that he'd used such offensive language!

The annoying thing was that when I called them both back later (after class) to engage in some mediation Belinda seemed unfazed, shrugged her shoulders and said, " ... it's just Adam ... that's how he is ...".

Part of the problem of addressing swearing with some students (adolescents most notably) is the "no-big-dealness" of it all. It can often help to raise the issue of swearing and offensive language more widely with the whole-class group through a classroom meeting (Rogers 1997). Ideally class teachers should have covered the issue of interpersonal communication, mutual respect and careless, thoughtless, disrespectful and abusive language within the classroom agreement (p. 27f.). A classroom meeting can re-affirm the issue of respectful language and reassess "how we communicate with one another here".

Swearing, at infant level, may mean something different to a child's perception. One of my colleagues recounts the occasion when a student came up to him with a most serious look on her face and said, quietly, "Sir ... Con said the F word."

"Did he Maria – really?"

"Yes he did."

"Are you sure?"

"Yes ... the F word."

The teacher thought he would check and asked, "Maria ... *what* did he say?"

Maria replied, with the utmost seriousness, in a whisper, "He said, he said ... *stewpid!*"; and covered her mouth as if to say "sorry I had to tell you he used the F word (stewpid)".

Conversational swearing

It is not uncommon, even in primary schools, to hear "conversational swearing"; I even hear it sometimes in classrooms (and staffrooms): "Did you see that fantastic f__ing game the other f__ing day. Shit! How was the f__ing score they got, eh? The other team; they're rat shit!"

Should we ignore this kind of swearing in the playground? Should we relegate it to the argument of, " …that's the reality now. That's how it is today – it's just street language …"? I have heard this argument many times now – principally from non-educators.

Ignoring such language (when we hear it on playground duty or even in the classroom as a *sotto voce* exchange) can easily send the message that we do not care how our students speak, or that such language is OK; or is even the norm (as a conversational exchange).

Of course such language is "street-language", but acceptance can easily excuse, even ratify, language norming. The issue for educators is how can we encourage our students to converse without lazy recourse to "f__ing and blinding …"?

A group of students are discussing the latest "f__ing film" they saw recently; some action-packed thriller with serious maim, gore and gratuitous … (well, gratuitous anything really). You can hear the descriptive qualifiers quite clearly, several yards away. It won't help if the teacher charges in moralising: "Oi!! I could hear *every* word you said!! Is that the kind of language you use at home – is it? You disgusting creatures!!"

It may well be they use such language at home, but a judgemental appeal to 'home environment' goes down like a lead balloon and may, in fact, get a hostile reaction.

The issue of conversational swearing can be addressed by a quiet, firm, acknowledgment, followed by a rule reminder about use of language (assuming the issue of thoughtful and respectful language has been explored across the school).

Sometimes a humourous question, or aside, can give a bit of self-checking. The teacher walks over and casually greets the students.

"How's it going?"

The returned, non-verbal body language suggests, "Well, we were going OK till you walked over – really." Their *actual* reply is, "OK."

The teacher leans a little towards them (as if to suggest he doesn't want others to hear) and asks a question about the "effing film" they had momentarily been discussing (without using the participle they used). "Seen any interesting films lately beginning with "F"?"

A couple of the students catch on with a weary smile and sigh. The teacher walks off with a pleasant "goodbye for now". Relaxed vigilance.

If some students habitually, and loudly, converse with strong swearing it is worth following up with these students at a later stage to discuss their behaviour and engage their responsibility for the way they communicate.

Most conversational swearing is an *unreflective habit*; some (of course) is peer-group, positional strutting, "Listen to me being 'tough', 'hip', 'with-it' …"

If the issue of conversational or banter swearing is typically frequent (particularly at upper primary and secondary level) it can help to run classroom meetings in tutor groups to raise the issue: define what is meant by bad, inappropriate or disrespectful language and swearing; discuss how feelings are affected by what we say and how we say it; and re-address core rights and responsibilities as per the classroom agreement (p. 27f.).

If you're not confident in running such a meeting, or if it is outside your experience, ask a colleague to conduct the meeting with you.

Most of all it is getting a balance between language probity, thoughtful discipline and education and modelling; our own modelling (as teachers) will go a long way in demonstrating that one can communicate frustration, even anger, without resorting to the lowest common language denominator.

Chapter 7
Managing anger in ourselves and others

That carries anger as the flint bears fire;
who, much enforced, shows a hasty spark
Shakespeare, *Julius Caesar* (iv, iii)

Managing anger

England is full of roundabouts – or so it seems to me. On one of my trips to the UK, a few years ago, I hired a car at Heathrow and was beetling down towards Basildon and a hotel. I had a map, but I was lost. At one of the large roundabouts I sat and waited to get into the circling mass of cars. To my right an old car pulled up, and with a brief glance I noticed two young lads, both drinking large cans of larger and smoking roll-ups. The lad nearest to my right-hand window wound his window down and said, "Oi – get going alright!" Apparently he could see it was easy for me to race into the traffic throng from the cusp of this roundabout! Sitting in this new car, with cars speeding past me, I was much more cautious.

My caution seemed to really annoy them, I was closer to the entry of the roundabout than they were. He called out again, "Just go, f___ing go, alright!!"

I thought their anger was disproportionate to the 20–30 seconds of caution on my part. I looked at him and shrugged (as if to say, "be fair, fellas ... I'm waiting for a break in the traffic ...").

"F___ you!" was the last I heard from the two lads and they shot off (having gunned the car) into the roundabout. But as they shot past my car they hit my right hand mirror and it did a 360° turn – Bang!

Having entered the roundabout, at last, I took a turn off to what I hoped would be Basildon. As I motored on I saw the two lads on the hard shoulder, standing looking at the damage to their car (where they had hit my mirror). I pulled over and parked about 20–25 yards in front of them, and got out (hoping I might get their number for potential insurance purposes ... an unwise move perhaps, but ...).

As I was "casually" examining my twisted side mirror, I noted (out of the corner of my eye) one of the lads walking towards me, with his can of lager. He looked tense; perhaps he thought I was going to create a scene. I turned side on (as casually as I could) and said (still looking as if I was examining my mirror) "You OK?"

He said, surprised, "Yeah."

"I'm glad", I replied. "Your car OK?"

"Yeah". Still surprised even wary.

"My mirror is jammed". I didn't verbally attack him, or judge him, or blame him (notwithstanding the fact that he'd arrogantly hit the mirror although I'm sure he didn't "mean" it).

He looked at the mirror – "It's jammed!"

("Course it's bleedin jammed!", I felt like saying). I didn't. A bit of "partial agreement", I thought. "You're not wrong, it's jammed".

He seemed less tense now. I was hoping my calmness would trigger some calmness in him.

"You can fix that easy" he said.

"Can you?" I wasn't too sure.

By this time the other lad had come over to see what was happening. I said "Hi". He grunted something. I added "I'm checking my mirror ...". He also noted the "bleedin obvious".

"It's jammed ..."

The other lad chipped in, "They're on a spring – you just pull it out and it goes back in the housing right. I can fix it if you like". They seemed marginally affable now. I hadn't verbally attacked them – it was as if we both had some basic human needs going at this point; we were beginning to see each other as more than a mere hindrance on the road.

He pulled at the mirror, groaned and grunted. I was hoping he wouldn't pull it out of its socket! He let go. It clanked back into place.

"Shit! I fixed it!" He seemed surprised and pleased.

Neither had admitted blame or even apologised. I didn't force it either. I looked at the fixed mirror – a few scratches on the plastic housing. No sweat!

"Good on you, fellas – thanks." They must have picked up on the Aussie accent. The first smile from the two lads.

"You an Australian?"

"Yes." I felt like singing the theme song from *Neighbours*. I didn't. "Fellas, I wonder if I could ask a favour." I noticed a little tenseness (perhaps I was going to ask for their license number). "I'm trying to find a hotel in Basildon." I explained where I was seeking to go to.

"I know where that is!" He ground his ciggie on the gravel. "It's ..." he started to explain.

"Could you draw me a map, fellas?"

"Nope – we'll take you there. You follow us – we'll show you where to go". I had a momentary thought they might lead me up the garden path. But no – they didn't. They went out of their way to help.

While I'd *never* advise stopping in such a situation, I know the situation could have been worse had I just let vent with some macho posturing.

I followed them to the Posthouse. As we parted they bipped their car horn. I think this was their version of "we're sorry".

While there is never any guarantee that our behaviour can positively affect another's in tense situations like this I believe that it helps if we calm ourselves before we seek to calm the other person, and take some thought of how we communicate with tense, frustrated or angry people.

Frustration and anger – in ourselves and others

Anger is a very powerful emotion. It can disturb, even destroy, positive-working relationships between ourselves and our colleagues, and ourselves and our students.

I have seen and heard teachers yelling or even screaming at individuals and whole classes as their frustration then anger reaches boiling point. I have intervened between teachers and students when I have sensed that the teacher is a few seconds away from hitting a student or getting into a self-defeating conflict. I have seen teachers eaten up with anger so that they behave in hostile and aggressive ways to peers and students alike. Anger, however, can also validate our feelings and needs, and can helpfully communicate those feelings and needs.

Understanding our anger

It is important to *understand* our own frustration and anger; to understand those situations, circumstances and people who lower our tolerance to frustration; to understand what we *characteristically* do in such situations, how we react and respond and manage *our* anger as well as seeking to help others to manage their anger. We can hardly do such reflection in the heat of the emotional moment. It is, however, worth generally reflecting on the emotion of frustration and anger in terms of our role as teachers.

Aristotle has taught us that "we must not forget that it is human to be painfully affected by anger and to find revenge sweet" (Thompson 1969: I, 100). He is not saying we should find revenge sweet; he is talking about the human tendency expressed by the familiar epithet, "Don't get angry, get even". A teacher with such a view of retributive justice is doomed to a short career!

Aristotle goes on, "Neither are we praised or blamed for the way we feel. A man is not praised or blamed for being angry; it is for being angry in a particular way ..." (*ibid.*: II, 63). He makes clear what we know in our more reflective moments: anger (or at least frustration) is a feeling we often *can't help*, it just comes, often when we're tired, hassled or trying to do ten things at once.

Aristotle also distinguishes between the *feeling* of frustration and anger, which we can't help or stop (like when you're in a traffic jam on the M25 and you're in a hurry and you forgot how useless a road system it is at peak times and so on) and the *behaviour* that results *from* our anger. He adds, "Being angry, or frightened, is something we can't help but our virtues are in a manner expressions of our will; at any rate there is an element of will in their formation" (*ibid.*: 81–2).

The *learned* bit in anger is what we do *when* we're angry. We have learned to get angry in certain ways; perhaps we have unhelpful habits of anger-behaviour, but we've learned these over time even though such learning may not be readily conscious. It is (as Aristotle says) the "element of will", the "expression of our will" that occasions any "virtue"[1] in what we do when we're angry.

> Anger may be produced by a variety of causes ... but, however, that may be, it is the man who is angry on the right occasions and with the right people at the right moment and for the right length of time who wins our commendation. (*Ibid.*: 127–8)

Is this a tall order? Of course! Aristotle never denies the humanity of our anger. What he is saying there are some fundamentals about the "rightness" of anger and how we express it.

The psychiatrist Scott-Peck makes the point that to "function successfully" in this complex world of ours we need to "possess the capacity not only to express our anger but also not to express it" (1978: 67). We are well aware of those occasions where a verbal outburst would (in hindsight) send the right message at the wrong time and, perhaps, severely damage a relationship with a friend, colleague or student. While there are times when an immediate brief, passionate expression of anger is right, at other times it is better, wiser, says Scott-Peck, "to express it only after much deliberation and self-evaluation" (*ibid.*: 67), as when we write an angry letter.

"I lost my temper!"

A frequently used phrase expressed by adults and young persons alike is, "I just lost my temper; that's all!!" We say this, later, to explain the high arousal that occurred at the time we were angry and to explain why we expressed our anger by shouting, yelling or being (unintentionally) nasty or vindictive.

It's an interesting choice of words. We don't actually "lose" our temper; we "find" it. The issue, really, is what we do when we've, very quickly, found it.

- Anger is normal; at times it's more than normal, it is *right*. There are occasions when justice demands that we clearly, unequivocally, communicate our anger to others.

  On many occasions, though, our anger is more typically the outcome of life's frustrations, irritations and what Lazarus (1981) calls "daily hassles", or what Shakespeare (in *Hamlet*) called "the thousand natural shocks that flesh is heir to". Shakespeare said "natural" shocks, and who wouldn't get frustrated (even angry) at intransigent, lazy, rude or arrogant student behaviour? Why wouldn't we get angry with an insensitive, unfeeling, "ill-considered" report from an OFSTED inspector (unlike, we hope, most OFSTED reports)?

  It is important to be aware of the situations, circumstances and people that lower our tolerance to frustration. The issue of secondary behaviours (noted in Chapter 1) is typical of a high level irritant for most teachers: when students speak in sulky, pouty, insouciant tones of voice; when their body language indicates they don't care (the shrugged shoulders, the eyes to the ceiling, the drawn out sighs). Awareness helps; so does skill. We can learn more effective ways to manage and communicate our anger and to help others when they are angry.

  I've talked with some men who say they "can't help getting angry when …". What they mean is that they can't help *characteristically* shouting, being immature or mean-spirited *when* they're angry – as if men are somehow hardwired in their social biology to only get angry in loud or physical ways. Angry *behaviour* is learned. Unhelpful and unprofessional angry behaviour can be unlearned, and other (more helpful and appropriate) anger behaviours can be learned.

- It is important to distinguish between anger as an emotion and the behaviour that comes from anger – particularly *impulse behaviour*. Anger is not of itself bad – how can it be? And we ought not to convey to children that they are somehow "bad" for having angry feelings or emotions, or "getting angry". As Conrad Baars points out, "it is necessary to realise that the high intensity of an emotion does not make it 'bad', even though its consequences may not be beneficial for that person or others around him" (1970: 68).

  Learning to guide our emotions with thought and skill will, in good part, help determine any constructive behaviour that proceeds from our anger.

- It can be helpful to distinguish between annoyance, irritation, being "cheesed off" and frustration; and between frustration, high frustration and anger; and between anger and aggression.

  Anger is at the high end of emotional arousal. Imagine, for example, saying to a student "I'm angry that you haven't finished your homework!" or "I'm angry because you're late!" Such behaviours (in students) might merit annoyance, or even annoyed concern, but do they merit anger? If we easily, quickly and characteristically get angry over such minor issues, when we *really* need to communicate anger we lose the emotional weight (or even the moral weight) of that which we might need to appropriately get angry about. Overuse of the word *angry*, or *anger*, will tend to devalue its currency.

- Allied to the previous point is the notion of "getting angry" on issues that matter or issues that count. In this way students can see, and hear, the relative justice in our expressed passion and behaviour.

  For example, if a supply teacher is badly treated by your class, and on your return from the flu you hear a litany of complaints from the head teacher about "your class" or "your students", this is an occasion where a clear, unambiguous communication of our anger (even disgust) is appropriate.

"I am very disappointed and angry about what I've heard from the principal today about members of our class and the way they behaved towards the relief teacher [name the teacher]. I cannot believe *anyone* in our class, or school, would say and do the sort of things some of you did when you ..."

In communicating our anger we are specific, but brief. Avoid using the language the students may have used – swearing or harassing language – while not shirking the inappropriate or even offensive language they used.

"I know it wasn't all of you. Those who said those things will be meeting with me and the principal soon (one at a time). I'm also appalled that many of you let the others, *in our class,* say those disgusting things and behave in the way they did. I think of you as responsible, capable, people."

Whenever I've had to speak like this to a class – with passion – with a firm and unambiguously serious voice, the students sit quietly with a look of perceptible chagrin. I suspect they are saying "we're in *really* serious poo here"!

In a case like this it is important that the teacher make clear that it is the behaviour that is totally unacceptable and that you (the teacher) will be "having a classroom meeting later to see if we can repair and rebuild the damage created by your behaviour yesterday".

When speaking to a group like this:
- be specific and as brief as possible;
- do not attack them: "You pack of animals, you're no better than pigs! Yes pigs!!". Tempting as such an attack might be, that is hardly going to win their understanding and cooperation; address their *behaviour.*
- work for some group restitution *and* an understanding that next time a supply teacher comes I expect that: "We (all of us) will ..." Then develop with the class a convention about working with supply teachers.

Communicating our anger

It is difficult, very difficult, in the heat of the moment to decide what we might do or say when we're angry. Some prior reflection, and general anger management awareness can help.

- Briefly calm yourself before you seek to communicate to the other person what you are angry about and why. This sounds deceptively easy; it isn't. Take a few deep breaths, but not too deep because the other party may think you're hyperventilating! Count a few seconds in your head, then communicate what is necessary.

  Brad Bushman (Iowa State University) has suggested that mere cathartic expression of anger increases habituation of angry or aggressive behaviours. In his study (involving some 600 volunteers) he observed that those who had practised calmness before expressing their anger were less aggressive in their expression of anger.[2]

- Focus *briefly* on the issue, circumstance behaviour you are angry about: "I am angry *because* you ..."; "I get angry *when* ...". If you are only annoyed or irritated use that word rather than "angry".

- Address the issue; don't attack the other person ("Who the hell do *you* think you are!! Don't *you* ever speak to me like that you little ....!!").

  If we need to use assertive language be assertive about the behaviour, briefly and unambiguously: "I don't *ever* make comments about your body or clothes. I don't expect you to *ever* make comments about mine. It stops *now*!" to a student who has made a gutless, sexist comment. The first time it happens do not ignore it; address it swiftly, briefly, unambiguously and assertively.

When we are assertive we need to look the other person in the eye, but don't stand too close and avoid the wagging, pointing finger. Extend an open hand and use a clear, firm, strong voice: "I don't swear at you. *That language is totally unacceptable here.* If you're uptight with me find another way of saying it" to a student who has sworn at a teacher (unprovoked).

Assertive language is to be distinguished from aggressive language, as when a person says, "*You* made me so angry with your stupid whining ...". By communicating with an "I" statement we let the other person know how we feel or are affected by their behaviour. Our non-verbal behaviour needs to be decisive without being hostile or aggressive. We model control (of ourselves) *while* communicating our fundamental right and at the same time addressing the other person's unacceptable behaviour.

- De-escalate the voice and the residual tension quickly. We may need to raise our voice (not shout) to initiate attention and assert a point. It is important to then drop the voice to a firm, controlled, more measured tone. Children are rarely adept at de-escalating emotional arousal when a situation is very tense. We, as adults, have to take the lead.

- After having communicated our anger some cool-off time enables both parties to calm down, perhaps even think and reflect. They are then more amenable to work for resolution.

- It is encumbent – professionally and morally – for the adult to initiate some repairing and rebuilding after the anger-arousing incident. Few children will come to their teachers and say, "Look, I'm sorry, sir. I've been tossing that incident around in my mind – you know when I lashed out at you and said ... well ... I'd like to repair and rebuild with you ... to re-effect that working relationship".

  As the adult, even if our anger is justified, we will still need to reach out with the olive branch to model the repairing and rebuilding behaviour that we hope they will exercise (perhaps one day).

We need to repair and rebuild because it is the right thing to do. Unresolved, residual feelings of animosity unnecessarily impair the teacher–student relationship. When we repair and rebuild we give the student the opportunity to share their feelings about the issue that led to the anger episode. Someone has to make the first move.

After cool-off time sit down with the student and:
- explain, briefly, what it was you were angry about *at the time* and why;
- invite the student's right of reply;
- tune in to their perception and feelings but refer back to the *fundamental right* affected by the student's behaviour;
- avoid forcing the student to share their feelings. If they choose not to share how they felt, or how they are feeling now, it can help to briefly suggest, "Perhaps you're feeling really annoyed about what happened the other day when ..." At times it is enough that we simply communicate that no grudges are held and "we move on from here";
- discuss how "we" might handle a similar incident "next time";
- separate amicably.

For a male teacher speaking with a female student it will be important to have a female colleague present for ethical probity.

Frustrated and angry parents

If you have ever had an angry parent storm into your classroom, or office, or try to buttonhole you in the playground you will know how stressful such an encounter can be.

Most parents are reasonable when they present to the school with concerns and problems relating to their children. They moderate or curb their feelings of frustration at what they perceive as being unfair, inappropriate or unacceptable treatment of their child.

When working with frustrated and angry parents it is crucial to acknowledge and affirm how they feel and what they (initially) perceive as "the problem".

Their perception may not be yours and may (in fact) be incorrect, but it is how *they* feel and perceive "things to be".

- Allow the parent some time to explain how they feel; avoid the temptation to butt in and defend the school. Allowing the parent to have their say may mean letting them "run out of steam".
- Invite the parent to sit down (it's harder to be overly angry sitting down).
- Listen first, then reflect back: "So you seem to be saying that …"; or "As you see it …"; "I can see you're really upset or angry about …". So, for example, if a parent believes their child is being harassed or bullied, one should be able to acknowledge and understand parental anger as well as refocusing energy towards appropriate mediation and consequences.
- Be sure to have the facts as the school sees them, and invite the parent to view the problems within the school's policy and due processes.
- At times compromise may be necessary without the school making promises or commitments they can't keep and without compromising the school's behaviour policy on rights, responsibilities, rules and consequences.
- Honesty is crucial; about how things are, what has happened and the most workable, sensible and fair options open to both "parties".
- Early support given to parents can often eliminate messy, and often inaccurate, disclosures in the public arena (gossip, the media).

Hostile and aggressive anger

I've taught with a number of colleagues over the years who have been reduced to tears by bombastic, arrogant and angry parents who bring no control to the wild, ill-formed accusations delivered in a barrage of four-letter words.

A colleague of mine, a principal (in Australia) had suspended a girl (Year 8) for punching another girl in the face. The victim had bad bruising around the jaw and face. The principal had given the other girl a non-negotiable suspension for three days, pending an accountability conference involving some mediation and restitution with the victim of this bashing.

The morning after the girl was suspended her mother stormed into his office (by-passing the school secretary).

"What d'you suspend my daughter for?! Eh?! Anybody calls my daughter a slut I tell her to f___ing punch her f___ing lights out …!!" The mother was hopping around, finger wagging and waving in the air. Droplets of saliva flashing around the office in the early morning sun.

By this time a few senior colleagues are hovering near the door ready to give moral support.

"And you can all p___ off!!" yelled the mother.

I asked him what he did to manage this *fracas*. "I know what I'd like to have said", he smiled wearily. "No wonder your daughter is off her tree with a mother like you!! Who the hell to you think you are storming in here yelling, screaming and abusing me you stupid _____!! Go home!! Take a valium sandwich and come back *if* and *when* you calm down. And don't you ever storm in here without making an appointment! Do you understand?! But I can't say all that can I? Tempting as it may be. If I do that I'm on the television news that night. The mother is standing there, now calm, looking seriously hard done by this cruel and heartless school. She faces the camera, dressed for the part, and says, 'You go to the school because you're concerned about your daughter. She was bullied you know – I can't repeat what she was called – and what did she get – no help at all but abuse, and from a school principal!'"

"So what did you do then?" I asked, although I'd already guessed.

"I let her 'run out of steam' as it were. She jumped around, yelled at me, effing and blinding. Eventually she calmed down. I was offering no resistance. Nor did I try, at this stage, to defend what I'd done. She stood there, somewhat 'out of breath'. I asked her if she'd like to take a seat. She sat, arms folded. I said, 'I can see you're really upset about Chantelle – about what's happened. I know you care about Chantelle so do we. If we talk this through, without attacking each other, we can support your daughter. After all that's why you're here. I won't yell and swear at you, Ms ___. I expect you not to swear at me. Thanks. Now ...'"

He then talked about the incident, getting the facts clear and straight.

"No, I'm not calling your daughter a liar, Ms ___", in response to her accusation that the witness reports were from liars in contrast to her daughter's honest account.

Eventually he got some understanding and assurance that the due-process of mediation (in three days' time – after cool-off time for all) would help. He didn't defend the school's policy on violence; just explained and reaffirmed it as non-negotiable and supportive to *all* parties.

It is hard to stay calm and professional in such situations, indeed sometimes the parent will fly off the handle again as the discussion of the problem challenges their view of rough justice. In these cases *continual* yelling and swearing by the angry and hostile parent is best dealt with by a firm assertion: "This meeting is *over*. It's not working Ms _____". He holds up a blocking hand. "It's not working. I've asked you to discuss this calmly. You're swearing and yelling at me. I'm not prepared to continue. Leave now; when you've had a chance to calm down please make an appointment and I'll be happy to talk with you – anytime." Show them to the door. If they refuse to leave (it happens!), it is better to leave yourself. They may harangue you all the way down the corridor, "You bastard!! You've never cared about our Chantelle. You're all a bunch of gutless ...!!"

If it is the mother haranguing you, go into the male toilet at this point if the (even if you're female!) "Go away – it's a male toilet." Meanwhile one of your colleagues will direct her to leave or warn her that the police will have to be called. These sorts of scenarios are rare (thank goodness) but they do happen, and in most cases teachers are incredibly professional in the way they handle such incidents.

- Calm yourself before consciously helping the other person to calm down. This will include consciously unclenching fists, and presenting open body language (which is easier said than done).
- It may help to let them "run out of steam" to aid their self-imposed calming.
- Invite them to sit down.
- Tune into how they may be feeling.
- Get to the facts (in writing beforehand – hopefully from records).
- Give an appropriate right of reply; listen, reflect back briefly.
- Emphasise that you're there to work on the problem – not attack each other;
- Always keep the focus on the core rights and responsibilities of the school policy as it relates to the parent's complaint.

- Work on a solution (if possible) or refer to the due process that needs to be followed. The focus should move to a solution that is mutually workable wherever possible.
- Separate as amicably as possible with an assurance that the parent can ring and make another appointment if necessary.

It is crucial that the colleague who has been on the receiving end of such parent behaviour has some de-briefing later with their peers. I've done this many times (a glass or two of workable Australian red can help). I've seen teachers unnecessarily blame themselves for the anger episode. A de-briefing can allow the teacher's pent-up frustration or anxiety, to be shared and provides the opportunity to validate their feelings and move on – hopefully learning something.

Many schools now have an internal school policy on managing complaining and angry parents. Such a policy needs in-servicing, reflection and review.

When the other person is angry

There are times when we have to manage a very frustrated or angry student. In a Year 8 class I taught, some years ago, a student had taken massive umbrage that I'd "taken over the class from another teacher". Within a few minutes of me being in the classroom Lisa stood up (in the front row) and in a raised voice, leaning forward, nearly shouting, she said, "What did do you have to come into our class for?! We don't need you!! This class was alright till you came!!" That was probably true! I'd come into this class as a mentor teacher to help re-focus their noisy, unfocused pattern of behaviour and now Lisa's power position was under *perceived* threat.

In such cases yelling back would be pointless (if tempting). I chose (in the emotional moment) to let her run out of steam. In a sense I took the wind out of her sails. A surprising and unexpected thing happened. The student next to her pulled down on Lisa's jumper and said, "At least he's listening to yer!!".

While I was letting Lisa run out of steam (as it were) I was scanning the eyes of the other students to non-verbally communicate to them that "you are part of 'this' too – as an audience you have a part to play". Fortunately the rest of the class was "with me". Lisa sat down, folded her arms, slumped back in her seat with a frown, a pursed mouth and a big grunt. The class watched. I thanked the student next to her, "Thanks Carmel". Turning to Lisa I said, "I *was* listening to you Lisa, but I don't yell at you. I don't expect you to yell at me". I wasn't nasty; just clear, brief and assertive.

When the other person is angry, and we have a management responsibility, we need to assist the other person to get back into some sort of control. At times this may involve a dignified time-out (calm-down) option. On this occasion the student settled.

"OK, folks," to the class, "the show's over." We carried on with the class discussion. Over several sessions my colleague and I worked with the class to help them re-focus how the class was (and wasn't) working and what we needed to do to change things (see pp. 139–44). Later I had a one-to-one chat with Lisa about the incident (with a female colleague "sitting in" pp. 71–4).

I also found out (later) that Lisa had an alcoholic father and that she had had run-ins with other male teachers. Having explained (to her) why I was the "new teacher", and also that I thought I understood a little of how she might be feeling about having a new teacher, and we discussed other ways of making one's feelings and concerns known, we made some progress.

In time Lisa and I got on reasonably well. She learned to moderate her more "bolshie" communication style and when I finished my time with her class we parted amicably, with some residual goodwill.

The rare situation – anger and aggression

There are some situations when an assertive command is necessary, as when two students are fighting. The sharp, brief command "Oi! Stop that! Move away *now*!" needs to make unambiguously clear that such behaviour must stop. The sharp tone is then reduced to a firm, controlled, assertive and calmer voice: "Move away *now*". We'll often need to repeat the command: "Move away now". The dropping of the voice gives a sense of calmness and control. If the voice is *kept* sharp and high it can create too much arousal. If the fighting students don't move apart we will need to decide whether to physically intervene (a risky course of action). Whatever we do in a fight situation we should *always* send for a colleague (for practical support and as witness) and direct the audience away (often the audience are just waiting for adult permission to leave the fight scene in a face-saving sense). Most schools have a policy for managing crisis situations.

In the rare circumstance where a student physically threatens a teacher (with a weapon, a chair or a fist) an assertive command may not be appropriate. Nor will it be appropriate to let them run out of steam!

A colleague had a student walk into her high school class with a large knife. He was clearly, visibly, angry; breathing heavily, rapidly, his eyes darted around the room. He was looking for someone. My colleague knew this lad quite well; that helped. She looked him in the eyes and in a *calm*, voice, amazingly controlled, said, "Ahmed (...), Ahmed (...), I know you don't want to hurt me or anyone else here. I can see you're very angry." She tuned into his feelings quickly, calmly, making a reference to herself in the situation. "I know you don't want to hurt *me* or *anyone* else here ..." She never took her eyes off him, as if by calm, sustained eye contact and the calm (reassuring) voice she could calm him. "Put the knife over there, Ahmed. Come on. We'll go outside now and we can talk. Come on." She walked slowly, with her arm beckoning gently. He put the knife down and followed her out. Thank God.

The class was sitting in stunned silence. By this time the principal had heard and rushed down to see the teacher walking with Ahmed towards the office area. Wisely, he too responded calmly, walking with the student and teacher towards the office. Halfway down the corridor my colleague collapsed. She had, she said later, used "all her emotional energy up" and just collapsed. The class and teacher had some de-briefing, and counselling – later. Ahmed, too, received counselling (after a formal suspension of one week). Apparently the knife was to scare another boy whom he had accused of stealing his girlfriend.

You may never have had, or will ever have, such an experience (I hope you don't). If you teach in EBD schools, or "Withdrawal Units", hopefully you will receive training for appropriate, professional responses in crisis-management situations. In mainstream schools such scenarios are, fortunately, rare. Spare a thought for teachers who regularly have to manage tense, hostile, aggressive students like that of my colleague noted here.

At the end of the day I share nothing here, about anger and anger management, that I do not struggle with as a teacher, father and colleague. What I am trying to share is that *all behaviour,* particularly in more challenging contexts, has a reciprocal effect for general good or ill. These comments and understandings about anger are an attempt to engage some reflection and, hopefully, more thoughtful behaviour.

Notes

1. Virtue (in this sense) means the *characteristic* direction of one's moral will.
2. Y. Merroberry and S. Farrer, *Sunday Times*, 9 May 1999.

Chapter 8
When things get difficult: hard class, hard times

People must help one another it is nature's law.
Jean de la Fontaine (1621–1695)

I like my isolation within easy reach of other peoples –
wide open spaces set me on edge.
Roger McCough (1993)

Your needful counsel which craves the instant use.
Shakespeare, *King Lear* (II, i)

Struggling teachers – the hard class

A few years back I was struggling with a really hard class. I'd tried being kind, I'd tried the "power-struggle" (*sic.*) approach … I'd kept kids back – even the whole class yet … I was also too proud and naive to attempt to discuss my problems with any of my colleagues who seemed to be handling things so well.

(cited in Rogers 2001)

From time to time the difficult class like this comes our way; a class that seems to sap at the energy and makes *that* timetable slot, or *each* day, a struggle. In the case of the colleague speaking above it was a seemingly recalcitrant Year 7.

All that we would normally do, and more, to manage such a class, saw him still struggling, halfway through Term 1: residual noise levels; students frequently off-task; calling out; cross-talking; lateness – all seemed to be too annoyingly and stressfully frequent.

A class like this can shake the confidence of even experienced teachers. I've worked with teachers who have felt they are a failure because they cannot manage *this* class, *this* year. Rather than seeing the failure as the annoying natural mix of challenging students and classroom dynamics, some teachers (struggling with such a class) will tend to blame themselves.

The term "struggling teacher" should not be a simple pejorative. When teachers experience a hard class, or several difficult to manage students, they sometimes feel that admitting that they are struggling or having a problem means that they are not able to cope (which is actually true but not a bad thing in itself). When teachers feel less effective they may also feel that an admission of their struggle means they will be evaluated or judged in some way. Hopefully, this attitude is not present in your school. If a teacher perceives his or her colleagues' support as having implied judgement, or strings attached, it may well constrain them from asking for early, valuable support.

Colleague support is crucial when coming to terms with the management of a harder than average class.

That support, in the first instance, needs to be offered and expressed in a "no-blame" way.

Offering support

> There's this ludicrous idea that when someone is really struggling we have this hands-off mentality – just in case we do, or say, the wrong thing. It's stupid really especially when we *know* they need help.
>
> (Senior teacher, cited in Rogers 2001)

The Elton Report (1989) has outlined this ambivalence about directly offered colleague support as it relates to behaviour management and discipline issues. On the one hand the offer of support may seem that one implies that a colleague is not coping; so, too, the request for support by a struggling colleague may imply that they cannot cope. So a teacher who is struggling with a hard to manage class may struggle on alone – unassisted.

> Teachers have tended to stay out of each others' classrooms and not talk about their own discipline problems. Too often teachers do not seek help because it feels like an admission of incompetence and they do not offer it because it feels like accusing a colleague of incompetence. As a result, the tradition of classroom isolation persists in many schools.
>
> (Elton Report 1989: 69)

This ambivalence, however, depends on how collegially supportive the school is (as a whole) and on how the school enables colleague support through both structure and forms of support that meet colleague needs.

"I don't have a problem with ..."

I've been in many, many meetings with colleagues to discuss issues relating to behaviour management and someone will say, "but I don't have a problem with [a particular student or class ...]". Even if what they say is true it hardly helps a struggling teacher. What can often result from such a comment is colleague rating: the struggling teacher unrealistically, unhelpfully, rates themselves against the "better" or more able colleague.

The sad thing is that the "more able" colleague who "may not [really] have a problem" may well be able to understand, support and give valuable assistance; the struggling teacher is, however, unlikely to listen when hearing that others "don't have a problem ...".

Tim O'Brien describes a typical scene where a teacher has had a hard time with a difficult student, comes into the staff room for a caffeine fix and bravely (and professionally) shares his or her struggle: "in the hope that empathy or advice will ensue. The response (sometimes) given is the verbal equivalent of a swift kick in the groin. 'He's alright with me ...'." Tim goes on to suggest (tongue in cheek?) that we should "ban the singular and plural versions of this morale wrecking phrase from our schools" (1998: 90). It's about shared identity.

Some teachers may say, "I don't have a problem ..." because they are anxious that if they speak up about management or discipline concerns they will be seen (or judged) to be "ineffective" or "weak" teachers. The masked assurance ("I don't have a problem ...") may also indicate the teacher's belief that request for support from senior colleagues may invoke offers of support with strings attached; and the request will be remembered in the teacher's ongoing service review. This kind of unprofessional culture tends to breed a degrading survivalism rather than professional empowerment.

Colleague support: stress and coping provision

Social support – colleague support – can affect stress levels and coping resources in a number of ways:

- In their research on job-related stress, Russell *et al.* (1987) note that social support can affect stress – even burnout – in positive, buffering ways. Job-related stress and feelings of stress and de-personalisation decreased as the level of *supportive* supervision increased. Individuals who have supportive collegial relationships are able to rely on others to aid and support them in dealing with stressful situations.

  Schools that consciously seek to address colleague support are aware that stress *and* burnout have a relational, social causation as well as psychological causation (Rogers 2001; see also Hobfall 1998).

- Positive support from supervisors was predictive of "measures of physical and mental health" (Russell *et al.* 1987).

- Teachers who indicate that when others (particularly senior staff) in their school acknowledge and affirm their skills and abilities there is a greater sense of personal and team accomplishment and that "feelings of de-personalisation" were lessened (Rogers 2001; see also Bernard 1990).

- Supportive collegiality seeks to address consciously the normative stress of day-to-day teaching by enhancing the "ecology of support" and strengthening the sense of supportive interdependency.

  The degree to which a school *consciously* acknowledges colleague support as an integrating factor in a school's culture (as well as its mission), and the degree to which a school leadership seeks to address the needs of its staff will significantly affect the dependability and reliability of ongoing support (Rogers 2001).

- The "buffering" and "coping" aspects of colleague support are enhanced when such support is given in a non-blaming, non-judgemental way, where the "ecology of support" in a given school seeks to meet colleagues' basic human needs as well as their professional needs (Rogers 2001).

In collegially supportive schools "reliable alliances" are nurtured through informal and formal sharing and teaming. These alliances can be informal, transitional and dyadic as well as expressed in more formal and systemic expressions such as teaming and policy imperatives.

Colleague support can:

- lessen the feelings of isolation ("I'm not alone here ..."; "It's not all my fault ..."; "I'm not totally responsible for all that happens ...");
- provide fundamental moral support, even in the many brief transactions of a school day;
- empower staff through the sort of teamwork that promotes committed and caring relationships among staff. Such team work can also increase an individual's confidence and risk-taking as they grow professionally;
- provide assurance that one is on the right track (in terms of one's teaching resources, strategies, approaches, and so on);
- provide a forum, a *collegial* context, for problem-sharing, problem-analysis, problem-solving and coping resources. This, in turn, reduces negative feelings of inadequacy (as one accesses wider resources beyond one's self);
- enable the essential stress relieving support in the management of attentional, disturbing and challenging student behaviours (Rogers 1996b, 2001).

Senior administration can effect significant support to their colleagues by allowing genuine needs analysis on those structural, organisational and role factors that contribute to stress in the workplace day-to-day: even so-called "minor" irritants like fluorescent lights not working, poor photocopier facilities, inadequate staffroom facilities, communication processes, procedures and systems, broken furniture in classrooms and so on.

A stress audit, each year, is a positive and practical way of legitimising genuine concerns or complaints of staff and enabling action planning to reduce the stress associated with such concerns. (Rogers 1996b)

Moral, structural, professional support

Colleague support can range from normative whingeing to active and constructive problem solving. Teachers need to "off-load", to whinge, to complain about individual children and classes that they find difficult. If that is all colleagues do, though, it will be of little help long-term with hard-to-manage students and hard-to-manage classes. Colleague support, in such situations, needs to be structural and professional in its ongoing application as well as giving the moral support we all need to be reassured and encouraged.

Structural support (Rogers 2001), in this sense, refers to those dependable "forms", "processes", "procedures", "action plans" and "policies" that can be depended on by colleagues when under pressure.

Professional support refers to the way we enable our colleagues to reflect on, and appraise, their professional obligations *and needs*, in light of the aims and objectives of their role in the school.

No one *expression* of colleague support stands alone, or is sufficient of itself. All expressions of support seek to meet colleague needs. When addressing the hard class issue a *collegial* action plan seeks to meet colleague needs with emotional and practical support through shared action planning.

Developing a collegial action plan for re-establishing a difficult to manage class

A collegial action plan provides a forum and a process for meeting the moral, practical and professional needs of a colleague struggling with a hard to manage class or several hard to manage students. When such a process is effected early in the cycle of concern, it can often re-engage the necessary hope, goodwill and energy of teacher and students alike.

- Begin with a year level, team meeting as early as possible before it becomes a habituated problem drifting into Term 2; early intervention is crucial. Once a profile of *group* behaviour is clear it will be important to have a meeting with *all* the teachers who work with the class in question.

  Issues to be addressed will include:
  - How many students are disruptive and it what ways?
  - How frequent and intense are the disruptive behaviours?
  - Who are the ring leaders?
  - Is the class "hard" for all teachers who teach this group or these students? No doubt there will be some whingeing in such a meeting. This can be cathartic, up to a point. It can be healthy to affirm our common struggle and validate common feelings, as long as colleagues avoid the easy "I don't have any problems with that particular student, or class". Any whingeing, though, will need to go beyond just the whingeing itself to problem analysis and shared action planning.

    It is also true that *some* teachers (by the way they characteristically treat individuals and groups) contribute to the "hard-class" phenomenon. At this first meeting it is important to allow some focused collegial attention to this reality.

- Develop a year-level plan based on thoughtful year-level needs analysis. Some of the issues that will need to be re-assessed in such a plan are:
  - a re-assessment of how colleagues established the class group in their first meetings, including basics such as: establishment of routines like seating plans (or lack thereof); classroom entry, settling and calming; noise levels; routines for asking questions, and obtaining teacher assistance; classroom rules for behaviour and organisation for learning and so on (see Ch. 2). The way a class is initially established has a significant effect on group behaviour norms (Rogers 1997);
  - a discussion of short-term options for immediate colleague support in areas such as time-out of provocative and persistently disruptive, students or even time-out options for the teacher (see p. 145 on colleague assisted time-out);
  - a clarification of procedures for tracking particularly difficult students, including how colleagues currently follow-up with such students beyond classroom settings (pp. 71–4);
  - a discussion of *any* issues of harassment of teachers (pp. 147–51).
  In developing a collegial action plan, it is important to elicit and engage the support of senior administration.

- Decide on possible approaches in enacting the plan. A common approach we've used, for example, is to have a classroom meeting with all the students of a given class group to discuss issues of common concern, and develop a shared plan to re-establish the class. In this sense the students are given a degree of ownership in the re-establishment or "fresh start" process.

Classroom meetings re-establish a difficult class
Any such meeting should address: the common behaviours of students currently causing concern to teachers (and probably to the cooperative students in the class); the rights being affected by disruptive behaviour; the responsibilities being ignored; and what needs to happen (as a class group) to address these issues.

In a more "open" meeting the teacher can direct the class focus to questions such as:
- What is working well (in our class) at this stage in our class journey?
- Why do you think such aspects of our class are working well?
If an issue or concern is too personal, or likely to cause embarrassment to the "respondent", or the teacher, it can be written down (anonymously) and read by the teacher at a later stage (assure confidentiality). The last question is:
- What can we do to change things in our classroom?
This question addresses individual and group behaviour) so that everyone's rights are enjoyed (and protected) and we take on our individual and shared responsibilities.

When we conduct an open meeting there is always the possibility that some mean-spirited students will use such an open forum to have a go at the teacher. If there is any suspicion this *might* happen these questions can (and should) be asked through a questionnaire format (Rogers 1997).

The emphasis behind such questions is the development of a learning community: we *all* share the same place, time, space, needs, resources here (p. 27), and that is why we need to work on these concerns and issues together. The questionnaire gives *all* students a voice, and an appropriate right of reply.

It is crucial after such a meeting that teachers (at a later stage) give feedback to the class on their responses and work with the class on developing a shared plan for key aspects of behaviour and learning – a re-establishing.

In a re-establishment plan we take the class back to:
- their *core rights* and *responsibilities*;
- the *rules* for classroom behaviours that affect those core rights and responsibilities such as the way we treat one another, the way we learn here and how we create a safe classroom/school community. Some rules may need some specific focus (e.g. use of shared equipment and property, movement around the room);
- the *routines* for the smooth running of the class, particularly procedural routines (pp. 26, 35–7);
- the *consequences* for affecting others' rights. These consequences will range from rule reminders to time-out options and even detention. Students need to know the consequences in advance. They also need to know that these consequences are fair and relate back to protection of rights;
- students also need to know the positive outcomes that will flow from students supporting each other, and their teacher, within such a plan. This is a crucial feature of any fresh-start. If the meeting is simply another opportunity to growl or moan at the class group it will further alienate the goodwill of the majority of the class who are probably quite cooperative and – when given a chance to a fresh-start – will support positive teacher leadership.

It is helpful to publish the plan on a couple of large posters with key headings. Use positive language wherever possible in the published outcome. The plan can also be published on A4 sheets and made available to all students.

Any such meeting, involving students, is best developed by those colleagues in the team who are both experienced and "comfortable" in running classroom meetings.

• Support each other (collegially) in the development of the whole-class behaviour plan. This will include ongoing shared collegial feedback and can also include cross-class visits (in our rare non-contact time) to see how students behave in other subject areas/settings. It can even involve some elective team teaching, observational feedback and mentoring (p. 152f.).

• Have a review meeting with the colleague team a few weeks into the re-establishment phase of the plan and discuss what is working well, what isn't, and see if there are areas where fine-tuning or change is necessary. It may be helpful to look at: how the time-out referrals have operated; how individual case-supervision (of students with challenging behaviour) is affecting the class dynamic (pp. 121, 122); and how teachers' perceptions about noise levels, time on-task, general student motivation, enthusiasm and cooperation have changed (if at all).

Any such review may need to include possibilities such as changing the structure and student placement in groups and even possible teacher rotation across groups. If, for example, one or two students are, effectively, holding the class to ransom, it will often be necessary to shift such students to other classes. This may be necessary both for the welfare of other students as well as the teacher. While this is a somewhat difficult organisational option, it will often need to be considered.

The fact that the senior administration have been a supportive part of this process will significantly affect how such an option is considered.

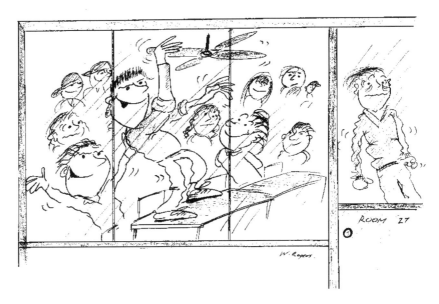

Time-out for the teacher

Walking past a classroom in the corridor one day I saw (and heard), through the corridor windows, some serious "catalytic conversion" going on: loud yelling, excited voices and raucous laughter. Looking through the window I saw a student standing on a table with his arm in an overhead rotating fan. He was laughing, his "mates" egging him on. The teacher looked quite stressed out. Should I intervene? How?

One *short-term* supportive strategy in such a situation is for the colleague "passing", or even a colleague teaching nearby, to knock on the door and offer either to withdraw one or two students (the ringleaders) or even give the teacher an opportunity for a dignified "exit".

- If a teacher walks past a classroom situation where a colleague is clearly struggling, rather than staring through the window with a look of judgement, or walking past, or walking in and shouting the class down, the support colleague knocks, enters and says, for example, "Excuse me, Mr Smith (…), I wonder if I could borrow one or two students?" This is "code" for "I'll take the two most difficult 'ringleaders' or 'power-brokers' off your hands for the rest of the class period". The teacher may feel like saying "One or two would be fine but eight would be better!"

The support colleague escorts the trouble-makers away to a time-out situation and talks through with them their inappropriate and unacceptable behaviour. A follow-through consequence may also need to be organised later that day. The support colleague may even escort the students to another classroom for some "time-out". This option will need to have been discussed, with colleagues, as a general school-wide option.

This approach is preferred to the visiting teacher walking in and shouting at the class, "Who the hell do you think you are!! I can hear you all from my office!! You pack of animals … !! I'm sick and tired of your stupid behaviour. Just shut it – alright?! You make me sick!!" Of course the students may well go "*stumm*", especially if the harangue is given by a senior teacher. While such a reaction is understandable, it hardly helps the class teacher's self-esteem. As the visiting teacher walks out on the now quiet class his non-verbal demeanour says, in effect, "That's how you deal with them." The class teacher may well feel unsupported even undermined.

- *Teacher time-out.* There are situations in the classroom where loss of control is so serious that the best short-term support we can give the teacher is time-out (for the teacher). This is what I did in the instance of the boy with his arm in the fan. I need to add his arm was in plaster; he was having a lot of "fun" using it as a brake in the fan ... and, of course, getting plenty of peer attention.

  The supporting teacher knocks on the door (loudly – it needs to be loud to be heard). "Sorry to bother you, Mr Smith. There's a message for you at the office." This is code for, "Get out of here ... I'll take over for now ...". The message at the office is simply, "Who's got your class?"

  Your colleague then has a breather, takes stock and re-composes.

  The supporting teacher's action is not merely some "white-knight" routine: it is a dignified collegial option in a crisis.

  The supporting teacher then meets with their colleague, later that day, to debrief and offer longer-term support. Our first thought though, in an immediate crisis, is for the emotional welfare of our colleague, followed, of course, by the safety and welfare of the students.

  When we take over in such a situation, it is important not to convey the message to the students that the regular teacher is ineffective, or can't cope: i.e. "OK!! The *real* teacher is here *now*. The one who has it all sorted (unlike the teacher who has just left ...)!!"

  Fortunately situations like this are rare. Any such colleague safety-valve support must be followed up by longer term needs analysis and strategic planning with the supported colleague and the class (p. 142f.).

There is a big difference between a testy class or bad-day syndrome and a class where there is a loss of control and a feeling of panic that order, purpose and focus cannot be regained.

If you have had such experiences then early acknowledgment that there *is* a problem is not a sign (or symptom) of weakness; it is a professional acknowledgement that you need colleague support. I've worked with teachers who have struggled for weeks on end with such classes and end up "breaking-down".

> "I didn't want people to think I couldn't cope ..."
> (Well you couldn't. That's not a sin, it's a recognition that something is wrong and you need support to reassess "where?", "why?", "how?" and so on.)
> "What will others think of me? Will it be a black mark against my career ...?"
> (Not in a supportive school ...)

I can understand why some teachers are reluctant to disclose their anxieties and struggles – but hopefully it won't take a crisis issue like that noted here to begin a process of support.

In some situations the only long-term recourse will be to regroup the teacher and the class. This is not the most elegant solution but it may be the necessary one.

Where colleague support (including ongoing mentoring) has seen no real changes in a teacher's ability to successfully work with a class it will be necessary to re-establish the class with a new teacher. The educational welfare of the students needs to be considered as well as the welfare of the current classroom teacher.

When passing the leadership of the class group to another teacher it will be important that the "new" teacher not convey, or impute, that their previous teacher was a "failure" or incompetent. A brief acknowledgment that it's time for *us* to move on is enough.

Harassment in the workplace

A provocative newspaper headline reads "Workplace is a war zone …". A closer reading of that research (from the Australian Institute of Criminology), conducted among police, doctors, nurses, taxi-drivers and teachers, indicates that these professions face the greatest risk of verbal attacks and even assaults; at least teachers are last on the list. The article used a broad term, "workplace violence", to include: "injury through employer negligence, physical and verbal abuse, racial abuse, bullying, sexual harassment and even malicious gossip" (*The Age* 2000). The article goes on to say that "we should not countenance such behaviours as 'permissible, systematic work-related risk'" (Santina Perore).

As this applies to classrooms, particularly in more "challenging" schools, a tacit acceptance of some expressions of hostile or verbally challenging behaviour as "boys-being-boys" or "this is the way kids are around here", or "some classes here are just difficult", may also mean an acceptance of psychological harassment of teachers. Worse, if we categorise harassing behaviour as merely "disruptive behaviour" that the teacher cannot control we may then, too easily, blame the teacher for the harassing behaviour of the students.

Harassment is more than merely unacceptable – it is wrong. It is an abuse of fundamental rights: the right to feel safe, the right to be treated with basic respect, the right to teach and the right to learn.

Blaming the victim is not an uncommon feature of bullying/harassing dynamics: "yeah, well she deserves it (the teacher) cause she's a useless teacher". This global, quick labelling then ratifies and even excuses the students' behaviour when they call out such things as, "don't listen to her", "she's rubbish", and "this is boring – boooring!!" Harassing behaviour can include the non-verbal suggestions that students use to refer to a teacher's sexual preference, or body shape, or clothing or anything they can pick on that will give ratification to their exercise of power.

I'm not talking here about reactive student behaviour. There are occasions when a teacher's behaviour sees understandable reactions from students. A teacher walks past a student's open bag on the floor, by the chair, and espies a packet of cigarettes in the bag. The teacher takes them stating, "You're *not* supposed to smoke here – I'll take them !!" The student's reaction is immediate, "Hey!! They're mine … don't you f__ing touch them!" The *student's* behaviour here is not harassment; it is an understandable reaction to a piece of unthinking, unnecessary behaviour by a teacher. What did the teacher think? Did she really think the student would just acquiesce? Did she care?

Harassment – addressing the issue

This is not an easy issue to write about. I have done so because I have observed it in some schools and have been involved in supporting colleagues to address it wherever it occurs.

• Harassment is not occasional bad-day syndrome behaviour. Some students will sometimes take the risk of "having a bit of fun" with a teacher (particularly a new teacher or a supply teacher). Most teachers recognise such behaviour for what it is; point out quickly that the student/s has gone too far and reign it in. Such behaviour will also necessitate the teacher conducting some follow-up (p. 71–4) to make the point clearly about the limits of "fun".

Harassment involves those intentional, selective and *repeated* behaviours of an individual or a group designed to hurt or abuse their victim. Bullies select people they perceive as weaker than they are (psychologically and physically weaker) and use bullying behaviour to confirm and ratify their social power (Rogers 1997).

- Bullies rely on collusive acceptance of or acquiescence in their bullying/harassing behaviour (by their peers). *Collusive bullies* may not directly harass a teacher but they do silently approve of, or give a non-verbal chorus to, the bullies' behaviour. Sometimes collusion can occur when students who are afraid of the bully go silent and will not speak out in (or out of) class. Bullies accept such collusion as confirmation of their social power.

  Bullies trade in secrecy – not from their peers but from adults. It is important to crack this secrecy code early.

- One of the problems inherent in any workplace harassment is that some teachers feel insecure about admitting that they are "having problems in a given class"; they believe that an admission that some students are "making their life hell" is a sign of their own weakness; that they can't cope; that they *should* be able to cope.

  "I didn't want people to think I couldn't cope …"; I've heard this many times – sometimes too late in the day. The point is that sometimes a teacher cannot cope with harassing behaviour on their own, nor should they have to.

  A more disturbing issue occurs when teachers feel that if they do "speak out" about harassment then nothing (effectively) will be done; that such student behaviour will not be seen as harassment.

  It is important to address harassment as early as possible in its cycle – to crack the secrecy code, confront the main perpetrators and the collusive perpetrators (where necessary) and support the victim (the teacher and perhaps other students).

  If you are ever in this situation or circumstance of knowing that the behaviour you are experiencing is more than merely a disruptive class on a bad day, or that you are going home disturbed, anxious or even angry about repeated disruptive or personally abusive behaviour, or you virtually hate coming to school when you have to teach a particular class, then you need to speak to a senior colleague *as early as possible* to address and confront the issue.

  If you are a senior colleague who senses that something is clearly wrong with a teacher's class, and suspect that harassment is a factor, it will be important to speak supportively with your colleague about your concerns and offer support.

  In such a meeting with a colleague it will be crucial to allay any anxiety about perceived judgement, or that in coming forward with their concerns they are a weak and ineffective teacher. A sharing of what you suspect about the class concerned (and the behaviour of some of its members) and an invitation to talk it through should lead to an early reassurance of support and the development of a plan to confront the perpetrators.

  Ideally, the first incidence, or suggestions of harassment, should have been nipped in the bud with an assertive comment by the teacher (p. 133) and immediate follow-up beyond the classroom (pp. 71–4). Some teachers, however, who lack assertive skill let such early behaviour go in the belief that it will go away in time. It rarely does.

- *Accountability conferencing*
  The concept of "accountability conferencing" can be utilised for any significant issue of concern that a teacher has about the way a student has behaved towards an adult (in or out of a classroom setting).

  Early intervention should include the teacher directly confronting the student with their harassing behaviour. Such an intervention needs the support of a senior colleague and thoughtful prior planning. By "confronting" I mean setting aside "one-to-one" time with the student, where the teacher makes *clear* to the bully what it is they have *specifically* been doing, saying or suggesting that constitutes the harassing/bullying behaviour. Such confrontation needs to be respectful, truthful and non-laboured. An opportunity is then given to the student to reply and account for their behaviour.

It is crucial that the facilitator (a senior teacher) plans this meeting with the teacher concerned beforehand, getting the facts clear (and written down) and going through the order of the meeting and how the different stages of the meeting might develop towards the outcome.

Such a meeting can reawaken quite emotional issues and concerns for the teacher, so it will be important to discuss what they will say and how they might respond to "discounting" and "avoidance" behaviours by the student. If the perpetrator is a female student and the "victim" a male teacher it may be wise to have a female senior colleague facilitate the process (for perceived ethical probity).

- The facilitator (a senior teacher) calls a meeting between the teacher and the student (the perpetrator of the harassment). The meeting is obligatory for the perpetrator.
- At the outset of the meeting the facilitator explains why it has been called. The tone of the meeting is serious; formal but respectful. If the tenor of the meeting is vindictive and merely an opportunity to attack the student, it will not work for the desired outcome. Nor should the meeting suggest that "this is *just* a little chat about a few problems in class".

  "I've called this meeting between you, Troy (the student), and Ms Smith because we are really concerned about ..." Here the facilitator briefly outlines the facts that relate to the student's *behaviours*. It is not an attack on the student as a person (tempting as that might be) The facilitator makes the rules of the meeting clear. We each listen to the other without interruption, giving assurance that there will be a right of reply, but the aim of the meeting is to determine what has been happening (in the classroom or wherever) and to make sure that the upholding of the rights and *responsibilities* of the individual, and of a safe, respectful classroom, are the outcome.
- The teacher who has been the recipient of this harassing behaviour is now given the opportunity to address their issues of concern about the student's behaviour *directly* to the student. The teacher outlines the behaviours that the student has been engaged in, *briefly* and *specifically*. It will help to have the typical incidents written down. It can sometimes help if the facilitator "models" some of the non-verbal harassing behaviour to increase clarity and understanding. This possibility needs to be discussed beforehand with the teacher concerned.
- The teacher *briefly* explains how such behaviour affects the teaching and learning in "our class ..." and how it affects "the teacher's right to respect". Avoid talking too much about personal feelings ("I went home last night and had eight aspirin, six Mogadon and some far-too-serious scotch and I've been tossing and turning all night"); such admissions may be unhelpful grist to the bully's power-seeking mill!
- The teacher points out that the behaviours detailed are *harassing behaviours* and must stop: "This behaviour (beckon to the list) has to stop so that I can get on with the job of teaching and the students in *our* class can get on with their learning ... and so that I can feel safe here and have that basic respect I seek to give to you ..."
- The facilitator then invites the student to respond and explain what they will do to "Make these behaviours stop ...". Many students (in response to the invited right of reply) will disclaim, discount or minimise their harassing behaviour: "I was only mucking about ...!"; "I was just joking ..."; "Others said stuff too!!"; "I wasn't the only one ...!"

The facilitator or teacher will reframe these discounting and avoidance behaviours: "Maybe you thought it was a joke, Troy, but it clearly wasn't for Ms Smith because ..."; "That kind of joke or mucking-around is never acceptable in our school – even if half the class laughed with you ..."; "Maybe you were not the only one who said and did these things ... I'll be speaking to other students in our class too ... At the moment I'm talking about what *you* did ... and *your* responsibility ...". This lets the student know that the secrecy code will be cracked across the classroom group, one-by-one, as necessary.

Sometimes students claim a kind of "right to silence". If they refuse to respond verbally, the facilitator can suggest to the student what they might be saying: "Perhaps you're saying in your head, Troy (because you're not speaking to us) ... perhaps you're saying that it is no big deal because you were just mucking around. It is a big deal *because* ... – it is extremely serious *because* ...". Here the facilitator reframes why such behaviour cannot be minimised or excused. The tone and manner (as stated earlier) is very important; firm but respectful.

"Troy, what do you need to do now and in the future to change this behaviour?" Here the teacher invites an apology and an assurance of behaviour change. A brief reminder about the fundamental rights and responsibilities inherent in the student's behaviour is outlined.

Some students will benefit from having a provisional plan about the behaviours they need to stop and the behaviours they need to start, relative to what has been happening. This provisional plan can form the basis for a discussion about behaviour change.

The key messages emphasised by the facilitator (the senior teacher) are:
- "You-own-your-own-behaviour; nobody makes you do X, Y and Z."
- "It's your choice every time you go into our classroom to decide whether you'll support fair rights or not."
- "It's all about what you *do* ..."

The facilitator will emphasise that the teacher is wanting to work these issues through with the student in a way that does not need to involve the parent(s) at this stage but does need the understanding, the accountability and cooperation of the student.

If, however, the meeting sees no response at all from the student, or sees a defiant unwillingness to acknowledge any responsibility, or accountability, the issue will need to be referred to a more formal harassment due process, within the school's harassment policy. The student will need to understand what the more formal due process will involve.

Point out, if necessary, the consequences of a refusal to acknowledge, and change, their current pattern of behaviour.

• If the student has grudgingly, or cooperatively, acknowledged their harassing behaviour and agreed to change, assure them there will be a review meeting (in a week's time) "to see how things are going back in your classroom [or wherever the harassing behaviour has been occurring]". This puts the student "on notice", but does so with the belief communicated that, "You can make things change ... You can support the rights and responsibilities here."

At the review meeting, if there is no change in the behaviour during that week, formal due process will need to be entered into quickly. We should give no indication that we will continue to tolerate such behaviour. If necessary, due process may necessitate suspension and even (on some occasions) expulsion.

- Separate amicably at the close of the meeting. Avoid any telegraphing of animosity, pay-back or threat. The relative success of this mediatory approach relies on early intervention, senior colleague support, thoughtful planning and teacher goodwill to work with the perpetrator to expose and confront the behaviour while inviting understanding and cooperation.

Special areas of focus for colleague support

While colleague support in some schools can often be incidental and based in loose (one-to-one) associations as well as more formal expressions (such as meetings and teams), there are key areas where colleague support cannot be left to mere goodwill or chance association:

Induction of new staff to a school

Each school has his own, unique, idiosyncratic culture and practices. A new teacher to a school can be assisted by having a "teaching-buddy", to help induct even experienced teachers into a new school. Such induction is not patronising to an experienced colleague; it is the offer of support from someone who can help make sense (through their availability) of the essentials one needs to know and be aware of when starting out in a new school. It is also important to introduce and welcome the new colleague formally at assembly – to the whole school – and even to their new classes.

First year teachers

I have heard too many accounts of newly qualified teachers having to engage their first year of teaching, and the new culture of their first school, without focused colleague support.

- Provision needs to be made for a "mentor" – an older, experienced colleague – to support the new teacher in their first term. Such support will involve regularly meeting with the new teacher to discuss any concerns, as well as being available at other times. Issues such as lesson-planning, classroom management and follow-up of students are typical concerns that will need to be addressed. The mentoring role may also involve in-class teaming to give the "mentee" an opportunity to observe a senior colleague's teaching practice and conversely gain supportive feedback from the mentor observing the mentee's classroom teaching and management (p. 152f.).
- An in-school peer support group can be formed to act as an emotional clearing house (without it being a total whinge session) and a forum for needs identification and problem solving.
- A network forum with other first year teachers (across several schools) to discuss common concerns, needs, experiences and strategies can be helpful.

It is also important to assist first year teachers with the basic essentials such as: a decent map of the school; a list of "break" times; discipline policy; time-out practice; detention policy; referral procedures; and playground management procedures. These "basics" are often so well entrenched in the organisational culture that senior colleagues may forget how different, even strange, the first few weeks in a new culture can seem for a newly qualified or new teacher.

Again, a "teaching-buddy" can give valuable assistance in coming to terms with these fundamentals.

Supply teachers

On the law of averages, supply teachers often take over the more difficult classes for one or several days. In some classes supply teachers are treated as fair game by students. They will need support similar to that offered to new teachers even if such support is only given for a day (map, break times, and so on). It can also help if a senior teacher introduces the supply teacher to the staff *and* their new classes to enhance the link between the administration and the "new" teacher.

Elective mentoring

Elective mentoring can provide the opportunity for a teacher to work with a trusted, supportive colleague over a period of time, providing a basis for ongoing professional reflection and skill development.

Mentoring has to be elective if a colleague is going to feel that they have some professional ownership of the support offered through such mentoring. Obviously the normative opportunity for such mentoring needs to be present in a school for colleagues to take it up as an option.

The emphasis of such mentoring needs to be seen within a supportive, professional development context rather than struggling-teacher context. Mentoring, in this sense, does not imply a superior–inferior relationship or an implied imputation of current failure in one's teaching and management practice.

Any mentoring, even with a trusted colleague, has some risk attached. Inviting a colleague to work with you, over time, in a difficult class means exposing one's self-esteem. Collegial goodwill and professional trust can minimise any perceived sense of inadequacy as both mentor and mentee focus on the common aims and needs as the basis for mentoring support.

For example, the mentee may be unaware of some of the factors in the classroom dynamics that their classroom management or even their normative teaching practice may be affecting. A key aspect of the mentor's role will be to enable a colleague's awareness of what is actually going on in their classroom. That awareness will involve supportive feedback that addresses such teacher behaviour where necessary.

The word "mentor" comes from Homer's *Odyssey*. In this epic myth, Mentor (the long-time loyal friend of Ulysses) is entrusted with the education of Ulysses and Penelope's son, Telemachus. He carried out this role so well that the word "mentor" has come down to us today as meaning "wise advisor and guide – one who gives support, encouragement and feedback". Ulysses, king of Ithaca (and known to the ancient Greeks as Odysseus), was one of the heroes of the Trojan War.

Before any feedback is given, however, the mentor will need to discuss the purpose of feedback, how it is likely to be given (supportively and non-judgementally) and how such feedback might be used in ongoing action-planning, particularly the development of one's teaching and management practice.

There are a number of stages in the ongoing professional journey of mentor and mentee. These are set out in Figure 8.1. Any mentoring will need to begin from a basis of perceived need on the mentee's part and a willingness to work in a professionally supportive way with a mentor.

Normative whingeing: "hearing" a teacher's frustration and concern

"Whingeing" can range from the occasional grizzle and moan to an ongoing state of being! At its most typical it is frustration battling with goodwill. It can also be a way of bonding with another ("in the same boat ... leaking, rusty, but roughly going in the same direction").

It is often a brief, transactional occurrence or chat in the corridor or staffroom or as we get into our car *en route* to partial freedom. It can enable a reframing of built up tension, particularly through shared humour, giving a little edge or momentary uplift in the day. It can also ratify a view of one's struggle; "you're not the only one".

Some whingeing, though, can be ongoing, laboured and even resilient to reframing and problem solving. When sharing with a colleague who frequently, even consistently, moans and complains it is important to:

- listen and acknowledge, first, before offering possible suggestions – *unsolicited* advice is not always well or easily received. Such listening is an affirmation of their feelings and needs; it doesn't have to validate all they are saying about a given incident or concern;

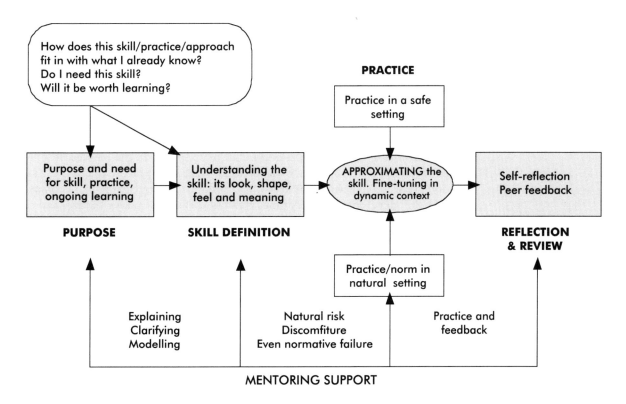

Figure 8.1 Skill development within a mentoring model (© William Rogers, 2000)

- be aware that sometime the whingeing is enough, acting as a kind of "off-loading" (even if you're the one who has been cornered for the off-loading);
- if the whingeing is a recurrent pattern, or keeps raising a recurrent theme, suggest a more focused form of support that includes some needs analysis, problem solving, resolution or some kind of workable plan to address the recurrent concern;
- if whingeing descends into a destructive moaning, inaction, destructive blame or dissenting behaviour that stymies any effective change or resolution options, make it clear to the colleague what it is they are doing *through* the whingeing, and let them know that productive support can help if the problem, issue or concern is addressed. Some colleagues, it seems, would rather keep whingeing about X, Y and Z than do something about them.

This sort of behaviour can sap at the good-will of supportive colleagues.

The mentoring process (Fig. 8:1)

Problem analysis
This is aided by the mentor making early visits to the class in question. Such visits need to be planned, particularly in respect to: how the mentor is introduced to the class (briefly); the mentor's role; how any management issues might be addressed by the mentor during the course of any lesson; and any cues or signals the mentor and mentee can use to indicate when (for example) the mentor could take a management lead during the course of a lesson. I have (on many occasions) chosen to calm a noisy class and refocus their attention during a colleague's struggle to manage whole-class behaviour. The cue for this (verbal or non-verbal) needs to be planned prior to any exercise of direct classroom control by the mentor. The last thing a supportive colleague needs to do is convey, publicly, that the supported colleague is an ineffective, incompetent teacher. The approach I normally use is give a brief, verbal cue at an appropriate time: "Excuse me, Mr Smith, do you mind if I (have a word to …) …?"

Goal setting
Mentor and mentee discuss and develop goals for the mentee to work on. These may be a particular approach to management (say – establishing whole-class attention more thoughtfully or more effectively), or particular skills in management and teaching, or even particular approaches to classroom teaching.

It is always important to remember that what seems patently obvious, and clear, to the mentor may appear difficult or confusing to the mentee. It will be important to clarify and discuss a particular skill; even practise the skill in a safe, non-classroom environment. It will also be important to reassure one's colleague that skill development takes time, effort and even normative failure, and that normative failure is OK (pp. 19–20). Goals need to be realistic, behaviourally focused, incremental and supported with ongoing feedback.

Skill development
The skills and approaches described and discussed in this book can form the framework for colleague mentoring (see also Rogers 1997). Skill development needs ongoing feedback to enable clarity, focus and direction (Fig. 8.1).

Feedback
For feedback to be supportive and effective it needs to focus on targeted areas, particular goals or particular skills. When giving feedback mentor and mentee should focus on the present *behaviour* or the present issues, specifically as well as generally, as they affect the colleague's teaching and management. While it is

helpful to *generally* note that a certain class is particularly noisy, and difficult to settle, it also helps if the mentor *specifically* notes what they believe contributes to that noise level and why, even if the mentee's behaviour (as the class teacher) is a factor. Before any feedback session it is essential for mentor and mentee to discuss the purpose and nature of colleague feedback by mentor to mentee and vice versa.

Keep any feedback descriptive and keep the focus of the feedback on aspects of teacher behaviour (including language.) For example, one of the factors that may contribute to ineffective discipline could be frequent use by the teacher of interrogative forms of language in a management context: "A*re you* calling out ...?"; "You're not supposed to be calling out *are you*?"; "*Why* are you talking?"; "*Are you* out of your seat ...?"; "*Can you* face the front *please?*";"*Haven't you* started yet?"

A teacher may be unaware of their characteristic language in discipline contexts; they may be unaware of their non-verbal behaviour, how they "come across"; they may be unaware of the interactive effect of their non-verbal behaviour; they may be unaware of how they address particular aspects of disruptive behaviour. In giving *descriptive* feedback the mentor is describing what they see, hear and perceive as a basis for shared reflection and shared action planning. Before developing any new skill repertoire a colleague will need to also be aware of their current behaviour. Descriptive feedback, supportively and sensitively shared, enables that awareness.

Examples of the typical questions used to raise awareness in feedback sessions are: "Were you *aware* that ...?"; "Did you *hear* yourself say ...?"; "Were you *conscious* of ...?"; "How did you *feel* when ...?"

- Avoid giving feedback that is too extensive or wide-ranging as it can easily dissuade or discourage a colleague. Overloaded feedback that covers too many factors about a colleague's management behaviour may make change look insurmountable. One can cope with incremental, supported, changes.
- Keep the feedback non-judgemental. The feedback should avoid any criticism of "personality" factors. Keep the focus of the feedback on behaviour.
- Encourage, develop and affirm a colleague's skill development within and from the feedback. Professional feedback, of any kind, is most useful, valued and effective when linked to common needs, aims and objectives.

Disengagement

There will need to come a time when the mentor will need to separate from the ongoing, supportive journey with the mentee. This does not mean a lack of further support; it means the professional mentoring journey now focuses the mentee on generalising their skills and adapting their skills into their own teaching practice. A school should have its own normative opportunities for ongoing professional sharing and even appraisal. Ideally, such opportunities are geared to enabling and encouraging personal and shared reflection on one's teaching and management in a spirit of professional goodwill.

Colleague support

Not all colleagues want or feel they need support from their peers, even in supportive schools. Some teachers will give support because the culture in the school makes the giving of such support easier; or perhaps because one perceives it as a personal or professional duty arising from "mutual regard". Within a school culture there are complex relationships that exist between personalities, structures and the demands of one's role.

Those who do give and give unstintingly of their time and energy to support their colleagues speak about the stress of *giving* support as well as the benefits of support enjoyed by the recipients (Rogers 2001).[1] It is important for school leadership to acknowledge these natural, creative tensions.

Further, colleague support cannot simply be mandated. Like any feature of school culture and practice, the things that really matter cannot be mandated or forced (Fullan 1993; Stoll 1998). Herein lies the anomaly. Teachers generally acknowledge that they want, need and benefit from colleague support, yet a school administration cannot simply mandate that colleagues give and receive support, or that it *will* operate. This does not negate external direction, policy initiatives, "forms" or expressions of support; but it does mean that what colleagues say they value and need cannot *simply* be built by policy imperative. Thoughtful procedures, plans and policies, while subject to the constraints of fallibility, can, however, be vehicles for human support and action. They can give a sense of shared purpose, dependable organisational structure, "back-up" and reciprocal interdependency. Of course such structures or "forms" need to be broadly and characteristically worthy of our trust. Time and usage will give the confirmation or refutation of such assurance and trust.[2]

When a school leadership seeks to address colleague support the focus needs to be on how the school, as a collegial community, can meet colleague needs. in this sense "form" always follows function.

Collegially supportive structures, "forms", processes, opportunities, "teaming structures" and so on can be enhanced by periodic colleague review. Such a review proceeds from the affirmation that the school values mutual regard and supportive interdependency.

Needs analysis and colleague support

- How *acknowledged* are the individual and collective needs of colleagues at your school? In what ways are they acknowledged? What current "forms", structures, processes or policies seek to address these needs?
- Where is the school, now, in terms of a general "consciousness of colleague support"?
- What changes will need to be made (or are functionally able to be made) to address and seek to meet identified needs?
- What changes to *current* "forms", structures, plans and procedures will need to be made to enable the meeting of identified needs?

(Rogers 2001)

Commitment to an "ecology of support" (Rogers 2001) depends on how a community of professionals chooses to operate, and cooperate. Choices that enhance and *enable* colleague support are more likely to occur when the school culture endorses and encourages colleague support and its individuals model collegiality within a belief and practice of mutual regard and colleague watchfulness.

Notes

1. In his autobiography, *Clinging to the Wreckage* (1989), John Mortimer notes that the world is divided into "nurses" and "patients".
2. Hargreaves (1994) notes that trust can be invested in persons or processes; in the qualities and conduct of individuals, or the expertise and performance of abstract systems. It can be an outcome of meaningful face-to-face relationships or a condition of their existence (1994: 39).

Epilogue

A cord of three strands is not quickly broken.
Ecclesiastes 4: 12

No doubt, like me, you went into teaching because you believed you could make a difference to the lives of your students in their educational journey. This is a profession that takes up a good deal of our time in and out of the classroom. You spend a good deal of your time outside classroom teaching, supporting your students by sharing time and assistance, being part of special events, and keeping on top of the ever present marking and feedback. Our profession is more than a job – it is a *noblesse oblige*, and a very challenging one at that.

This book has a parallel text, beyond classroom management, discipline and effective teaching: that of colleague support. Without colleague support – reasonable, basic support– our profession is made more difficult and more stressful.

Colleague support can meet our basic needs for belonging and affiliation as well as our professional needs for affirmation, assurance, shared professional identity and supportive feedback.

From the transitional whinge and offloading to the brief assurance that we're on the right track; from the shared identity through to shared teaming and appraisal, colleague support affirms and enables our coping, our morale and our professionalism.

To some of you (if you've read this far) I will have said more than enough about the sorts of management, discipline and teaching issues you face each day as a teacher; to others I will not have said enough. There is always more that can be said to qualify, extend and clarify. I hope that what I have shared has helped your *personal* reflection on your day-to-day teaching and management.

I wish you well in your teaching journey – all sanity and grace, day-to-day.

Kind regards, Bill Rogers

My daughter, Sarah, did this drawing when she was 11 years old. The rings under the eyes show that these are teachers. She has tried to demonstrate colleague support: note the long, collegial arm!

Bibliography

Baars, C. W. (1979) *Feeling and Healing your Emotions*. Plainfield, NJ: Logos International.

Beck, A. T. (1976) *Cognitive Therapy and the Emotional Disorders*. New York: International Universities Press.

Bernard, M. (1990) *Taking the Stress out of Teaching*. Melbourne: Collins Dove.

Carr, W. (ed.) (1989) *Quality in Teaching: Arguments for a Reflective Profession*. London: Falmer.

Clark, M. (1991) *The Quest for Grace*. Ringwood, Victoria: Penguin.

Clarke, D. and Murray, A. (eds) (1996) *Developing and Implementing a Whole-school Behaviour Policy*. London: David Fulton Publishers.

Cornett, C. E. (1986) *Learning Through Laughter: Humour in the Classroom*. Bloomington, IN: Phi Delta Kappa Educational Foundation.

Cummings, C. (1989) *Managing to Teach*. Edmonds, WA: Teaching Inc.

Denenberg, V. H. and Zarrow, M. J. (1970) "Rat pax", *Psychology Today* 3(12): 45–7, 66–7.

Dodge, K. A. (1981) "Social competence and aggressive behaviour in children", paper presented at Midwestern Psychological Association, Detroit, Michigan, USA, May.

Dodge, K. A. (1985) "Attributional Bias in Aggressive Children". In P. C. Kendall (ed.) *Advances in Cognitive Behavioural Research and Therapy* 4. Orlando, FL: Academic Press.

Doyle, W. (1986) "Classroom Organisation and Management". In M. C. Whitrock (ed.) *Handbook of Research on Teaching*. New York: Macmillan.

Dreikurs, R. (1968) *Psychology in the Classroom*, 2nd edn. New York: Harper & Row.

Dreikurs, R., Grunwald, B. and Pepper, F. (1982) *Maintaining Sanity in the Classroom*, 2nd edn. New York: Harper & Row.

Edwards, C. (1997) "RET in high school", *Rational Living* 12, 10–12.

Ellis, A. (1977) *Anger: How to Live with it and Without it*. Melbourne: Sun Books.

Elton Report (1989) *Discipline in Schools, Report of the Committee of Inquiry*. London: HMSO.

Faber, A. and Mazlish, E. (1982) *How to Talk so Kids will Listen & Listen so Kids will Talk*. New York: Avon Books.

Frankyl, V. (1963) *Man's Search for Meaning: an Introduction to Logotherapy*. New York: Simon and Schuster.

Fullan, M. (1993) *Change Processes: Probing the Depths of Educational Reform*. London: Falmer.

Fullan, M. and Hargreaves, A. (1991) *What's Worth Fighting For?: Working Together for your School*. Toronto: Ontario Public School Teachers' Federation.

Geffner, R. and Brians, S. (1993) *Effective Teaching Approaches for ADHD Children*. Texas: ADHD Association of Texas.

Gillborn, D., Nixon, J. and Rudduck, J. (1993) *Dimensions of Discipline: Rethinking Practice in Secondary Schools*. London: HMSO.

Glasser, W. (1986) *Control Theory in Classrooms*. New York: Harper & Row.

Glasser, W. (1992) *The Quality School*. New York: HarperCollins.

Goffman, M. (1972) *The Presentation of Self in Everyday Life*. Harmondsworth: Penguin.

Green, C. and Chee, K. (1995) *Understanding Add*. Sydney: Doubleday.

Guskey, T. R. (1986) "Staff Development and the Process of Teacher Change", *Educational Review* **15**(5): 5–12.

Hargreaves, A. (1994) "Restructuring restructuring: postmodernity and the prospects for individual change", *Journal of Education Policy* **9**(1): 47–65.

Hart, P. M. (1994) "Teacher quality of life: integrating work experiences, psychological distress and morale", *Journal of Occupational and Organisational Psychology* **67**: 109–39.

Hart, P. M., Wearing, A. J. and Conn, M. (1995) "Wisdom is a poor predictor of the relationship between discipline policy, student misbehaviour and teacher stress", *British Journal of Educational Psychology* **1195**(65): 27–48.

Hobfoll, S. E. (1998) *Stress, Culture, and Community: The Psychology and Philosophy of Stress*. New York: Plenum Press.

Howell, K. (1993) "Eligibility and need: is there a difference between being disturbed and being disturbing?" In D. Evans, M. Myhill and J. Izard (eds) *Student Behaviour Problems: Positive Initiatives and New Frontiers*. Camberwell, Victoria: ACER.

Jarman, F. C. (1992) "Management of hyperactivity: multi model interventions", *Practical Therapeutics* August: 31–8.

Johnson, D. W. and Johnson, R. T. (1989) *Leading The Cooperative School*. Edina, MN: Interaction Book Co.

Jons, P. and Tucker, E. (eds) (1990) *Mixed Ability Teaching: Classroom Experiences in Experiences in English, ESL, Mathematics and Science*. Roseberry, New South Wales: St Clair Press.

Kounin, J. (1971) *Discipline and Group Management in Classrooms*. New York: Holt, Rinehart And Winston.

Kyriacou, C. (1981) "Social support and occupational stress among school teachers", *Educational Studies* **7**: 55–60.

Kyriacou, C. (1986) *Effective Teaching in Schools*. Oxford: Basil Blackwell.

Kyriacou, C. (1991) *Essential Teaching Skills*. London: Basil Blackwell.

Lazarus, R. S. (1981) "Little hassles can be hazardous to health", *Psychology Today,* July: 58–62.

Leiberman, A. (ed.) (1990) *School as Collaborative Cultures: Creating the Future now*. Basingstoke: Falmer Press.

Mcgough, R. (1993) *Defying Gravity*. London: Penguin.

Mcgrath, H. and Francey, S. (1993) *Friendly Kids, Friendly Classrooms*. Melbourne: Longman.

Mcinerney, D. M. and Mcinerney, V. (1998) *Educational Psychology – Constructing Learning*, 2nd edn. Sydney: Prentice-Hall.

Miller, A. (1996) *Pupil Behaviour and Teacher Culture*. London: Cassell.

Mortimer, J. (1984) *In Character*. London: Penguin.

Mortimer, J. (1989) *Clinging to the Wreckage*. London: Penguin.

Nias, J., Southworth, G. and Yeomans, R. (1989) *Staff Relationships in the Primary School*. London & New York: Cassell.

O'Brien, T. (1998) *Promoting Positive Behaviour*. London: David Fulton Publishers.

Pearce, H. (1997) "Groupwork in the classroom". Unpublished notes.

Perore, S. (2000) "Workplace is a war zone", *The Age* (newspaper), 22 February: 8.

Relf, P., Hirst, R., Richardson, J. and Youdell, G. (1998) *Best Behaviour: Starting Points for Effective Behaviour Management*. Stafford: Network Educational Press.

Robertson, J. (1997) *Effective Classroom Control: Understanding Teacher–Pupil Relationships*, 3rd edn. London: Hodder and Stoughton.

Rogers, B. (1995) *Behaviour Management: A Whole School Approach*. London: Paul Chapman Publishing.

Rogers, B. (1996a) *Behaviour Recovery*. London: Pitman Publishing.

Rogers, B. (1996b) *Managing Teacher Stress*. London: Pitman Publishing.

Rogers, B. (1997) *Cracking the Hard Class: Strategies for Managing the Harder than Average Class*. London: Paul Chapman Publishing.

Rogers, B. (1998) *You Know the Fair Rule and More*. London: Pitman Publishing.

Rogers, B. (2000) "Effective teaching – some fundamental considerations" (in print).

Rogers, B. (2001) *"I Get By With A Little Help" Colleague Support In Schools* (in print).

Russell, D. W., Altimaier, E. and Van Velzen D. (1987) "Job related stress, social support and burnout among classroom teachers", *Journal of Applied Psychology* 72(2): 269–74.

Rutter, M., Maughan, B., Mortimer, P. and Ousten, J. (1979) *Fifteen Thousand Hours: Secondary Schools and their Effects on Children*. London: Open Books.

Sacks, O. (1990) *Awakenings*. London: HarperCollins.

Schwab, R. L. And Iwanicki, E. F. (1982) "Who are our burned out teachers?", *Educational Research Quarterly* 7(2): 5–16.

Scott-Peck, M. (1978) *The Road Less Travelled*. London: Arrow Books.

Seligman, M. (1991) *Learned Optimism*. Sydney: Random House.

Stoll, L. (1998) "Supporting school improvement", paper presented at the OECD conference "Combating Failure at School", Christchurch, New Zealand, 1–5 February 1998.

Thompson, J. A. K. (trans.) (1969) *The Ethics of Aristotle: The Nichomachean Ethics*, London: Penguin.

Woodhouse, D. A., Hall, E. and Wooster, A. D. (1985) "Taking Control of Stress in Teaching", *British Journal of Educational Psychology* 55: 119–23.

Index